ANGRY MEN, PASSIVE MEN

UNDERSTANDING THE ROOTS OF MEN'S ANGER AND HOW TO MOVE BEYOND IT

(Formerly titled: *In the Company of Men*)

MARVIN ALLEN

WITH

JO ROBINSON

FAWCETT COLUMBINE · NEW YORK

A Fawcett Columbine Book
Published by Ballantine Books

Copyright © 1993 by Marvin Allen

All rights reserved under International and Pan-American Copyright Conventions. Published in the United States by Ballantine Books, a division of Random House, Inc., New York, and simultaneously in Canada by Random House of Canada Limited, Toronto. Originally published as *In the Company of Men* by Random House, Inc. in 1993.

This edition published by arrangement with Random House, Inc.

All of the names and identifying details of the men described in this book have been changed to protect their privacy.

Library of Congress Catalog Card Number: 93-74506

ISBN: 0-449-90811-9

Cover design by Judy Herbstman

Manufactured in the United States of America

First Ballantine Books Edition: June 1994

10 9 8 7 6 5

This book is dedicated to the
thousands of courageous men who
have consciously embraced a new kind
of manhood that honors vulnerability
as well as strength, and who
steadfastly refuse to oppress women,
children, other men, or the planet.
My brother Lewis and my son
Chesley are two of those men.

ACKNOWLEDGMENTS

My work in the men's movement hasn't always been smooth sailing. Through it all, Allen Maurer has remained a valuable colleague and supportive friend. By his actions, he taught me that men, as well as women, could be supportive and nurturing. I am forever indebted to him for this and his many contributions to my well-being.

I thank Dick "Coyote" Prosapio, my friend and associate, for teaching me a spirituality that includes the cry of the hawk, the wind in my face, and the dirt beneath my feet. I also thank him for being part of a friendship in which two middle-aged men like us could let down our guards and just be ourselves with each other.

As a mentor, John Lee went out ahead and blazed a trail that I could follow. He continued to be an inspiration and model for me in my early years as a writer and speaker. Later, as a partner, John generously shared his talents, his energy, and his ideas with me. I thank him for his generosity and his many gifts.

Although I love to write, finishing this book has been the hardest thing I've ever done. Without Jo Robinson, my collaborator, I'd probably still be trying to figure out which paragraph follows which. Like a good collaborator, Jo helped to organize the book into a structure that was easy to read and understand. But she didn't stop there. She believed in the healing value of men's emotional work and became dedicated to the book and its vision. And in the midst of everything, with compassion and wisdom, she counseled me past my perfectionism and my critical inner voice. Although it wasn't part of the bargain, she became my friend and cherished mentor. I owe her more than I can say.

My sister Anna is another woman to whom I owe more than I could ever say. Anna has been a political, intellectual, and emotional mentor to me for most of my forty-eight years. There have been times in my life when I felt as if she were the only person in the world I could count on to really listen to me and my feelings. Without her validation and support through those early years, I'm not sure where I'd be today. I left home at sixteen, a scared, angry young man attracted to right-wing extremist politics. Through countless conversations, discussions, and yes, arguments, Anna has gently and consistently guided me from the politicization of my rage, fear, and ignorance to the politicization of an informed mind and open heart.

I would also like to acknowledge my wife, Carol. Her goodwill, cheerful attitude, and generous heart have helped to create a marriage safe enough for me to practice being vulnerable. She has willingly taken on more than her share of household chores so that I could have more time to write. She has been my friend, my lover, and my wife. She has loved me and she has let me love her. I couldn't have asked for more.

Finally, I would like to thank my parents for giving me life. My childhood was pretty difficult and for a long time I blamed them for hurting me and causing my life to be so painful. Thank God I'm finally moving through that stage. With much of the rage and blame worked through, I can honestly say I know that, given their awareness, their circumstances, and their emotional development, they did the very best they could do. For that I will be eternally grateful.

CONTENTS

A PERSONAL INTRODUCTION

This is a book about men, from stockbrokers to bricklayers, who are learning to find more success and joy in their daily lives. It's not a fanciful flight into the world of myths and symbols or a treatise on masculinity. It's a book about the men I have counseled in private sessions, men's groups, and weekend retreats called Wildman Gatherings. In these pages I've tried to capture their courage and determination as they've learned to become soulful fathers and passionate partners. I've done my best to describe their struggles to create a new definition of manhood that frees their souls but doesn't imprison others.

As you will see, this is a personal, emotionally revealing book. It slips beneath the social smiles, stiff upper lips, and three-piece suits to explore men's innermost thoughts and feelings. It goes below the drinking problems, the work obsession, the loneliness, the emptiness, and the depression to examine the roots of these common maladies.

I'd like to begin by telling you something about my own life because my life illustrates many of the problems I'll be talking about later in the book. There's not much that has happened to my clients that hasn't already happened to me. Also, the therapy process I've developed for men that I describe throughout the book is a direct outgrowth of my own struggles to recover from a difficult childhood. By hearing my story, you'll have a better understanding of my unique approach to men's therapy.

I grew up in a one-story house with a big front porch in a modest neighborhood in Fort Worth, Texas. I have an older sister named Anna and a younger brother named Lewis. We were a working-class family. My dad worked on the assembly line at General Dynamics, and my mother was a bookkeeper in a meat-packing plant.

My father, a wiry man with receding hair, was the dominant force in my life. He was passive most of the time, but when he became upset he would move very quickly from annoyance to violence. One minute he would be watching TV; the next minute he would be whipping out his belt. More often than not, I was his scapegoat. When he was angry at me, he would bare his crooked, discolored teeth and yell obscenities. When he was furious, he would lay into me with his belt.

The first time I saw my dad laugh, I was eleven years old. The five of us were on vacation in Colorado, and we were sitting in a café eating breakfast. My brother said something funny, and all of a sudden my dad laughed out loud. I stared at his crinkled face in utter amazement. Until that moment I had no idea he found any pleasure in life.

A year later my father did something else out of character. My prize possession at the time was a hunting bow, and I used it to play an Indian version of Russian roulette. I shot my arrows straight up into the sky, then I ran around trying to dodge them. After a few weeks I would lose all the arrows, and I would have to scrounge up some money to buy new ones. This particular day my dad came up to me and asked if I wanted to go for a drive in the car. "Why?" I asked, surprised that he wanted my company. "We're going to get you some arrows," he said. I couldn't believe my ears. "You mean, you want to take me to town and buy me some arrows?" I asked. He said, "Yeah, that's what I said." I was compelled to ask again, "You want to get some arrows for me?" My stunned disbelief was making him furious. "Look, do you want to go or not?" My shock was justified. This was the first time in my life I could ever remember him going out of his way for me.

My mother was the self-proclaimed spiritual leader of the household and made reluctant Baptists out of all of us. Sunday-morning preaching, Sunday-night services, and Wednesday-evening prayer meetings were deemed necessary to keep our wretched souls just one step ahead of the devil. Momma didn't allow Dad to drink in the house, and she tried to keep him from cursing. Although she was afraid to confront him directly for fear of stirring up his anger, she got her way through skillful manipulation.

My mother seemed to favor me over my brother and sister and gave me an extra measure of attention. But she also gave me the hidden message that I had to earn my privileged status. Just being me didn't make me worthy of love, so I did everything I could to win her approval. I would hurry home from school so I could clean the house before she came home from work. I remember trying to do an extra-special job so she would be extra specially pleased. Sometimes my labors paid off. She would come home and say, "Marvin, you did a great job. You don't know how much your mother appreciates you when you clean up like that!" But other times she would say nothing at all, and I would be crushed.

From my adult perspective I can see that my mother was consumed with worries much of the time, which was why she couldn't give me the steady love and reassurance I needed. But I didn't see it that way as a child. When she ignored me, I felt unloveable, so I would redouble my efforts to win her approval. Although I had no way of knowing it, my compulsive need to earn her love set up a lifelong pattern of trying to please women.

Another pattern that appeared early in my life was the need to prove my self-worth by earning money. I can still remember the first time I got paid for working. I was about ten years old. I'd been working all day for my Uncle Richard, hanging up some laundry, mowing the grass, helping him plant a couple of trees. I was working because I'd been told to, not because I thought I'd be paid. At the end of the day my uncle called me into his study. "Marvin," he said, "I've got some-thing for you." He walked over to his wall safe and slowly worked the combination on the lock. I watched in breathless anticipation as he opened the door to the safe and took out a dollar bill. He handed me the money. "This is for helping me," he said. I was speechless. For the first time in my life I had money all my own. I could spend it any way that I wanted. So much of the time I felt worthless and empty inside. Now I had power. With that dollar bill in my pocket I was somebody.

One of the most significant events of my childhood took place when I was fourteen years old. For some minor offense that I can no longer recall, my father began hitting me with his belt. My older sister came to my defense and tried to push my father away from me. Enraged by her interference my father turned his anger on her and started pushing her around the room. I ran into the kitchen and listened in horror to the sound of my sister's screams. I was afraid my father was going to kill her. Without thinking I pulled open a drawer and grabbed a meat cleaver. I had no idea what I was going to do with the cleaver, but I felt safer with it in my hand. I heard my sister run outside, then I heard my father stomping toward the kitchen. He threw open the kitchen door and saw me holding the cleaver. His face went as white as a sheet. For five seconds he stood absolutely still, then he screamed out to my mother: "Come look at your son," he yelled. "He's trying to kill me." I was so frightened I couldn't utter a sound. My dad began to taunt me. "What kind of son are you, anyway?" he jeered. "Just look at you, trying to kill your own father." I stared at the floor, my face hot with shame, and I slipped the cleaver back into the drawer.

Although that incident was never mentioned again, it marked the end of my father's physical abuse. He could no longer be assured that I would submit to his beatings without defending myself. He had taught me one of the masculine credos: might makes right.

In my early teens I took whatever job I could find to earn money. I wanted to get away from my father and find some way to bolster my self-esteem. When I was fourteen, I worked all summer long at my uncle's dairy shoveling manure. It was hot, smelly work. Through the long, hot days of the Texas summer the blisters on my hands turned to calluses. As a part of my payment my uncle gave me a baby pig. That next school year I raised the pig and had her bred. When the pig was eighteen months old she gave birth to a litter of eleven little piglets. I sold all twelve pigs for three hundred dollars and used the money to buy my first car—a black, ten-year-old Cadillac Coupe de Ville with power windows. I took excellent care of that car and only drove it to school a couple of days a week. For some reason, my father was annoyed that I was so careful with it. He said to me, "Why'd you buy the goddamn thing if you're not going to use it?" I never could make him happy.

My dad and I reached the breaking point one night when I was sixteen years old. I had gone to the movies with a girlfriend and had arrived home twenty minutes past my eleven o'clock curfew. My dad started yelling at me as soon as I walked in the door. I explained that the movie didn't get out until ten-thirty and it had taken me forty-five minutes to take my girlfriend home and drive back to the house. He said, "I don't give a goddamn! If you're too big to come home when I say, you're big enough to pack your bags and get out!" The next morning I threw my clothes in a suitcase and left home. I never went back.

As I look back on that first, grim chapter of my life, I see a young boy struggling with fear, shame, loneliness, and rage. Although I felt all those emotions very strongly at times, it wasn't safe for me to express them. My mother was too preoccupied with her own needs to listen to me, and my father was too quick to attack or ridicule me. Gradually, I learned to control my feelings so well I didn't even know I had them. Except for occasional bursts of anger, I felt strangely dead inside.

A happier chapter of my life began the day I left home and moved in with a couple of men in their early twenties who were renting a small house. Most of the men in my life have, when given the chance, abused me or taken advantage of me. Fortunately, these men were exceptions. For the next year I went to high school in the morning, worked in a grocery store in the afternoon, and cleaned house and cooked for my two friends at night. In exchange for my work around the house I was given free room and board.

People may feel sorry for me because I was on my own at such a young age, but at the time I felt as if I'd been summoned to Paradise. My friends didn't yell at me, hit me, shame me, or lay down oppressive rules. They treated me like an equal and gave me complete freedom. They didn't give me the guidance and protection that I needed, but at least they left me alone. I began to feel much older than my sixteen years and gradually lost interest in school dances and sports. All that seemed like child's play. I didn't even go to my own high school graduation. On the outside I felt more like a man than a boy.

On my seventeenth birthday my two friends bought me my first sexual experience in a hotel in Fort Worth. Although it took me less than ten minutes from the time I entered the room until I was back out the door, I felt as though I'd been born anew. I had no idea that sex with a woman could be so wonderful. I was only seventeen years old, but by that time I had already discovered my three primary motivations: pleasing women, earning money, and making love. Like many men whom I counsel, I spent much of my life heeding these urgent calls.

It wasn't long after that, at age eighteen, that I got involved with a girl named Sandra. Sandra was only sixteen years old and still in high school, but we wanted to get married. Her parents wisely argued against our marrying so young, but we were determined. We got married in the summer of 1963. We had our first child, a daughter, eleven months later.

At first my teenage bride and I tried to maintain a cheery warmth on the surface of our relationship. But it was like tending a small fire on top of a glacier that is slowly moving toward the Arctic Ocean. By the end of our first year of marriage the flush of romance had faded, and Sandra and I began to enact a repeat performance of my childhood. Before long I was feeling unappreciated, unloved, and resentful—the very feelings I had struggled with as a child. The two of us were quietly miserable, but our little girl and my hidden fear of abandonment kept us glued together.

I dealt with my misery in typical male fashion—by turning to work. My friend, John, and I got together and formed a small construction company. We had no business experience and knew next to nothing about the construction industry, but we were determined to make money. To my relief I discovered that the longer and harder I worked, the better I felt. At work I felt as though I belonged somewhere. I felt important and needed. Soon I was working as if my entire life depended on every business transaction.

A year later my partner and I were still scratching and clawing, but success was on the horizon. We worked well together, and our mutual desire to make something out of our lives spurred us on. Then John was drafted to fight in the Vietnam War and I was forced to manage the business all on my own. John was killed in action a year later.

Instead of mourning John's death, I numbed my feelings and became even more obsessed with work. His death was just another trauma to put behind me. There was a period of a year when I was working at my business during the day and moonlighting by painting the interior of apartment buildings at night. I'd come home from work, have dinner, and Sandra would drive me to my painting job. There were times when I would work all night long. To keep myself going I would tell myself, "Wait until Sandra picks me up and sees how much work I've done. She won't believe how hard I've worked!" The little boy who had worked so hard to please his mother was now a young man desperately trying to please his wife.

After several years the money started trickling in. When I was twenty-four years old, I was able to walk into a car dealership, write a check, and drive away with a brand-new, 1968 Cadillac Coupe de Ville hardtop convertible. Three days after I'd bought it, I drove home in triumph to my parents' house. I wanted my dad to see what his black sheep had done. I pulled into the driveway wearing sunglasses and smoking a King Edward cigar, just as I had seen men do in the movies. My dad didn't say anything at first, but about a half hour into the visit he said, "Looks like you're doing real good, Marvin Jr." I had struggled for years to hear those words. I'd been convinced that if I could just earn a few words of praise from him, my life would change forever. I smiled at my dad and said thanks, but to my disappointment I didn't feel much of anything. I didn't feel proud. I didn't feel happy. My father's meager words of praise were too little, too late. I drove home feeling confused and depressed, wondering if I would ever find happiness.

Not knowing where else to turn, I continued to seek salvation in work. Two years later, at age twenty-six, I had eighty-five people working for me, most of them older than I was. Now I owned a boat, a motorcycle, a sports car, and a big house—all the toys that are supposed to separate the men from the boys.

I also had another child—a boy. While I had been building my business, I had been neglecting my family. I spent very little time with my children, and although I was dependent on my wife for validation and a sense of well-being, I offered her little in return except more and more of what money could buy. Gradually her anger over my physical and emotional absence began to grow and our marriage brought us more pain than pleasure. About the same time, my satisfaction with work began to diminish. My business had grown beyond my ability to manage it, and I was feeling overwhelmed by my never-ending responsibilities. I felt trapped in my business and trapped in my marriage. I desperately wanted out of both of them, but I was terrified to do without either one.

As time went on, my misery in my marriage increased to the point that I had to get out of it, but I was afraid to make the first move.

Eventually I did what many men in my position have done: I made life so miserable for my wife that finally, one afternoon in our eleventh year of marriage, *she* asked for a divorce. Even though I had all but forced her to leave me, her announcement devastated me. I ran out of the house in a panic and fell to my knees on the driveway. With my face on the concrete, next to my Cadillac, I broke down and cried for the first time since I was a child.

After my divorce I was even more cut off from people. Like so many men I counsel, I felt as if I were always on the outside looking in. When I was married, I would look in the taverns and dance halls and see people dating and having fun, and I wanted to be there. When I was divorced, I would look in the windows of the suburban houses and see happily married couples with their children, and I wanted to be there. But wherever I happened to be, I felt only isolation and anxiety.

In desperation I began to look for comfort in the arms of women. In every woman I slept with, I looked for a lover who would make me feel manly and a momma who could make me feel safe and loved. What I found instead was a string of women who were looking for something from me. What they seemed to want was a "relationship." For me that word had *trap* written all over it. To keep from having to make a commitment, I would date several women at once so I wouldn't become too involved with any of them.

If work and sex could heal and enlighten anyone, the next few years would have made me a saint. But all they did was keep the dragon from my door one more day and one more night. They kept me busy enough to stay distracted and exhausted enough to stay numb. But in those rare moments when I wasn't preoccupied with work or women, I would be overcome with despair.

Like most men, I felt that I had to solve my problems on my own. I couldn't confide in others, and I certainly couldn't get any psychological help. To go to a therapist was to admit I was crazy. But between the time I was twenty and twenty-eight, I had periods when I was so desperate and so miserable and so frightened that I was forced to look for help. I saw two different psychologists with whom I had unproductive relationships, as I describe in more detail later in the book. The third person I saw was another psychologist. I worked productively with her for a number of years. She helped me gain insight into many of my childhood issues and started me on the road to recovery. She also encouraged me to go back to school. Going to college made me realize I had some internal worth other than my ability to earn money and seduce women. It also changed my career. After graduating from college at age thirty-five, I began working on a master's degree in psychology and counseling. I had decided to be a therapist.

Yet my own recovery was far from complete. The work I had done with the third therapist had only skimmed the surface of my underlying problems. The kind of therapy she practiced was traditional talk therapy. This meant that I spent most of my time in her office talking about my emotional problems, which did not fully resolve them. I needed to *experience* my emotions in order to heal, and she was unable to help me do this. The bulk of my feelings of anger, rage, and grief remained trapped inside me, frustrating any further growth.

I finally was able to release my emotions and complete my recovery by turning to nontraditional therapies. A fear-of-flying class and a men's group devoted to anger-release techniques allowed me to begin letting go of the emotions I had kept locked inside me for almost forty years. Significantly, both of these experiences were group therapies. For reasons I explain later on, getting therapy in a group setting, particularly a group of men, was one of the keys to my recovery. I took part in a third therapy group as well. This one was designed for therapists and was devoted primarily to identifying self-defeating relationship patterns. This group gave me additional insights.

I describe my convoluted healing journey in more detail in the second half of this book. I also explain how I combined my traditional training in counseling with the lessons I learned in the three group experiences to create a new therapy for men, one that addresses their unique needs and hastens their healing. In the final chapters of this book I invite you into my therapy sessions to see how men are using these techniques to transform their lives. As is true for me these men are beginning to experience all the feelings that make life worth living.

But this book is more than just a new approach to men's therapy. It's an exploration of the thoughts and feelings that most men keep hidden. I hope that all men who read this book will gain new insights into their own inner world and the thoughts and feelings of other men. As they acquire these insights, perhaps they will no longer feel so isolated. I hope that all female readers will gain new compassion for their husbands, fathers, and sons.

PART I

MEN AND THEIR EMOTIONS

CHAPTER 1

WHY MEN CAN'T FEEL

Of all the various professions psychotherapy seems to offer the most ready access to the inner lives of men and women. Sociologists examine broad trends and patterns. Physicians work with tissue and bone. Philosophers ponder universal truths. Linguists dissect words and phrases. But therapists are privy to the hidden fears and secret longings of their clients.

Being a therapist who works primarily with men has given me some insight into the male condition. By counseling hundreds of men in private practice and thousands of men in weekend retreats called Wildman Gatherings, I have broadened my view of men's emotional problems. More important, I've used what I have learned to develop a gender-specific therapy to help men resolve them. Through a series of techniques especially adapted for men, I've helped hundreds of men diminish their emotional pain and lead richer, more joyful lives.

In the early years of my practice most of my clients were women, so the insights I had about men came secondhand. I didn't go out of my way to attract female clients. It just happened that they were the ones who showed up. I would sit in my office day after day and listen to women talk about men. I heard all the familiar complaints: "My husband is emotionally dead." "My husband won't listen to me." "My father was always working." "My boyfriend frightens me with his violence." "My husband is too passive." "My boyfriend loves me but he doesn't want to get married." "I am the only real friend my husband has." "My husband is having an affair." "My husband is depressed." These women felt that the men in their lives had difficulty connecting with them on an intimate level. The men were either too passive or too domineering, too angry or too repressed, too clingy or too wary of commitment. For one reason or another they struggled with emotional intimacy.

As women began to bring their husbands in to me for marital counseling, I saw grounds for their complaints firsthand. The men seemed to find it much harder to express their feelings than the women. I could imagine how difficult it would be to live with these stoic men. One couple stands out in my mind because they were such a study in contrasts. John and Karen were both in their mid-thirties. John was a witty man. He enjoyed humor and light conversation and would dominate the discussion at the beginning of each session. However, when I managed to maneuver the conversation around to their marital struggles, John would retreat and let Karen do most of the talking. She was much more comfortable in the "feminine realm" of feelings and relationships than he was. As she talked, I noticed that John would watch her impassively, no matter what she said. He rarely changed his facial expression, not even when she cried. It didn't surprise me that one of Karen's chief complaints was that he was cold and indifferent to her.

During one session Karen finally realized that John was determined to file for divorce. She started to cry. It wasn't unusual for her to shed a few tears during a session, but this time she was crying so deeply her whole body shook. She was grieving for the end of their eighteen-year marriage. As she sobbed, I noticed that John continued to look at her with the same blank expression.

When Karen stopped crying, I asked John what he'd been feeling as he witnessed his wife's misery. "I know this seems brutal," he said, "but I felt absolutely nothing. I know I should have felt something, but I didn't." A thought popped unbidden into my mind: Was this man one of those "unfeeling bastards" I'd heard so many women describe?

I pressed John to tell me what he might have felt had he been able to feel. He said, "I don't know. I guess I should have felt sad because she was crying. Maybe I should have felt guilty, too, because I'm the reason she's so unhappy." Then, to my surprise, John stood up and said, "I can't do this. It's not going to work. I'm sorry."

I asked John to stay with us for a few more minutes and explore his feelings. He sat down reluctantly, and I asked him to talk about the powerful emotions that were making him want to flee the room. "I'm not feeling anything," he said. "It's like there's this barrel around my chest and nothing can get out of it. I've tried to feel and I can't. Nothing gets in and nothing gets out."

John's discomfort was so intense he had a hard time staying for the remaining minutes of the session. He wanted out of the chair, out of my office, out of his marriage. His wife's pressure on him to express his feelings and my unwitting collusion with her were almost more than he could bear.

HOW BOYS ARE TAUGHT TO SUPPRESS THEIR EMOTIONS

As I began to work with an increasing number of male clients, I discovered that a majority of them were emotionally blocked. It took them months to display the same openness that most women revealed in their first few sessions. Even then the men's emotional range was more restricted. Their thoughts and feelings seemed to be dampened by their intellect. It's as if they were living life from the neck up.

Why are so many men repressed? I was talking with two men the other day and one of them said, "I've been mad, scared, or numb since the day I was born." The other commented, "I've been lonely and isolated all my life." To them it seemed as if their emotional problems were evident at birth. I assured them that, when they were born, they were emotionally whole, just like all other babies. A few weeks ago I spent an afternoon with a seven-month-old baby boy and his mother. I found myself fascinated by the little boy's expressiveness. His face was constantly in motion, reflecting everything that was happening in him and to him. A gas bubble, a hunger pang, the comfort of being held, the fear he felt when his mother handed him to me while she answered the phone, the relief he felt when she came back to reclaim him—all of these sensations and emotions registered instantly on his face. He didn't filter his thoughts or stuff his feelings.

Most babies are allowed to be free with their emotions until they are around one year old. Then about the time they begin to walk and talk, their parents start to clamp down on them. The degree to which parents repress their children varies from household to household, but there are some overall patterns. In our culture parents tend to discourage so-called "negative emotions" such as fear, sadness, and anger. We harbor a naïve belief that if we can make our children *act* happy and well behaved, they will become truly happy and well-adjusted adults.

To some degree this management of emotions applies to both sexes. When boys or girls show feelings that their parents deem inappropriate or that threaten to reveal the dysfunctional nature of the family, their parents find some way to stifle them. Parents do this in a variety of ways. Depending on their parenting style they may ignore their children ("Go play with your toys"); contradict them ("You do *not* hate your baby sister"); invalidate them ("There's no way you could be feeling sad on such a sunny day"); shame them ("When you cry like that, you sound like your baby sister"); ridicule them ("If you stick your lower lip out any farther, you'll trip on it"); "educate" them ("Yes, you *do* want to share that with your brother. Some day he will be your best friend"); bribe them ("Please stop crying, honey. Want a cookie?"): distract them ("Did that big doggy scare you? Look, there's a bird!"); punish them ("How *dare* you look at me that way! Go to your room!") or physically abuse them ("All right young man! You're going to get the belt!").

It is the rare child who is not subjected to some form of parental repression. But as a rule, little boys are required to restrict even more of their emotions than little girls. Men in this society are assigned three traditional roles: providing, protecting, and procreating.[1] In order to fulfill those roles little boys are required to repress more of their emotions. Our culture maintains—and rightly so—that men are more efficient workers and warriors when they are not inconvenienced by tender feelings. To this end boys are raised according to a masculine code, a complex set of beliefs that influences how they think, feel, and behave. The masculine code is not taught through institutional or

1. I first read about these three terms in David Gilmore, *Manhood in the Making* (New Haven: Yale University Press, 1990).

formal means. Boys learn how to be men by absorbing the thousands of messages about manliness that filter down to them through parents, siblings, peers, ministers, teachers, scout leaders, comic books, cartoons, TV shows, action movies, and commercials. Taken as a whole these messages encourage boys to be competitive, focus on external success, rely on their intellect, withstand physical pain, and repress their vulnerable emotions. When boys violate the code, it is not uncommon for them to be teased, shamed, or ridiculed. Society's goal is not to cause emotional injury to the boys but to harden them to face the difficulties men have always had to face.

MEN AS PROVIDERS

Of the three traditional masculine roles, providing and protecting demand the most stoicism. As a provider a man is the primary supporter of the family. He rarely has the luxury of working when it pleases him or selecting only those tasks he enjoys. The weather, the economy, or his boss dictates what he does, when he works, and how long he toils. Historically men have had to put aside what they really wanted to do and spend most of their waking hours providing for their families. This has required them to shut down their senses, dampen their emotions, and focus on the task at hand. This fiercely channeled masculine energy has built our railroads, logged our forests, tilled the soil, and forged the steel that has made this country a world power.

Most men today expend even more energy in the role of provider than is required for their family's survival. Having bought into the cultural notion that external success is the manly road to happiness and security, they do whatever is required to hone a competitive edge. In order to gain power, status, and wealth, they unwittingly sacrifice their leisure, their health, and their love relationships. All too many men follow an exaggerated version of the Puritan work ethic, which leaves them exhausted and emotionally drained.

Traditionally women have also had to work long and hard in their age-old roles as wives and mothers. As much or even more than men, they've been required to put aside their own desires and tend to the needs of others. They, too, have rarely been able to do what they wanted, when they wanted. But there is a fundamental difference between a woman's traditional role in the family and a man's traditional role as provider—a difference that has had profound consequences for both sexes. Historically a woman's role in the family has required her to be *emotionally responsive.* One of her time-honored functions is to monitor the feelings of family members and create strong family ties. She pays as much attention to the ebb and flow of relationships as a fishermen pays to the tides. Her role in the family may exhaust her and leave her little or no time for herself, but for the most part it allows her to express a wide range of feelings. She can cry, show compassion, display tenderness, reveal her weaknesses, ask for help, and broadcast her joy—emotions that few men would feel comfortable displaying in the workplace.

Many women today play a dual role in society, working both inside and outside the home. As they make this transition, they may be required to adopt a more masculine posture on the job. Mimicking male values and behaviors is regarded by many as the best way for women to succeed in a male-dominated workplace. But when a woman opens the door to the family home at night, she immediately becomes the emotional hub of the family. The fact that she leads two lives may deplete her energy reserves, but it has not seemed to diminish her capacity to feel. Now, as always, women have the luxury of greater emotional wholeness.

MEN AS PROTECTORS

It is the role of protector that has taken the greatest toll on men. Throughout history and in virtually every culture, people have relied upon men to protect them because of men's superior size and strength and because of their testosterone-fueled aggressive nature. To fulfill this crucial role men have been required to hide their fear and display tremendous courage. The primary function of the masculine code is to create this warrior mentality.

I got a renewed appreciation for the rationale behind the masculine code when I spoke recently with David C. Mossman, a World War II veteran who was a second-class gunner's mate on the light cruiser USS *Detroit* during the Japanese attack on Pearl Harbor. His ability to mask his fear allowed him to perform his duties and safeguard the lives of his men throughout the devastating battle.

There was chaos aboard the *Detroit* at the beginning of the surprise attack, and Mossman had to struggle to maintain order. He had seven recruits directly under him—young men in their late teens who had seen only four days of active duty. They'd had only one loading drill, and now they were in the midst of a war. Although Mossman was only twenty-two himself, he had four years of military experience. He said, "I looked at these kids and realized I was their security blanket. I had to act like a machine. If I allowed any feelings to come up, I might crack up—and so would they."

Minutes into the attack an airplane crashed into the water right next to the *Detroit*. The concussion of the blast flung Mossman across the deck. He was slammed into one object after another. When he finally came to rest, he was numb from the neck down. At first he was afraid to look down at his body to see the extent of the damage. His initial concern wasn't about dying or being maimed—it was about losing control. He said, "I was afraid that if I looked down and saw that I was ripped in two, I was going to scream. I didn't want to panic the boys." Sensation slowly returned to his body, and he was able to get back into the fight, setting an example for his frightened gun crew.

His efforts to keep his men from losing their nerve suffered a setback later that evening. The captain came on the public address system to deliver a chilling message: "All men topside. I want you to take a good look at the sunset. Few of you will live to see the sunrise. This ship was not built for modern warfare and it will not stand up to modern warfare. But we will attack and continue to attack until we are sunk."

The captain's dire announcement fanned the fears of his crewmen. Throughout the long night that followed, the young men came to Mossman one by one, desperate for reassurance. Although Mossman was exhausted, in pain, and fearful for his own life, he was able to joke with the boys and keep up their spirits.

Throughout history we have called upon men to show this rare courage, not only in wartime but during times of disaster. I read an account of the sinking of the *Titanic* and learned how bravely many of the men went down to their death. There were only enough lifeboats on the ship for half of the passengers, and as tradition decrees, women and children were evacuated first. Once the lifeboats were filled, the men who remained on the liner had an hour to contemplate their death as the huge liner slowly filled with ice-cold seawater. One man, declaring he was going to die "like a gentleman," went to his stateroom and put on his tuxedo. A group of four men retired to their cabin for a final hand of cards. It is this ability to conceal fear and endure what needs to be endured that we have long admired—and cultivated—in men.

At the end of my conversation with Mossman, I asked him how he had managed to act so bravely. He told me he'd been taught by both his father and his older brother: "My father reminded me over and over that the mark of a man is his ability to control his emotions. And I wanted very, very much to be a man in my father's eyes." His brother, Fritz, taught him not to cry out in pain. Whenever Mossman hurt himself and Fritz was around, Fritz would squeeze his arm and say, "Don't cry, Dave. Don't make a sound. Bite your teeth, bite 'em hard. Don't ever cry." Mossman said that when he was lying on the deck of the *Detroit* paralyzed from the crash of the plane, it was the thought of his brother that helped him maintain his stoicism: "I knew Fritz would want to know how I died," he said. "I didn't want him to hear that I'd lost control."

BOOT CAMP BEGINS AT HOME

Most men have gone through an indoctrination similar to the one Mossman received from his father and brother. Whether or not they were ever called upon to fight in World War II, Korea, Vietnam, or the Persian Gulf; whether or not they have had to perform any of those dangerous and difficult deeds that men have long been required to do—face the rigors of life at sea, protect the homestead from marauders, mow a field of hay in the blistering sun, track down predatory animals—they were raised by the same masculine code. Even if the only hardship they face is struggling to support a family during a recession or going through the pain of divorce, they have learned to "take it like a man." War or no war, men are trained to face the world with masculine stoicism punctuated by an occasional flare-up of rage.

As in Mossman's case boot camp begins at home. At a recent Wildman Gathering I asked the men to reveal some of the messages they had received about manliness from their fathers or brothers. The responses came quickly:

"Don't feel."
"Big boys don't cry."
"You have nothing to cry about."
"Think out your problems."
"That didn't hurt."
"Get that look off your face."
"Tough it out."
"If you don't stop crying, I'll really give you something to cry about."
"Stop your whining."
"For God's sakes, get yourself under control."
"Use your brain."
"Stop being a sissy."
"You're acting just like your sister. Should we put a dress on you?"

But a boy doesn't have to be the target of caustic remarks such as these to be persuaded to "act like a man." The most powerful lessons are taught by example. Said one man, "My father didn't have to say a damn thing. I just looked at my mother and father and I got the picture: women feel; men don't."

As this man observed, all a little boy has to do to grow up to be a stoic man is to be raised by a stoic father. Imagine this exchange between a well-meaning but repressed father and his six-year-old son. The little boy is awakened in the middle of the night by a crash of thunder. He runs to his parents' room for comfort. His father tries to reassure him. He touches the little boy on the shoulder and says, "Hey, little man, don't cry. You're getting too old to cry. It's only thunder. There's nothing to be afraid of. If you'll stop crying, I'll explain some things about lightning."

This father is doing his best to allay his son's fear of the storm. But unwittingly he's teaching him to ignore his feelings—even to fear them. The message that filters down to the boy is this: "If you want to earn my respect, you have to stop crying and hide your fear. I am proud of you when you hide your feelings. If you don't stop crying, I may get upset with you and send you back to your room."

Virtually every little boy in this situation will stifle his tears, because if he continues to cry, he fears he will lose his father's protection. He discounts his own reality in favor of his father's. When this happens over and over again, voluntary *su*ppression turns into involuntary *re*pression, and the boy grows up feeling just as numb as a child who has had his feelings shamed or bullied out of him.

Recently I told the anecdote about the little boy and the thunderstorm to the men in one of my therapy groups. One man said, "So what should a father do? He can't just let the boy cry." Like many of us he was so used to the notion that "big boys don't cry" that he couldn't imagine a different way of handling the situation. I volunteered that a father who was less repressed might have acted quite differently. First, he might have gathered his son in his arms and reassured him he was safe: "Daddy is here to protect you. The thunder won't hurt you." Then he might have validated his fear: "That *was* a loud noise, wasn't it? When I was a little boy, I was scared of the thunder, too. I'm not afraid anymore, but I can remember when I was." Then he might have held and rocked his son until he stopped crying of his own accord. Finally, if the boy still needed comforting, he might have taken him back to his room and sat beside him until he calmed down. In this way the father would have acknowledged his son's feelings and given him permission to express them. The boy would eventually learn that tears are not a source of shame—they're a natural response to fear and a built-in way to relieve stress.

However, few boys in this culture grow up with such enlightened fathers. Their fathers and their fathers before them learned to repress emotions at an early age. They were taught to be tough, not to flinch, to keep a stiff upper lip, to shoulder a heavy weight, to be a shoulder to lean on, to pick themselves up by the bootstraps, to tighten up, to stop their bellyaching, to be a "real man." It's only natural that they pass on this hard-earned legacy to their sons.

If for some reason a boy escapes this indoctrination at home, he is likely to be given remedial lessons in manhood from the guys on the block. This can be even more devastating to a child, because peers socialize with the subtlety of a sledgehammer. If a ten-year-old boy cries on the playground, his friends may call him a sissy or a "girl." If he picks a bunch of flowers, they may call him a "queer." If he refuses to jump off a garage, they may taunt him for being "yellow" or a "scaredy cat." There seems to be a built-in injunction that if you were not allowed to express your own feelings, you can't tolerate them in others. I remember being in junior high school and watching a group of bullies surround a younger boy who was more sensitive and bookish than the others. They were calling him a "momma's boy." As the circle tightened around the boy, the most macho member of the group began slapping him in the face. I remember being grateful that I wasn't in the center of that cruel initiation, that I had developed my own "mask-ulinity" years before.

LIVING IN THE MAN BOX

Few men are aware of the extent of their gender conditioning. It's too subtle and all-pervasive for them to see. To help the men in my groups gain more insight I tell them that it is as if society requires them to live in a box labeled MAN. Scrawled on the outside of the MAN BOX are dozens of rules: "Compete." "Succeed." "Perform." "Don't feel." "Don't reveal any weakness." "Get a grip." "Tough it out." "Ignore your physical symptoms." "Win at all costs." "Have all the answers." "Fix the problem." And so on and so forth. Some of these directives work to their advantage. For example, their gender conditioning re-wards them for being tough, uncomplaining, and courageous—quali-ties that can help them succeed in life. But others go against their very nature and wound them psychologically and spirtually. Nevertheless, "real men" are trained and conditioned to stay in the box.

In fact, society has done its best to convince men that staying in the box is not only a duty but a privilege. Because they were born male, they are rewarded with higher-paying jobs, greater chances for ad-vancement, domestic privileges, and more political power. If for some reason a man begins to examine the hidden price of his social advan-tage and dares to poke his head outside of the MAN BOX, people begin to question his masculinity.

Women also live in a box. Their box, labeled WOMAN, has its own rules written all over the sides. "Don't compete." "Nurture." "Smile." "Be nice." "A woman's place is in the home." "Cooperate." "If you're not married by twenty-five you're an old maid." "Put other people's needs first." "Don't be smarter than a man." "Children are a woman's greatest fulfillment." "Act like a lady." "Stand by your man." And on and on. But in the past few decades women have managed to punch gaping holes in the sides of the WOMAN BOX. They have obliterated many of the old rules and modified others. Today a woman's place is not only in the house but the Senate. She presides over the kitchen and the Supreme Court. She nurtures her children and runs a small business. Although many women are burdened by the multiplicity of their roles, there is air circulating inside the WOMAN BOX that is allowing them greater freedom.

To some degree watching women rewrite their gender conditioning has allowed men to question the cost/benefit ratio of the masculine code. Men are finally beginning to see that the patriarchal system that has long oppressed women, children, and the planet Earth has also been oppressing them.

The reason it has taken men so long to see the negative effects of the masculine code is that male and female gender conditioning operate in different spheres. A woman's gender conditioning limits her activities, her "doings" in the world; it disenfranchises and disempowers her. By contrast, a man's gender conditioning inhibits his emotions, his "being" in the world.[2] In exchange for the mantle of privilege, he is required to repress many of the emotions that might expose his vulnerability. The masculine code may make him a deadly fighter; it may grant him power and privilege; it may give him access to the Senate, the boardroom, and the presidency. But it can also destroy his health, his healthy anger, his empathy, his sensitivity, his compassion, and his joy. It decreases the pleasure he finds in his daily life and keeps him isolated and alone.

THE "ISOLATED MALE"—THE PRICE OF MASCULINE PRIVILEGE

One of the ironclad rules written on the MAN BOX is "Big boys don't cry." This key part of the masculine code keeps men from showing their vulnerability in dangerous and tense situations. It makes them appear to be formidable foes. But it also prevents them from dealing with the serious losses that come their way, such as a divorce or the death of a family member. Although few people today would fault a

2. I first heard this concept explained by Roy Schenk in an audiotape of one of his lectures, titled "The War of the Sexes."

man for shedding tears in these situations, many men find themselves unable to do it. Because they've suppressed their grief over and over again, they have lost the ability to *experience* grief. Feelings of sorrow don't well up in them when they should. Their feelings are blocked off at the source like a spring that's run dry. It's not unusual for a man to go to his mother's funeral on Saturday and be back to work on Monday, never having dealt with the loss. Many of my male clients have told me they haven't cried since they were little boys. They've repressed the pain of all of their hardships since they were four or five years old.

Tragically, when a man suppresses his vulnerable emotions, he also deadens his capacity for joy. It's not possible to surrender part of the psyche and leave the rest intact. It's like going to the dentist to have your tooth filled. In order to stop the pain of one tooth, the dentist has to numb the whole side of your jaw. Similarly, a man who intends to numb just his fear and grief blunts his other emotions as well. This leads to what I call the Isolated Male Syndrome, which is the inability to understand or even be aware of the feelings of others. A man who suffers from the syndrome finds it hard to sympathize with his wife when she cries. He does his best to understand her problems with his rational mind, but it's as if they were on separate planes; they can't connect. When his children are upset, he either ignores them, minimizes their feelings, or rushes in and tries to fix their problems. He can't identify with their pain. When his friends are having a rough time, he finds it hard to empathize. His own formula for dealing with emotional problems is to ignore them, so he ignores his friends' problems as well. Such a man may be a good person to have around when a ship is going down, but he can be a difficult man to have as a husband, a father, or a friend.

Stuart—Living Life in an Emotional Coma

Most of the men I see in therapy display some elements of the Isolated Male Syndrome. Stuart, a forty-seven-year-old pharmacist, is a testimony to how barren life can become when a man loses his ability to feel.

Stuart came to see me because his wife had convinced him he needed therapy. I saw him individually for a few sessions. He told me he had

gone for years without having a discernible feeling. I found this difficult to believe, but he maintained it was true. "I'm just not a very
emotional person," he said. As the weeks went by, I learned that he
had no hobbies and no friends whom he saw on a regular basis. "What
do you do for fun?" I asked. He said that he and his wife played bridge
twice a month and that he watched TV.

I encouraged Stuart to join one of my men's groups. In the group he
displayed many of the narcissistic qualities that people have come to
associate with men: it took him months to learn everyone's name, even
though there were only nine other men in the group; he had a habit of
interrupting other people while they were still talking; he didn't listen
very carefully when the other men talked. All he seemed to care about
was himself. But underneath these self-centered behaviors Stuart was
a good, kindhearted man. It's just that he was so out of touch with his
feelings he found it impossible to empathize with others. Like many
men, his emotional connection with the outside world was so tenuous
that he was slow to pick up on social cues.

For a few months Stuart continued to seem emotionally dead. Even
though he was having a lot of marital problems, he didn't appear to be
bothered by them. One evening he told us about a particularly cruel
comment his wife had made to him, but he delivered the story in his
customary flat tone of voice. He displayed no reaction whatsoever to
the verbal abuse.

In frustration I asked Stuart if the rest of us could show him how we
felt about his wife's remark. He said we could. At the count of three,
we all bellowed out in anger. Stuart was stunned by our reaction. What
was there to get so upset about? His wife said things like that to him
all the time. He'd gotten used to it. But I could see that Stuart was
pleased by our response. It must have been gratifying to him to have
such vocal allies in his twenty-five-year battle with his wife.

During the next few sessions Stuart brought up similar cutting remarks from his wife, and we obliged him by dramatizing our reactions.
However, after we had acted out Stuart's feelings for him for five
sessions I told him that the group was no longer going to play that role.
If he wanted his emotions, he was going to have to express them
himself. The next week Stuart was able to summon up a few angry
feelings about his wife, but his response seemed mechanical, almost as
if he were mimicking our reactions. He surprised us a few weeks later

by picking up the plastic bat that was stationed in the middle of the group and landing several hard blows on the pillow. There was genuine anger flowing through his body. We cheered him on.

Stuart's next step, standing up to his wife, took another couple of months. Before coming to the group his only defense against her had been to complain in a meek tone of voice. He didn't have enough angry energy to gain her respect. One night he finally worked up the courage to blurt out to her exactly how he felt. He said, "I won't have you talking to me that way. It makes me really angry." He told us that, as he said those words to her, he was feeling fear as well as anger. That was one of the first times he had ever confronted her directly. But when he described the encounter to us, there was a grin on his face. He was coming alive.

Stuart had a twenty-year-old son who was away at college. As he inched his way out of his shell, he decided to visit his son and ask him what it had been like to have him as a father. His son was glad to talk to him, but what he had to say hurt Stuart to the quick. "Dad," he said, "I don't want to hurt your feelings . . . but you were never there."

"What do you mean?" he said. "I was there every evening. I never went anywhere!"

"I know, Dad," he said, "but it was like there was nothing to you. You never got mad. If you were ever sad, I never knew it. You never seemed happy. You were like a zombie. I didn't know who you were. You were like a stranger to me. I hate to say this, but most of the time I felt like I didn't have a father."

When Stuart related this conversation to us, he broke down in tears, which was the first time he had cried in over forty years. "Can you believe it?" he asked. "I was there every damn day of his life, and he felt I was invisible."

Eventually Stuart got past his dismay over his son's revelation and went through a surge of emotional growth. He seemed like a man coming out of a coma trying to make up for lost time. He joined an outdoor club and went on weekly hikes. He took his son white-water rafting and deep-sea fishing. But mixed in with the joy of his recovery was a great deal of bitterness. He told us one night, "I'm so angry. So much of my life has been wasted. And what I really regret is that I've hurt my son—not because I ever did anything mean, but because there was so little inside of me for him to see."

HOW THE MASCULINE CODE FRUSTRATES A MAN'S CHANCES FOR SUCCESS

Ironically, when a man rigidly follows the masculine code, he not only isolates himself from his family and friends, he also reduces his chances for financial success. At first glance it would seem that living in the MAN BOX would only enhance a man's ability to succeed at work. The mere fact of being a man gives him easier access to high-paying jobs, upper levels of management, bank loans, the boardroom, and the Good Ol' Boy Network. It's one of the many advantages of being born male. On top of that, his gender conditioning trains him to compete, work hard, postpone gratification, ignore the feelings of others, and, if necessary, jettison his relationships in the pursuit of power, money, and prestige. Being a "man's man" appears to be the ideal recipe for financial success. *But although a man's gender conditioning may give him numerous advantages in the business world, it also limits the amount of functional intelligence he brings to his work.*

Ultimately, what helps a man succeed at his job goes beyond how easily he can borrow money, how hard he works, or how well he can network. What he needs most of all is "functional intelligence," which I define as the ability to see a wide range of options and choose the most suitable solution in any given situation. A man's gender conditioning narrows his field of vision, obscuring all those choices that are not in line with the masculine code.

I had a chance to see to what degree this masculine myopia can interfere with a man's work life when Ray joined one of my groups. Ray was reeling from a one-two punch. Both his marriage and his plumbing-supply business had collapsed in the previous year. Part of the reason his business went under was that he had had a dispute with his partner, and his partner had taken most of the assets and left him with all of the bills. Ray put in a year's worth of grueling, seventy-hour weeks to try to recover from the debacle, but he wasn't able to make up for the loss. His twenty-year-old business failed.

Shortly after he had to close the doors on his business, his wife left him, complaining that he had walled himself off from her. She knew he was going through a hard time, but she was fed up with his unwillingness to communicate. The more upset he became about his business, the more he would drink and the less he would talk to her. She was tired of living with a shell of a man.

In the group Ray slowly gained some perspective on both the collapse of his marriage and the failure of his business. He saw for the first time that he had had a wide range of options in dealing with his marital problems. When he realized his wife was deeply upset, he could have: (1) suggested marriage counseling, (2) read a book on relationship skills, (3) asked a friend for advice, (4) started sharing more of his feelings with her, or (5) numbed his feelings with alcohol and retreated into himself. He chose option number five, the manly choice. His gender conditioning had kept him from showing his pain, asking for help, and confiding in others.

He'd had a similar range of options in his business dealings. At the first sign of financial trouble, he could have: (1) hired a business consultant, (2) sold the business and tried something new, (3) gotten a loan and reorganized the business, (4) asked his employees for their suggestions, or (5) tried to solve his problems by resorting to the "work, work, work" ethic. Choice number five had loomed large in front of him. Keeping him from seeing all his other options was a series of masculine platitudes: "Don't admit you need help." "Do it yourself." "Don't let this get the best of you." "Succeed at all costs." "Keep on pushing." Ray had blindly followed the masculine code, which had reduced his functional intelligence and contributed to the failure of his business.

THE HEALTH CONSEQUENCES OF THE MASCULINE CODE

Living in the MAN BOX not only compromises a man's love relationships and interferes with his ability to succeed in business, it can wreak havoc with his health. Millions of men in this country have learned to play hurt on the playing field and to ignore physical pain in their daily lives. I remember a time years ago when I came down with the flu. I was scheduled to paint the interior of an apartment building. I went to work despite the fact that I felt dizzy, was sick to my stomach, and had a high fever. I managed to paint for an hour before I was too weak to stand up. Then, instead of going home to bed, I scooted along on the floor and painted the baseboards.

It was stupid for me to work when I was feeling that sick, but it didn't kill me. I was a young, healthy man filled with ambition. But when a man abuses his body year after year, the consequences can be deadly. The plight of two middle-aged men, Bob Edwards and Don Earley, was recently aired on the television news program *20/20*. Both men had refused to see a doctor despite ominous warning signs. Bob had ignored frequent chest pains, and Don had refused to acknowledge the telltale signs of colon cancer. Both men chose to tough it out, ignoring the urgent messages from their bodies and the pleas of their wives. The words they used to explain their reluctance to seek medical help came right off the sides of the MAN BOX. Bob said to the interviewer, "You are the man. You are the person. You can't be sick. You cannot let yourself be sick. That's weak. You can't be sick. You've got to work, work, work. You have to run that business." Echoed Don, "I feel as if I'm almost indestructible. I just can't get sick. If I get sick, I took care of it myself."

Dr. Georgia Witkin, an assistant professor of psychiatry at Mt. Sinai Medical School, was also interviewed on the program. She summarized the results of her research into why so many men avoid medical care: "Many men told me they actually feel shame when they have physical symptoms. They feel they have allowed their lives to get beyond their control. They haven't been taking care of business the way they should have. So they hide their symptoms." Men are not only supposed to control their emotions, they're supposed to control their physical symptoms as well.

It is amazing how tenaciously these two particular men denied their illnesses. Don, the man with the colon cancer, refused to go to the doctor despite the fact that he had chills and fever for six long weeks. His wife pleaded with him to get help: "Do I have to watch you lie here and die?"

When the interviewer asked Don if his symptoms had ever worried him he said, "Yes. But I still put it to the back of my mind, you know." When he finally sought medical help, the doctors discovered he had a malignant tumor in his colon. They operated to remove the tumor and found that the cancer had spread to his liver. Don's liver cancer may be too advanced to respond to treatment.

Bob was equally determined to ignore his chest pains. He said, "You watch it on TV and you see them say football players and basketball players have got to play hurt. Well, that doesn't matter if you're in a sport or in everyday life. You have to play hurt."

Bob succeeded in ignoring his pain until he had a mild heart attack. It was a wake-up call, but not one he was willing to heed. He followed his doctor's orders for "about three days. I took the medicine, then you're back to the same routine. And you just go." Taking care of business was more important to him than taking care of his health. Four years after his initial heart attack Bob had a much more severe one. His wife rushed him to the hospital and he lay in the backseat of the car, rolling from side to side with pain.

The heart specialists at the hospital discovered that Bob's heart condition had deteriorated so much since his first heart attack that they recommended immediate bypass surgery. Bob survived the heart attack and the surgery and then began the slow process of recovery. Sadly, it took him so long to get back on his feet and to recover from the depression that followed the heart attack that he was forced to declare bankruptcy. His "work, work, work" ethic had cost him his business and had nearly cost him his life. As the *20/20* camera crew filmed him wandering around the vacant building of his concrete business he said, "There's nothing left but me and a lot of memories. That's all."

Both men would have had a much better prognosis if they had gone to a doctor at the first sign of illness. But like so many millions of men, Bob and Don were unable to acknowledge their physical weaknesses or admit they needed help. The rules of the masculine code were like so many coffin nails shutting them into the BOX.

Victoria: The Heartache of Living with a Repressed Man

A man's gender conditioning influences every sphere of his life, including his quest for health, wealth, and happiness. It can also take a toll on every member of his family. Recently I had a poignant reminder of how much a man's emotional isolation can distress his wife. I was on a wide-bodied jet flying home from a Wildman Gathering I had held in Seattle. I was sitting next to a good-looking, well-dressed woman in her early forties. The woman had a beautiful and regal name, so I'll call her Victoria. A few minutes into the flight Victoria noticed I was reading a book on relationship therapy. She asked me if I was a therapist or if I was having trouble in a relationship. "Both," I said, and we laughed.

At first glance she seemed demure and emotionally fragile, so I was surprised by her eagerness to talk with me. She asked if I worked with couples, and I said yes, but that I worked primarily with men. She told me in a confidential tone of voice that she had been a battered wife for ten years before she had finally broken away from her first husband. After working to rebuild her self-esteem she had fallen in love with her current husband, Herb. "Herb's a really good man," she said. "He treats me really nice, and he's never even touched me in anger. I was so lucky to find him."

Despite her words of praise, I sensed some hidden pain. A struggle welled up inside me. I was tired and didn't want to be her therapist, but I didn't want to close her out entirely. She seemed to need to talk. I decided to create an opening. "I'm glad you got yourself out of that abusive relationship," I said. "And how lucky for you to be married to a good man. You must be a happy woman."

"Oh, yes. I'm very happy," she said. "It's just that . . ." she paused, and I almost knew what she was going to say, ". . . it's just that my husband is so busy I seem to find myself alone quite a bit. I know he loves me. It's not that. Not at all. It's just that he's gone so often, I don't get to be with him as much as I'd like. And when he's home, he's always talking on the phone or working on the computer." She explained that Herb owned and operated four pizza parlors, and that kept him very busy.

I asked her what it was like when they did spend time together. She lowered her voice even further. "Well, it's nice, but Herb doesn't talk all that much, so I never really know what's going through his head."

"Does he show his feelings around you?" I asked.

"What do you mean?" she asked.

"Well, does he ever laugh out loud, or get sad and cry, or get angry or things like that?"

"Oh, no! Not Herb. He's steady as a rock," she said proudly.

"Doesn't that bother you, that he doesn't show any feelings?"

"I guess I never thought about it that way before."

She leaned back in her seat and was quiet for a few minutes. Then she touched my shoulder. "Marvin," she whispered, "could I ask you just one more question?"

"Sure," I said.

"I feel so guilty and selfish saying this . . ." I looked at her and saw her eyes were bright with gathering tears, ". . . but I feel so all alone in this world. I feel so very, very lonely. What I want to know is, what's wrong with me that I could feel this way and have a husband who's so nice to me and takes care of me in so many ways?"

I took a deep breath, and hoping I was doing the right thing, tiptoed deeper into the dark, unhappy waters.

"Victoria," I said, "you keep saying your husband is nice to you. How is he nice to you?"

Now the tears broke loose and slid down her cheeks, taking some of her mascara with them.

"He shows his love by buying me things," she said. "That's how he's always done it. He's very generous. And when I ask him if he loves me, he says, 'Of course I do.' But somehow, even when he's around, I still feel lonely. I finally told him how I was feeling and asked if maybe we could spend more time together. He said I sounded depressed and that I should go to our doctor. The doctor gave me something to help my moods and something to help me sleep. The pills helped, but they weren't enough. Then Herb got the idea that I needed to find something to keep me busy, so you know what he did?" She broke into a smile. "Last year, for my forty-second birthday, he surprised me by buying me my own pizza parlor to manage. Can you believe that?" Her tears had stopped and she wiped away the mascara with a tissue. "Since I've had the pizza parlor, I've stayed busier and I don't have as much time to be lonely. And now Herb and I have something to talk about. We compare notes on our profits. I guess things will work out for the best. I hope so."

She took my hand and squeezed it. "You are such a good listener," she said. "Thanks for letting me cry on your shoulder."

I smiled and wished her well.

For the rest of the flight and for several days afterward I thought about Victoria and all the suffering that goes on in the world because so many men have lost the ability to feel.

ADDING UP THE COST OF THE MASCULINE CODE

As I lecture around the country, I discover that many people, men and women alike, fail to understand the far-reaching effects of male gender conditioning. They ask me, "What are men complaining about?" "Don't they have all the power and privilege?" "So what if men can't cry?" They don't get it.

I explain that a man's inability to feel is not just a momentary inconvenience that keeps him from crying at sad movies. His repressed state impoverishes his life from the moment he wakes up in the morning until he falls asleep at night. He finds it difficult to create a close, lasting love relationship. He remains distant from his children. He jeopardizes his health. He fails to see all his options at work. If he manages to succeed at his job, the success fails to bring him pleasure. When he takes time off from work, he can't glory in the beauty of the world around him. When there's a tragedy in his life, he can't grieve. Each emotional injury is added to the one that precedes it. Much of his life he feels as if he were roaming around on a flat, gray landscape without color or texture. He finds little pleasure in his daily activities and, tragically, has no idea where to look for it.

In the next chapter I talk about a problem common to most men—the inability to express their healthy anger. For many men, anger is one of the few emotions left in their tool kit, but they don't use it appropriately. They either fly into a rage or become passive and ineffective. As you will see, anger problems are more troubling to many men than their inability to experience fear or grief.

CHAPTER 2

ANGRY MEN/PASSIVE MEN:
The Kick Ass/Kiss Ass Syndrome

The men I've worked with across the country have had a wide range of emotional difficulties, but some problems have struck me as close to universal. For example, most of the men have had problems with intimacy: their relationships with their wives, girlfriends, parents, and children were either perplexing or painful to them. A majority of men have had problems with work: they either felt imprisoned by their jobs, worked too compulsively, or were frustrated by their inability to reach their goals. And a large number of men have been struggling with some form of addictive or compulsive behavior, whether to alcohol, drugs, sex, sports, food, or TV.

But virtually every man I've ever worked with has had problems with anger. The problem has been manifested in one of two totally opposite ways: either the men have had difficulty controlling their anger, which has made them frighten or alienate the people around them; or they have had difficulty *expressing* their anger, which has rendered them passive and ineffective. I call this the Kick Ass/Kiss Ass Syndrome. It is the rare man who is strong and assertive when necessary but keeps his anger from bubbling over into destructive rage.

In an effort to understand why so many men have anger problems researchers have been examining the role played by male hormones. In a study of a group of adolescent boys researchers found that boys with high levels of testosterone reacted more vigorously to provocations and threats. They also were more impatient and irritable than boys with more normal levels.[1] A related study of over four thousand men demonstrated that high levels of testosterone were associated with delinquency, drug use, promiscuity, conduct disorders, abusiveness, and violence. It could be that many men with out-of-control anger have higher levels of certain hormones.

But it's not just hormones that create male violence. Our culture plays a supporting role. "Might makes right" is one of the rules written in bold letters on the MAN BOX. From early childhood many little boys are taught that violence is the male solution. Their fathers tell them to beat up on neighborhood bullies. Their mothers heap their Christmas stockings with guns, missiles, and military action figures. I was at a toy store last December and happened to see a formative scene between a mother and her little boy. The boy appeared to be about four years old. He had slipped away from his mother and was sitting in an electric car. I watched him happily spin the wheel on the car and make sputtering engine noises. I smiled to myself as I remembered how much I used to enjoy playing with cars. Suddenly his mother spotted him. "What are you doing in that car?" she cried out in alarm. "That's a girl's car!" I looked more closely and saw that the car was a white sedan with a Barbie doll logo on the side. "Are you a girl?" his mother taunted. "Here," she said, pulling her son by the arm and dragging him toward a camouflaged jeep. "This is a *boy's* car. This is a G.I. Joe Jeep. Do you want to be a girl?" The little boy looked shamed and confused. His sense of joy had evaporated.

That encounter took place almost a year ago. My guess is that by now the little boy has learned to steer clear of white and pink and gravitate toward the black, green, and beige toys. This is but one small example of how parents fan the flames of stereotypical male conditioning, pushing their sons toward competition and aggression.

The lessons that a boy gets about violence from his family are

1. Olweus et al., "Circulating Testosterone Levels and Aggression in Adolescent Males: A Causal Analysis," *Psychosomatic Medicine,* 50 (1988):pp. 261–72.

reinforced by the media. A grade school boy wakes up on Saturday morning and turns on the TV. He sees more violent incidents per hour on cartoon shows than on any other kind of program on television. After lunch he watches a rerun of a cowboy show. He watches the cowboy wearing the white hat slug the cowboy wearing the black hat. The cowboy with the black hat slumps to the floor and is dragged out of the bar by his heels: problem solved. At night he watches still more TV and sees as many as ten to twenty episodes of violence per hour. Over 80 percent of prime-time programs feature men who are involved in some form of violent behavior. When he goes to the movies, he will see yet more violence. Movies have been steadily increasing in violence since the 1930s, neatly paralleling the increase in violent crimes reported in the FBI's Uniform Crime Report.[2] In virtually all the movies and TV shows a boy sees, men are the ones who commit most of the mayhem. In one study, television criminals were 84 percent male and 16 percent female.[3]

The jury is still out on whether violence in the media makes people more violent in real life, but there is mounting evidence that it does. In another study ten preschoolers were divided into pairs. Before playing together one of each pair was shown an aggressive cartoon, the other was shown a nonviolent cartoon. "In all five pairs, the child who observed the aggressive cartoon engaged in more hitting, throwing of objects at others, kicking, and so forth."[4] The same effect has been observed in adult men, but with more dire consequences. David P. Phillips, professor of sociology at the University of California at San Diego, has observed that the homicide rate goes up by as much as 11 percent in the three or four days following a widely televised boxing match. Significantly, if the losing boxer happens to be a black male, the murder of black males increases, but not the murder of white males. If the losing boxer is a white male, the murder of white males goes up, but not that of blacks.[5] It appears that the televised boxing matches are

2. Comstock et al., *Television and Human Behavior* (New York: Columbia University Press, 1978), p. 81.

3. Ibid, p. 40.

4. Ibid., p. 239.

5. Curt Suplee, "Berserk! Violent Employees Obsessed with Revenge," *The Washington Post* (October 1, 1989), p. D10.

providing not only some of the incentive for violence but also the actual script.

Another even more disturbing correlation between violence in the media and violence in real life shows up in extremely violent men. Serial killers, in particular, seem to take careful notes about what they read in the paper and see at the movies. Nathaniel White, a man alleged to have killed six people while on parole, recently told reporters that his murders were inspired by the hit movie *RoboCop*. "The first girl I killed was from a RoboCop movie . . . I seen him cut somebody's throat then take the knife and slit down the chest to the stomach and left the body in a certain position. With the first person I killed I did exactly what I saw in the movie."[6]

Needless to say, the vast majority of men who watch televised fights and action movies do not go out and commit violent acts. But it cannot be denied that the media reinforces the notion that violence is the manly solution. It is interesting to speculate how men's behavior might change if there were more TV shows like *McGiver* in which the protagonist finds creative, nonviolent solutions to problems. What if Hollywood had a sudden change of heart and started producing movies called *Arbitrator II* instead of *Terminator II*? What if Bruce Willis starred in *Tryhard* instead of *Diehard*? One thing is for certain: if boys grew up seeing more of their heroes choosing nonviolent ways to safeguard their lives, protect their property, and defend their honor, they would have a wealth of new options for managing their aggression.

MEN WHO CONFUSE GRIEF WITH ANGER

Society contributes to male violence in a subtler fashion by making it socially unacceptable for men to grieve. When men can't cry over a severe disappointment or loss, they have a tendency to become angry instead. At first it may be hard to understand why men resort to anger to resolve their grief, because the two emotions are entirely different. Anger hardens us and allows us to protect ourselves from harm. Grief

6. "Do Movies Trigger Violent Acts?" by Steve Garbarino. *Newsday*, Monday, August 10, 1992, City Edition, Part II, p. 38

softens us and allows us to accept the injuries we've already sustained. But when a man is not able to cry, he is filled with emotion that is looking for expression, and for some men the only feeling they can access is rage.

I remember a session I had with Henry, a sixty-year-old real-estate broker who was cut off from both his healthy anger and his grief. The work of this particular session focused on an incident that had taken place over the weekend. In a fit of rage, Henry had kicked two large dents in the door of his beloved classic car, a 1956, two-door Chevy hardtop. With a pained expression, he filled me in on the details. A week earlier, he had taken the car to a body shop to have it primed and painted. He had instructed them to use original red and white factory colors. When he went to pick up the car, he saw at a glance that the red was not the original Chevy color. He asked the painter to repaint the car. When he came back the second time, he was furious to see that the painter had ripped the front seat upholstery. It would have to be re-covered. The upholstery had been original fabric in excellent condition and was one of the reasons his car was so valuable. Henry was pushed over the edge. Before he knew what he was doing, he walked up to his car and kicked the door as hard as he could. When he saw the enormous dent he had created he was so enraged that he kicked the door again, creating an even larger dent.

When Henry finished his sad tale I commiserated with him. "I can understand how you feel. I've traveled down that road myself several times. Let's see if we can figure this out. First of all, what or who was the enemy here? Was it your Chevy?"

"No," he said. "It was the goddamn painter. When I looked at the tear in the upholstery, I felt like kicking him. But I had enough sense not to do that. So I took it out on my car."

"What did you eventually say to the painter?" I asked him.

"I called him that afternoon and told him I was taking my car somewhere else. And he would have to pay for re-covering the seat."

"My guess is that you weren't just mad at the painter, you were also mad at yourself. It must have been frustrating to have chosen such an incompetent person to work on your car."

Henry admitted that he had chosen the painter because he had given him the lowest bid. He was also mad at himself for not having expressed his anger to the painter when he had used the wrong color of paint. "I can't be angry at someone without blowing up," he said, "so I tend to underplay my hand. When I look back on it, I don't think the painter really knew how upset I was that first time around. Knowing me, I probably gave him the silent treatment. If I'd showed more authority, he might have taken more care with my car." Henry acknowledged that an ounce of healthy anger might have saved him a pound of rage further on.

"Now, how about your grief?" I asked him. "What did you do with your grief?"

"What grief?" he asked, looking perplexed.

"Your grief over the damage that had been done to the upholstery."

As I said this to Henry, an image flashed through my mind of a time when I was twelve years old and had just lost my last arrow. I had been so angry at myself for losing that arrow that I had broken my precious bow in two over my leg. If I had been able to mourn the loss of the arrow, I wouldn't have had to destroy my bow.

After some discussion Henry was able to see that damage to the upholstery had been a significant loss to him. He loved his car. But like many men, he hadn't been able to express his pain. His anger at the painter, his frustration at himself, and his unexpressed grief had turned into a rampage against his beloved Chevy.

THE DIFFERENCE BETWEEN ANGER AND RAGE

In order to understand why men rage, it's important to understand healthy anger. Anger is a positive emotion that is designed to protect you and those you love from harm. It's a clean, immediate, protective response that tells other people: "You are threatening my well-being." Anger can be likened to an immune system for the psyche. It's always on guard, always ready to be activated whenever there is danger. It's a healthy, natural, life-affirming reaction.

Think for a moment about the animal world. A dog growls at another dog that is trespassing on his property to convey two pieces of information: (1) You're invading my territory, and (2) I don't like it. The dog's anger is evident. His hair is raised, his legs are tense, his teeth are bared, his head is lowered and ready for action. Most dogs will read these signals and make a wise decision to back off. By making a visible show of anger dogs are able to protect their turf much of the time without shedding blood.

The same is true for humans. By showing our displeasure to each other in our speech and body language we protect our boundaries without causing physical harm. Our anger lets other people know what we need, what we want, and how we expect to be treated. It earns us safety, power, and respect. When we show our healthy anger, it's as if we are pulling a sword out of its sheath and showing off its gleaming edges to the would-be intruder. Once the intruder appreciates the fine edge on the blade, we can put the sword back in its sheath. There is rarely a need to go further.

In any discussion of healthy anger it's important to state what anger is *not*. Anger is not malice. It's not revenge. It's not violence. It's not hostility. It's not punishment. It's not rage. Of all these related emotions men seem to have the most difficulty distinguishing between anger and rage. Recently I was giving a talk to seventy-five men, and I asked who would volunteer a definition of the two emotions. One man spoke up. "Anger is when I'm frustrated or annoyed," he said. "Rage is when I'm ready to punch somebody out."

Like this man, most people view anger and rage as points on a continuum: anger is being a little bit mad and rage is being extremely mad. But, in reality, anger and rage are quite different things. Anger is an expression of authority and power, while rage is an expression of hopelessness and helplessness. Men rage when they're boxed in a corner and can't get out. They rage when they're feeling afraid and are too "manly" to show it. They rage when their anger has been ignored. They rage when they've been denied the healthy expression of their anger and have no way to defend themselves. They rage when they're in a desperate situation and are too proud to ask for help. Rage, unlike anger, is not a simple, timely transmission of information; it's an impotent, misguided fury.

When a man's feelings of loss and helplessness are extreme, his grief tends to be expressed as extreme rage. People who work with battered women have observed that a woman is most vulnerable to physical abuse when she makes an attempt to leave a love relationship. Her male partner is driven into a frenzy by the thought of losing her. This year, in my area alone, ten women have been murdered by their husbands or boyfriends. Not long ago, in San Antonio, a man confronted his wife in a cafeteria. "You're coming back with me," he said to her. "No, I'm not," she replied. He pulled out a gun and killed her on the spot. In another incident in west Texas, a man was furious at his ex-wife for moving in with another man. In retaliation he killed his ex-wife's mother, her father, their eighteen-month-old child, her brother, and himself. He left his ex-wife alive so she would have to live in emotional pain for the rest of her life.

Men who abuse their wives are often motivated by feelings of helplessness and grief. On the surface they appear to be powerful and controlling. But underneath they're terrified by the thought of living alone, wounded by the loss of love, too proud to admit their dependency, too self-sufficient to ask for help, too "manly" to cry. The only option left to them is violence. Arlette Ponder, a counselor at the Family Violence Diversion Network in Austin, Texas, works with men who batter their wives. She says that many of the men are "afraid of being alone, afraid of the unknown, afraid to come home to an empty house."

THE FUTILITY OF RAGE

A month ago I ran across a news story that is a tragi-comic illustration of the futility of rage. In a recent one-year period, fourteen people, all of them men, were crushed to death by soft-drink machines. It doesn't take much imagination to figure out what happened. In fourteen separate incidents the men must have plunked a few coins into a soft-drink machine that refused to dispense a drink or relinquish their money. At first the men probably reacted in typical male fashion by muttering to themselves, punching the buttons, and jerking the levers. But they didn't stop there. When the machines continued to defy them the men's frustration escalated into rage. The soft-drink machines had become a symbol of how powerless they felt in their lives. The whole world was rising up against them and had assumed the shape of a Coke machine. The rage created an overwhelming rush of energy that made them kick and pound the machines and scream obscenities. Still no soda and no coins. The kicking became more violent. As the men battered the machines, they realized they were doing more damage to their fists and their feet than they were to the metal casing. In a final rush of fury they grabbed the machines with both hands and rocked them so violently that they tipped them over, crushing themselves to death.

I'm sure there are some of you who have never felt the urge to savage a soft-drink machine, but others of us know exactly how it feels to want to punch a fist through a wall, drive a car into a telephone pole, kick in the TV screen—and yes, manhandle a soft-drink machine. We know the shame of venting our frustration on helpless animals. We know what it's like to project a lifetime of anger onto whatever is frustrating us at the moment—the driver who makes us miss a green light, the secretary who garbles a message, the garbage man who leaves behind a trail of litter. We don't like flying into a rage; it fills us with shame. We have no idea why we do it. All we know is that there are times when we are out of control.

I have battled with rage much of my life. In the past decade or so, after much work, I have been gratified to see that my emotional temperature rarely reaches the boiling point. A few months ago, however, I blew it. It was a day filled with annoying phone calls, broken promises, and agonizing setbacks. After a hurried lunch and an immediate attack of acid indigestion I glumly returned to my office. As I surveyed the chaos on my desk—piles of unanswered mail, half a dozen messages from people I didn't have time to talk to, stacks of clippings and articles that needed to be filed—something in me snapped and I attacked my desktop as if it were my mortal enemy. With one violent sweep of my arm the desktop was perfectly clean. I felt a rush of gratification. I felt powerful. I had vanquished my foe. Seconds later, reality set in. I looked down in despair at the whirlwind of paper, the shattered pieces of clock, the crack in the telephone. It took me thirty minutes to undo the damage and several hours to recover from the shame.

Randomly venting our rage does not diminish the reservoir of pain stored inside us, nor does it empower us, raise our self-esteem, or earn us respect. What it does is etch a destructive pattern of behavior a little deeper into our psyches. Ultimately, our rage is no more effective in meeting our needs than the explosive behavior of the fourteen men who died fighting the soft-drink machines.

THE KICK ASS SYNDROME

Most men I know have occasional episodes of violence, but, like me, they manage to vent their rage on safe objects like office desks and living room walls. They stop themselves before they destroy much property or injure themselves or others. But some men routinely display rage and hostility and are less selective in their targets. They are examples of what I call the Kick Ass Syndrome. Men who fall into this category are almost always deeply wounded individuals who grew up in a dangerous and hostile environment. It's not just testosterone and gender conditioning that fuel their anger, it's also a dark history of childhood abuse. Arlette Ponder says that "the common denominator among the men treated at the Family Violence program is violence in the family of origin. Most of them were abused as children or witnessed a great deal of violence between their parents."

It takes years for the Kick Ass Syndrome to develop in a little boy. At first when a child is physically or verbally abused, he responds with healthy anger. His anger is a built-in, life-affirming response: "Stop hurting me!" "Take care of me!" "Pay attention to me!" However, his parents are likely to punish him for showing his anger, which makes him turn his anger inward, where it accumulates. When the boy is pushed over the limit, his anger explodes into rage. But his rage is rarely understood for what it really is—a desperate plea for help. Instead, it is viewed as yet another act of willful disobedience.

In addition to rage, most boys who are abused by their parents display hostility—the desire for harm to come to others. At first the boys' hostility is directed at the most logical target: their parents. But most abusive parents will not let their little boys even the score between them. They punish their children for their hostility even more severely than they punish them for their anger and rage. Out of desperation the boys adopt yet another strategy: they make an unconscious decision to numb their feelings. This way they won't have to experience any pain. They put on suits of masculine armor. But underneath the armor the hostility lives on in their fantasies, fantasies that provide comfort and the illusion of protection from abuse. Sometimes, without warning, a little boy's hostility spills over from his fantasy to the real world, and he vents it against safe objects like toys, pets, or younger siblings. To him his violence may feel a lot like power, but it has its roots in terror and helplessness.

When the boy becomes a young man and finally escapes the abuse of his home, he learns to his dismay that his rage and hostility come along with him. It's as though his mother and father had used a fierce and punishing sword on him for years, then handed him the bloody steel to carry on the family tradition. The beautiful little boy with the innocent eyes, trusting smile, and dimples in his cheeks grows into a man with darting eyes and a wounded soul. When he has a family of his own, he begins to abuse his wife and children. But it isn't a conscious thing. It isn't something he plans while driving home in the traffic. Somebody says something. Somebody does something. He drinks too much. Something happens. And suddenly his furious sword is flailing about. From the time his brain receives a message to mobilize until the adrenaline dumps into his bloodstream is about three seconds—not enough time to think things over. Over the years this violent reaction to frustration becomes a deep-seated habit.

A couple of years ago I had a tall, slender twenty-five-year-old client named Fred who was filled with rage from the mistreatment he'd received as a little boy. Like most of the hostile men I've known, he had a hostile man for a father. Monkey see, monkey do. His father would come home drunk, yelling, and looking for someone to attack. He was physically and verbally abusive to all members of the family, but especially to Fred. Fred hated his father and was terrified of his violence. But when he married, he emulated him by verbally abusing his own wife. Although he rarely hit her, he would terrorize her by punching his fist through the living room walls, leaving fist-sized craters.

When Fred came to me for therapy, he wasn't interested in exploring his childhood—that was "all in the past." And he wasn't interested in talking about his attacks of rage. What he wanted to do was talk about his wife, Janis, and how she was the cause of most of his problems. He accused her of being clingy and needy. He especially resented the fact that she always needed to know where he was. He called her his "ball and chain" and "jailer." He went out of his way to fan her fear of abandonment. For example, he would play pool until midnight without letting her know where he was.

When I asked Fred if he thought his treatment of Janis was abusive, he said, "No. She deserves it. Besides, it's not physical abuse like it was with my dad. It's only words."

During the first three months of therapy Fred continued to blame Janis for virtually all of his problems. He claimed that he was only staying married to her for fear of how sad she would be if he left. Finally, a few days before Christmas, he left her and rented an apartment on the other side of town. At first Janis was heartbroken and terrified—just as Fred had predicted. But after weeks of anguish she began to develop some confidence in her ability to fend for herself.

Meanwhile, Fred quit therapy, believing he had solved his problems by leaving Janis. He began dating other women and playing pool five nights a week. At first he was reasonably content, but after ten months of separation he discovered that being single was not that much better than being married. In fact, when he spent any time by himself, he was bored and anxious. Reluctantly, he decided to move back home. To his astonishment Janis wouldn't let him move back in. She'd discovered that life was much more pleasant without him. Besides, she informed him, she was seeing another man, someone who treated her much more kindly.

Fred was devastated. He went through a terrible ordeal of loneliness and abandonment anxiety that lasted for months. He even considered suicide. He called me up in desperation one day and signed up for another round of therapy. This time Fred was ready to do some work and was able to get in touch with the repressed pain of his childhood.

During one session he recalled a violent fantasy he had relied upon as a small boy to give him psychological protection from his father's abuse. His father had had a real Indian hatchet mounted in a glass box on the wall of his bedroom. When Fred went to bed at night, he would imagine himself creeping into his father's bedroom, smashing the glass with his fist, grabbing the hatchet, and "slicing" his father. The fantasy gave Fred a sense of power and safety. But as soon as it was over, he would be overcome with intolerable guilt and would have to "pray to the Lord for forgiveness." Finally, having protected himself with an imaginary rampage against his father and then having atoned for his sins, he would be able to fall asleep.

As Fred and I discussed this painful ritual, he was able to see for the first time how his father's rage had stirred up an answering rage in him, a rage that he had vented on his wife fifteen years later.

After this particular session Fred's inner rage began to break like a long, chronic fever. He began to see how much Janis had suffered from *his* mistreatment. At long last he was in touch with his own pain and could empathize with hers. As the therapy deepened, he gained another insight. He realized that underneath his rage he was just as scared, just as needy, just as clingy as Janis was—maybe more so. The only difference was that he had learned to disguise his vulnerability by attacking others. Like his father before him he had used a loved one as a punching bag to absorb his overflowing fear and rage. Both men were prime examples of the Kick Ass Syndrome—only Fred had succeeded in breaking the cycle.

THE KISS ASS SYNDROME

What about the other half of the Kick Ass/Kiss Ass Syndrome—those men who are unable to assert themselves? What happened to *their* healthy anger? To gain insight into the increasing numbers of "soft men" in our culture, it helps to subdivide them into four additional groups: (1) Passive Men, (2) Paralyzed Men (3) Passive/Aggressive Men, and (4) Pleasing Men. Although the men in each of these categories have suppressed their healthy anger to one degree or another, they have done it in different ways and for different reasons.

The Passive Man

One of the distinguishing characteristics of Passive Men is that they have muted all of their emotions, not just their anger. Typically, they were raised in households where strong feelings were not allowed. They learned to compensate for their repressed emotions by becoming highly rational. Their emotions atrophied and their intellect grew overly large. A little girl growing up in the same household will have the same tendency to repress her feelings, but it is likely she will hold on to more of her vulnerable emotions than her brother. She may not be permitted to yell or get angry at her parents, but she may be able to cry and show tenderness. Her brother not only has to contend with the repressive nature of the household but also the overlay of the masculine code. He is not allowed to show his anger *or* his vulnerability. As a result, he loses much of his ability to feel.

Typically, Passive Men fail to experience much of an emotional connection to the world around them. I remember going to New York with a business associate who was a Passive Man. Neither of us had been to the Big Apple since we were small boys. We had only two days and nights in the city, and I was determined to see and do everything possible. I was like a kid in a candy store. My friend seldom laughed and appeared to be uninterested in just about everything we did. A barrier began to grow between us. After the first day I asked him if something was troubling him. I was worried that I might have done something to upset him. He told me that nothing was bothering him and that he was having a good time. I found it hard to believe. Because he wasn't expressing his emotions, they were invisible to me. I couldn't share in his reality, and it seemed he couldn't share in mine. Although we did nearly everything together those two days, I felt strangely alone. The experience gave me renewed sympathy for all my female clients who complain about stoic husbands.

Another characteristic of the Passive Man is that he rarely knows what he wants out of life. He doesn't have strong enough feelings to serve as an internal compass. What handicaps him most is his reduced capacity to experience joy. Joy is like magnetic north on your inner compass. It tells you when you're on track and where you want to go. The Passive Man lacks this inner direction. When his wife asks him if he wants to go to the movies, he says: "I don't care. You decide." And it truly makes little difference to him whether he goes or not because he feels pretty much the same wherever he is. He is a piece of flotsam carried in and out on the family tide.

The Passive Man's inability to feel also makes it difficult for him to protect himself from abuse. When someone mistreats him, his response is to either ignore what happened or to try to figure out what happened and why. At some point in his life he gave away his sword, and he has no way to protect himself. At a dinner party not long ago my attention was drawn to a man and his wife. The man appeared to be very passive. His wife was clearly the more dominant member of the duo. Through-out the dinner I noticed that this woman made frequent cutting remarks about her husband. He seemed to have little reaction. He would watch her with a bemused smile. Toward the end of the evening she went into great detail about how long it had been since he had had a promotion and how difficult it was to live on his salary. Once again I saw almost no reaction. There wasn't even a glint in his eye to warn her to stop the public humiliation. His passivity invited her abuse.

Even though Passive Men experience little pleasure in life and tend to endure more than their share of mistreatment, they rarely have much incentive to change. Unlike men with violent tempers they don't frighten themselves or others. There are no embarrassing scenes to make them remorseful or propel them into counseling. If for some reason a Passive Man decides to get help—or more likely, is maneuvered into getting help—he rarely puts much energy into his personal growth. In the early years of my practice I didn't know how to work with these men. They dropped out of therapy just as they had dropped out of life.

Darrell, a muscular, fair-haired Passive Man, was coerced into getting marital counseling by his wife, Marion. Marion came to the first appointment power-dressed in a tailored pantsuit sporting a scarf for a tie. She was clear about Darrell's problems and even clearer about the fact that she wanted them resolved in a very short amount of time. "I've given him six months," she said. "That's as long as I'm willing to hang in there. I've had it." Among other things she complained that Darrell was an underachiever whose salary and job title were far below his potential; that he never shared his feelings with her; that he exerted no authority as a father to their three children; and that he was always tired or depressed or lost in a fog.

It's uncanny how they always seem to find each other—the Passive Man and the Powerful Woman. At first she is attracted to him because he seems so stable and grounded. She thinks of him as being "rock solid." Later she does an about-face and sees him as weak and boring. He goes through a similar reversal in his thinking about her. At the beginning of the relationship he sees her as a spark plug that gets his engine firing on all cylinders. He thrives on her drive and energy. Later she becomes an electric cattle prod, zapping him every time he turns around.

When Darrell and Marion interacted with each other in therapy sessions, they were a study in polarization. The more subdued Darrell became, the more aggressive Marion became. As Darrell withdrew into his shell, Marion reached out farther with her claws. One way or another she was determined to get some reaction out of him. During one bitter exchange Marion was perched on the edge of her chair, her lean body tense with energy. Looking Darrell squarely in the face, she said to him: "You can't accomplish anything. You're always screwing things up at work. You really screwed up the insurance adjustment on the car. When you come home at night, all you do is sit and read. You're always hiding behind a book. You ignore me. You ignore the children. I may as well be a single parent!" Darrell responded by slumping down in his chair and lowering his eyelids over his eyes.

Struck by the contrast in their body language, I asked Marion how she was feeling. She said that, to be honest, she felt like leaving Darrell. I asked Darrell how *he* was feeling, and he said he wasn't feeling a thing, except maybe a little sleepy. He looked for all the world as if he was about to take a long, restful nap.

The next week I saw Darrell by himself, and I suggested that he join one of my men's groups. He agreed to give it a try and said he would join the Tuesday-night group. He came for two sessions and then quit. Like many Passive Men, he didn't have enough motivation to change, and, regrettably, I didn't have the skills at that time to reach into his muted world of daydreams and fantasies.

The Paralyzed Man

Superficially, the Paralyzed Man can be confused with the Passive Man, because both of them have trouble asserting themselves and protecting their boundaries. The main difference between them is the amount of anger hidden beneath the passivity. A Passive Man has little rage inside him. The Paralyzed Man is repressing a lot of rage. He's like a pressure cooker with no safety valve. People around him have the feeling that sooner or later he's going to explode.

Mark, a member of one of my men's groups, shows many of the characteristics of the Paralyzed Man. When he first came to the group, he said he thought he might be very angry inside, but he wasn't sure. All he knew was that he was having a lot of negative thoughts about his wife. He revealed to the group a number of unusually violent fantasies. To help him release some of his pent-up rage I asked him to participate in an exercise designed to help him connect with his emotions. He declined, saying "I just can't do it." What he eventually learned was that he was terrified of his own anger. He was afraid that if he started feeling any anger toward his wife, he would go crazy with rage. He had been stoic so long that he was sitting on a mountain of anger. If he started chipping away at that mountain, he was going to crack into tiny pieces and never be able to put himself together again.

Unlike the Passive Man, the Paralyzed Man has a sword, but he's afraid to use it. He has bloody fantasies of what might happen to himself and others if he takes it out of the sheath.

Despite the extent of their repressed anger, most Paralyzed Men go through their entire lives without committing a single act of serious violence. But there are a few Paralyzed Men who "snap" and lose all control. An extreme example of the Paralyzed Man is the guy who has no police record, but one day walks into the factory with an automatic rifle and opens fire. Neighbors and coworkers shake their heads in bewilderment: "He never did a violent thing in his life."

For a short time I worked with a Paralyzed Man named Tony who had all the ingredients necessary for extreme violence. He came to see me on the advice of his doctor. He had a chronic ulcer and his doctor recommended therapy to help relieve his tension. Although Tony was always polite and respectful, I felt uncomfortable around him. A Passive Man is like a limp piece of spaghetti; a Paralyzed Man like a high-tension wire. When Tony wasn't talking, he would often grind his teeth or rhythmically knead his biceps. When he laughed, it was a curious-sounding "heh, heh, heh" that sent a chill up my spine.

Tony's mannerisms began to make sense to me when I learned about the extreme abusiveness of his father. At first I didn't believe his stories. I'd heard numerous tales of abuse before, but Tony's stories seemed too extreme to be true. For example, one day he told me that his father had poured lighter fluid on the clothes he was wearing and set his shirt aflame with a cigarette lighter. Another time he said his father had caught him playing with his screwdriver and had jabbed it into his leg, piercing him to the bone. Tony said, "The screwdriver would have gone all the way through my leg if my father hadn't hit the bone." Then he laughed, "Heh, heh, heh."

Initially I didn't believe either of those stories, and, one day, in an effort to get more honesty into our relationship, I decided to test him.

He had just brought up the lighter-fluid incident for the second time, so I said to him, "I bet that left you with a nasty scar."

"Yeah, it did," he said.

"Do you mind showing it to me?" I asked.

"No," he said.

He unbuttoned his shirt and I saw a swath of red, puckered skin covering his torso. It wasn't long after that that he came to an appointment wearing shorts, and I saw the indented scar left by the screwdriver.

I had little success getting Tony to express any feelings about his father's abuse. This was before I had developed specific techniques to help men release their rage. In frustration I referred him to another therapist.

The Passive/Aggressive Man

Like the Paralyzed Man, the Passive/Aggressive Man is burdened with repressed rage and hostility. But he comes from a less abusive upbringing than the Paralyzed Man so he has less archaic anger to repress. In addition, he keeps his frustration from building up by venting it in quick little bursts. He has a safety valve on his pressure cooker that lets out a burst of steam whenever the temperature rises. However, he doesn't vent his anger in healthy ways. He lets out his steam in sneaky, subtle ways, scalding the people around him. For example, he might torment his children and then criticize them for not being able to take a joke. He might tell his wife he's going to do a chore, then forget to do it, do it late, or do a poor job. Ask a Passive/Aggressive Man what he wants to do, and you'll never get a straight answer. For example, if you ask him if he wants to go to a movie, he'll say something like, "Why not? It's better than hanging around here." Does he want to go with you or not? You're not sure. If you end up going to the movies, he'll find some way to irk you. He might make you fifteen minutes late or play the role of movie critic, spoiling all the tender scenes. In retrospect you would have been much happier if he had just said, "No thanks. I'm not interested in a movie." But the last thing you'll get from a Passive/Aggressive Man is a direct answer. He needs to keep you guessing and keep you off guard. He needs a ready target for his hostility.

The Passive/Aggressive Man has a sword but he keeps it concealed. When your back is turned, he whips it out and nicks you. When you turn around to protect yourself, his sword is back in its sheath. "Why are you upset?" he asks. "I'm unarmed." If the sword of the Passive/Aggressive Man is sharp enough, you may not even notice you're wounded until you see the trickles of blood running down your leg.

Carlos is a Passive/Aggressive Man whom I saw in couples counseling. Carlos had made a career out of frustrating his wife, Anna. He baited her by making demeaning remarks about her in public where she was too embarrassed to defend herself. He took advantage of her gullibility by telling her outrageous lies and then mocking her for believing them. What angered Anna most was his failure to follow through with his commitments. She would ask him to do something and he would say, "Sure." Then he would find some way to sabotage it. For example, at one point she asked him to take over the family bill paying, to which he agreed. But he ended up paying the bills late and not recording the amounts in the checkbook. In exasperation, she took back the job.

Carlos told me about an incident from his childhood that provided a clue to the origin of this lifelong pattern of hidden aggression. The event took place when he was about six years old. On that particular day he had eaten a few pieces of candy that had been set aside for company. When his mother discovered the "crime," she lectured him about eating food without her permission. To reinforce the lesson, she placed three pieces of the forbidden candy in front of him. "Do you like this candy?" she asked him. Carlos nodded his head up and down. "No, you don't like it," she corrected him. "This candy is for adults. You don't like it." "But I do like it," he protested. "No," said his mother. "Let me explain it again. This candy is not for children, so you don't like to eat it. You'd rather eat a graham cracker or an apple instead." Carlos remembers that she kept up the brainwashing until he gave her all the correct responses. No, he didn't like the candy after all. No, it really didn't taste any good. Yes, he was very sorry he'd eaten it.

It is likely that this was just one of a thousand encounters in which his overly controlling mother had succeeded in bending his will to hers. To survive he learned to be compliant on the outside and let his rage leak out in subversive ways, a pattern he clung to in adulthood. A child who is not allowed to express his true feelings will learn to be devious.

The Pleasing Man

The Pleasing Man has more positive energy than other men who repress their healthy anger. He may even display some passion. However, like other Kiss Ass men, he doesn't assert his needs or express his anger in a straightforward manner. He goes with the flow—provided it makes others happy. And that's the main identifying characteristic of the Pleasing Man: he needs your approval. Ask a Pleasing Man if he wants to go to the movies with you and he'll say "Sure—if that's what would make *you* happy. You want to take me to see Bambi? For the third time? Great. I'd love to go." What the Pleasing Man would really like to do with his Saturday night remains a mystery not only to his partner, but also to himself. At some point in his life he elected to renounce most of his needs.

It is not uncommon for a Pleasing Man to be the oldest child in the family. More than his younger siblings, he felt a responsibility to live up to his parents' expectations. He followed their dictates rather than his own. Other siblings had more freedom to display their independence because older brother was dutifully following the party line.

Other men become pleasers by being overly reliant on their mothers. Their fathers were either distant, absent, critical, or abusive—as so many men are in this culture—making Mom vital to their survival. Meeting their mothers' needs gradually became so important they repressed their own. Making Mom happy, earning her praise, or keeping her from being sick, angry, drunk, or depressed became their primary motivation. Later in life, this pleasing manner was transferred to other people—employers, friends, and coworkers—but primarily to the women in their lives.

I have a friend who, before completing therapy, was an archetypical pleasing male. He was madly in love with an older woman and courted her for four years. She kept saying to him, "If only you would do _____ I would love you more," each time filling in the blank with a new request. My friend would do his best to comply. "I wish you could be more giving," she said to him, and he brought her expensive gifts. "You need to get into your feelings," she said to him, and he joined the men's movement and started expressing his feelings. "If you just discussed books more . . ." she said, and he went out and bought books and scattered them around on the tables. Because he was dyslexic and a slow reader, he bought crib notes on all the classics so he could discuss them with her. Finally, when my friend thought he had jumped through all the hoops, she said to him, "I think what I am really looking for is that man over there"—a macho Neanderthal who wore a gold chain around his neck and drove a Corvette.

The Pleasing Man may be able to keep a woman happy over the short term. But as time passes, she finds her relationship with him to be frustrating and disappointing. Typically, she will either leave him for someone else or lead him around by the nose. An even deeper tragedy is that despite all his efforts to please the women in his life, the Pleasing Man rarely feels loved. He doesn't know whether women like him because of his continual efforts to make them happy or because of his inner worth. Before the Pleasing Man can have a rewarding love relationship, he has to reclaim his healthy anger.

MEN WITH COMPLEX ANGER PATTERNS

Few men fit perfectly into any one of these categories. Most men display complex anger patterns. For example, some men alternate between being passive and passive/aggressive. When things are going well, they don't show much hidden aggression. When they're feeling stressed, they resume the needling. Other men are pleasers some of the time and passive some of the time. But the most common variation is for men to alternate between some form of passivity and rage.

It makes sense that a passive man would have episodes of rage because it is difficult to completely repress one's negative emotions. They build up, despite our attempts to keep them under control. My father was a prime example. He would be dormant for days on end, allowing himself to be manipulated by my mother and cowed by his friends. Then he would erupt with little warning. This is what I call a volcanic pattern of anger. From my vulnerable position as a child I was most vividly impressed by my father's outbursts of rage, but the truth is, most of the time he was fairly passive.

Throughout much of my life I have displayed a rather unusual pattern of anger, for I would alternate weeks of pleasing behavior with episodes of rage. This Jekyll and Hyde nature was most evident in my relationships with women. An example stands out in my mind. Years ago, after divorcing my first wife, I lived with a woman whom I desperately wanted to please. I would work during the day at my construction business and come home in the evening and clean the whole house. I cleaned the counters and the sink until they shone, then I would wad up the dishrag and leave it by the side of the sink. By the next morning the dishrag would start to smell. One evening my girl-friend complained about the dishrag in a polite, sensitive manner. But for some reason I started to rage. How dare she complain about something so trivial as a smelly dishrag when I washed all the dishes and did this and did that! She was ungrateful! Lazy! Thoughtless! I stomped out of the house, slamming the screen door. One minute I was doing my best to please her. The next minute I was a tyrant, shaming her for being ungrateful. I sympathize with the women who put up with me in those early years.

ANGER AND MEN'S THERAPY

Helping men release their rage in a safe setting has become an essential part of my work with men. Anger-release techniques allow passive men to become more assertive and hostile men to reduce their rage. Traditional therapy, in which men merely talk about this anger, is much less effective. Men can talk for years without draining off their rage. Burdened by repressed anger, they find it difficult to experience other emotions. I talk about my anger-release techniques in the second half of the book, and show how they help men reclaim their healthy anger.

The next chapter focuses on the relationship between fathers and sons, an essential but often overlooked component in a man's emotional development. Significantly, the six categories of fathers I will be describing parallel the anger patterns discussed in this chapter. As it turns out, how fathers handle their anger is a determining factor in how they raise their sons. Whether a man withdraws into himself and becomes a Passive Man, expresses his anger as hostility, or allows his rage to leak out in passive/aggressive spurts has a profound influence on his little boy.

CHAPTER 3

GROWING UP IN NO-MAN'S-LAND: Exploring the Father-Son Relationship

The relationship between fathers and sons has become the subject of much interest in recent years as the psychology of men has gained more attention. But this wasn't the case when I was in graduate school studying to be a therapist. The little research that there was about fathers focused on physically or sexually abusive men. The primary emphasis was on the mother and her legendary failings. But after mulling over my own childhood and counseling hundreds of men I began to sense how deeply boys are influenced by their fathers.

One of the reasons that the father role has been overlooked for so long is that a boy's initial connection is with his mother, first through the umbilical cord, then after his birth through a hundred daily interactions—the soothing sound of her voice, her loving touch, the looks that pass back and forth between them, and the nourishment that comes from the breast or the bottle. The mother's role is to build an interpersonal bridge for the boy that bonds him to another human being. Child psychologists believe that if a baby boy develops a strong, healthy attachment to his mother, then he is more likely to develop secure relationships with other people later in life. Good mothering is an essential component of a child's well-being.

However, we are now discovering that the father has important roles to play in a boy's life as well. Ideally, one of those roles is to assist the mother in building that interpersonal bridge for the baby boy, helping him feel safe and connected to other people. But the father has an additional role to play, one that is uniquely his. When a baby boy becomes a toddler and is ready to gain a little distance from his mother, the father promotes his independence by building a new kind of bridge for his son, a bridge that leads to the world that is Not Mom. This bridge is built brick by brick, day by day. The father creates this vital link by playing games with his son, patiently answering his questions, taking the boy on short excursions away from the house, and inviting him to walk in his masculine shadow as he works around the house. At first the boy will stay in his father's world only a short time before running back to the softer, more familiar world of his mother. But as he grows older, he will want to spend more and more time with his dad.

Under optimal conditions, the boy learns to view both his mother and father as safe, loving people. But he begins to notice some fundamental differences between his parents. Some of these differences are differences in behavior. His dad may seem more abrupt, less coddling, more physically active. His father and mother may also have different interests and attitudes. Some of the differences the little boy sees are physical. He notices that his father has a larger stature, a beard or stubble on his face, a deeper voice, more hair on his arms and legs, and blood vessels that stand out on his hard muscles. The little boy also observes that his father's genitals are a grown-up version of his own, which tells him that when he grows up, he will be more like his dad than his mom. As this gender identification begins to sink in, he begins to pattern himself even more strongly after his father. Ideally, by the time he has gone through puberty, he will have a secure sense of his own masculinity.

BOYS WITHOUT FATHERS

What happens to boys who grow up without fathers? Since mothers are not men, it is difficult for them to help their sons develop a masculine identity. If a boy's father is absent or emotionally unavailable, and if there is no surrogate father to take his place, then the boy will spend most of his time in his mother's world. Unwittingly, his mother may instill "feminine" qualities in him by rewarding him for being sweet, gentle, cautious, and well behaved. She may be reluctant to test his physical abilities or challenge his courage and endurance. Although women display a broad range of behaviors, interests, and emotional patterns, a mother on average is more likely to introduce her son to passive activities such as music or reading than traditional male activities such as sports, cars, machinery, hunting, and fishing. Her son's safety and good manners may matter more to her than his athleticism. But even if she makes a conscious effort to reinforce traditional masculine qualities in her son, she will model for him in a thousand ways her more feminine approach to the world.

Because my father spent very little time with me, I turned to women for support and validation, like so many men I know. I enjoyed being around my mother and grandmother, my aunts, my female teachers, and the mothers on the block. The women were interested in how I was doing, and, sometimes, even in how I was feeling. They complimented me on my blue eyes, quick mind, and sense of humor. But despite the fact that I thrived on all of this female attention, I yearned for my father's approval. There seemed to be an innate programming pulling me away from my mother and toward the masculine world. It was as though my genetic structure contained an inner man or masculine archetype that was waiting to take form. All I needed was a father or mentor to give it life.

As was true for me, most boys who spend a great deal of time in the feminine world develop an urge to push away from their mothers. The time-honored way to do this is by being rude—farting, belching at the table, swearing—or by being disobedient. Boys use rudeness to draw a crude but essential line separating themselves from their mothers. Meanwhile, they take it upon themselves to build an alternate bridge to the masculine world. Some boys turn to sports or fast cars to find their rightful place among men, or, if they are emotionally troubled, to gangs, juvenile delinquency, drugs, or alcohol.

But these unguided forays into the imagined realm of manhood are rarely successful. Boys who do not have a strong father figure wander around in a kind of No-Man's-Land. They don't belong in the masculine world because they don't have a safe bridge or a guide to take them there. They don't belong in the feminine world because of the simple fact that they are boys and not girls. They're stuck in a No-Man's-Land where the sand is always shifting beneath their feet. Unconsciously, they search for a firmer foundation to stand on, a way to prove their manhood, but they are uncertain what being a man is all about. Is it the opposite of Mom? Is it being like the Lone Ranger or Clint Eastwood or Rambo? Is it getting drunk or getting laid or tearing up a creek bed in a four-wheel Bronco?

Late one Sunday night after the end of a Wildman Gathering I sat on the porch of a cabin in upstate New York talking with a young man named Paul. Paul was a good-looking man, in his late thirties, with blond curly hair that came down to his collar. As we talked, he beat softly and rhythmically on his drum. The other men had gone home hours before, but Paul had lingered at the campsite. He talked briefly about his failing marriage. He'd only been married one year, but he and his wife were already separated. He missed his baby son. He also talked about his struggles for manhood. "My father died when I was four years old," he told me. "I have no memories of him. It's like he didn't exist. I think that gave me a broken heart, only there was a metal plate there, in front of the breakage, and I wasn't able to spill out my feelings. I tried to make up for the loss by absorbing other men's personalities—teachers, neighbors, scout leaders. I could see that I was doing this and I would get down on myself. I wanted to be myself. I wanted to know where I was at, where my heart was. But I always felt like I was faking it, taking on some other man's personality.

"When I was a teenager, I would do wild and crazy things to impress other guys. I'd get in a car and I'd drive like a crazy man. I dreamed of being a stock-car driver. I got into rappelling. I got into hang gliding. Hang gliding was a way of showing the guys that—hey, I'm a man. Look at me. Look at how much of a man I am. Can you jump off a sixteen-hundred-foot cliff?"

Before coming to the retreat Paul had viewed his desperate need to prove his manhood as a personal failing. But this night, after having spent two days at the Gathering exploring the father-son relationship, he was beginning to sense how hard it is to cross over to the masculine world when there's no one there to show you the way. Like many young men without fathers he had tried to become a man by following an exaggerated version of the masculine code. He had followed all the rules on the box but was unable to capture their essence. There had been no one to give the masculine code any life or meaning.

Days later, as I was mulling over Paul's remarks about his need to prove his worth as a man, I realized that I had heard comments like his from hundreds of men, not just from those who had lost their fathers through death or divorce. Many of the men I had counseled felt adrift in the world and attributed at least some of their confusion to a lack of love and guidance from their fathers. There were a variety of reasons for their fathers' neglect. Some fathers worked twelve hours a day, six days a week, leaving too little room in their busy schedules for their sons. Some were alcoholics who spent more time with Jim Beam than Jimmy Jr. Some were Passive Men who had allowed the job of parenting to be commandeered by their wives; they weren't fathers— they were just men who happened to live in the house. And sadly, many of my clients grew up with physically or emotionally abusive fathers. Their fathers weren't patient, loving guides ready to lend a helping hand; they were towering monsters to run away from.

As I reflected on my conversations with thousands of men, I reluctantly came to the conclusion that legions of men have grown up without the love, attention, and guidance from their fathers they so richly deserve.

SIX TYPES OF DYSFUNCTIONAL DADS

To help men gain more insight into this paternal void in their lives, I've come up with six categories of Dysfunctional Dads: (1) the Critical Father, (2) the Smart Ass Father, (3) the Passive Father, (4) the Self-Centered Father, (5) the Hostile/Abusive Father, and (6) the Neglectful Father. In presenting this rogues' gallery of fathers I don't want to give the impression that these men had any intention of hurting their sons. Most fathers start out with the best of intentions. But for a number of reasons, not the least of which is their gender conditioning, they develop dysfunctional patterns of behavior that turn them into dysfunctional fathers. A culture that tells men that the way to find happiness is to strive for perfection, focus on external success, numb their feelings, and repress their needs creates fathers who are compulsive, perfectionists, self-centered, distant, neglectful, and critical. When we scrutinize our individual fathers, we must keep in mind the narrowness of the box in which they were obliged to live.

I also don't want to give the impression that fathers are to blame for all of a man's ills. Fathers are a major influence in a man's life, but they're not the only influence. Mothers are just as influential, and I take a fresh look at the mother-son relationship in the following chapter.

Finally, although it is important for men to get a clear picture of what happened to them in childhood, it's essential that they don't get mired in the "healing and feeling" stage of the recovery process. Once men have released their feelings about their childhood abuse or neglect, I encourage them to create healthier relationships with their parents in the present. (A discussion of how the men in my groups are reconciling with their parents appears in Chapter 9.) This effort has a positive effect on all of their other relationships.

The Critical Father

Last fall I found myself admiring a neighbor as he raked all the leaves on his hundred-foot-square lot. He was very thorough. By late afternoon his lawn was immaculate. I counted nine large bags lined up at his curb, each one neatly filled with leaves and tied off with yellow twists.

It turned out I wasn't the only one who had been monitoring his progress. As my neighbor was about to put away his rake, his father, a man in his seventies or eighties, came out of the house, leaning on his cane. He began a silent, meticulous scrutiny of his son's work. Finding nothing to complain about in the yard he walked out to the street and spotted a few sodden leaves nestled against the curb. With a disapproving look he tapped at the curb with his cane and called out to his son, "Gerald. Here. Over here. You've missed some." I wondered how many tens of thousands of times my neighbor had failed to live up to the expectations of his Critical Father.

One of a father's many responsibilities is to help his son learn to master his environment. He sets ideals for his son and gives him the support and reassurance he needs to attain them. But the Critical

Father sets standards his son can never reach. He starts out with the boy's interests at heart. But in setting "manly" performance standards, the Critical Father fails to take into account the experience and skill level of the little boy.

Another failing of the Critical Father is that he teaches by pointing out mistakes rather than by highlighting successes. Instead of being mentor and guide, he is judge and critic. This gives new meaning to the term *trial and error*. The boy feels on trial whenever he attempts to master a new skill or practice an old one; he is in error if he doesn't satisfy his father's expectations. Unwittingly, the Critical Father ends up destroying his son's motivation, his confidence in himself, and his joy in learning.

Competitive sports bring out the worst in some Critical Fathers. They take their own obsession with external success and project it onto their sons. It's as if they were taking the same MAN BOX that limits their own chances for happiness and lowering it onto their little boys' shoulders. One client paraphrased for me the bruising lecture his father gave him every time he struck out in Little League: "I've told you a hundred times, Kevin—hold the bat in the ready position! And watch the damn ball. How can you expect to hit the ball if you're not looking at it? And how many reminders do you need to widen your stance? Do you ever listen to what I say? Is it that you're not listening to me or that you just don't have what it takes? Maybe that's it. Maybe you just don't have what it takes."

Kevin recalled spending one particularly painful Saturday afternoon playing left field in a regional Little League game. No one had hit the ball to him for several innings, so he relaxed his vigil and glanced up at a helicopter that was maneuvering in the distance. Just then he heard the crack of the bat. He scanned the sky for the ball, but he didn't see it until it landed a few yards in front of him. Over the cheers of the other team he heard his dad's voice booming out, "Watch the god-damn ball Kevin! What are you *doing* out there?" After the game his dad summoned him to the car and delivered a grave lecture on the responsibility boys have to their teams and their families. "We're all pulling for you, son. I have to tell you, though, I felt pretty let down out there today. Sometimes I just don't know what's the matter with you. You have a chance to do something and then you just . . . I don't know." His dad started the car engine, shook his head, and sighed, "I just don't know." Kevin can still remember feeling hot with shame as they drove home. He'd worked so hard to make his dad feel proud of him, but nothing was ever good enough for him. After that day Kevin never wanted to play baseball again. Although he played out the season and tried hard not to make any mistakes, the fun was gone.

Talking with Kevin brought back memories of the fishing trips I went on with my dad and my brother, Lewis. I loved to be out on the lake, but I hated to spend so much time around my dad because he was so critical of us. It was a crime if we tangled our lines. It was a capital offense if we snagged a limb.

The big bass that we were trying to catch hung out around the partially submerged stumps and bushes near the shoreline of the lake. We would try to cast our lures as close to the bushes as possible without getting snagged. I remember feeling so proud when my lure plunked in the water at the base of a stump. My dad never noticed those times. But he always noticed when I got hung up on a bush. He would sigh heavily and say something like, "Goddamnit. If I've told you boys once I've told you a thousand times—watch what you're doing!" He would mutter to himself and row the boat toward the bush to retrieve the lure. When he got it loose, he would toss it back to me without saying a word. I would feel scared and ashamed that I had caused him so much trouble. After several fishing trips my brother and I finally caught on to the fact that it was more important to steer clear of his anger than to catch a big fish. We began to cast our lures far away from the bushes.

There seems to be a little bit of the Critical Father in virtually every dad. Criticism has become one of the most prevalent teaching models for men in this culture, perhaps because it's so quick and easy. It's more efficient to bark out a correction to your son than to take the time and energy to give a detailed demonstration. A man who is obsessed with his work is always looking for parenting shortcuts.

A Critical Father fails to realize that a boy who is taught through criticism will automatically criticize himself throughout his life. He takes his Critical Father along with him as an internalized parent. No matter where he goes, he is dogged by the demeaning voice of his father. It is tragic how many fine men I know who have taken up where their dads left off and become their own worst critics and taskmasters: "Why did you do that?" "What's the matter with you?" "Quit daydreaming and get back to work." "Did you really deserve that promotion?" "Can't you do anything right?" "When are you ever going to grow up?" The inner voice of the Critical Father leaves no room for supportive or validating messages.

The Smart Ass Father

The Smart Ass Father is the paternal version of the Passive/Aggressive Man I described in the preceding chapter. He is often bright, well educated, and highly verbal, but he uses his formidable talents to belittle his son and make jokes at his expense. Most little boys are too naïve and trusting to fend off the caustic wit of the Smart Ass Father. Even a wary adult would have difficulty protecting himself from this cynical man.

The Smart Ass Father is an angry, embittered man, but he is rarely straightforward about it. He has a complicated anger pattern that goes like this: frustration → sneak attack → denial. He'll take out his frustration by making a cutting remark to his son, then deny he intended any harm. He'll top it all off by humiliating the boy for being offended: "What's the matter with you. Can't you take a joke?" "You're a little sensitive, aren't you?" "Relax. I'm only kidding." Through his caustic wit he erects an invisible barrier between himself and his children. Although he can be charming and amusing at times, he is rarely affectionate or caring. Most of the time he is remote and unreachable.

Here's a typical interaction between a boy and his Smart Ass Father. The boy comes home from grade school with his report card. The report card shows one *A,* two *B*'s, and three *C*'s. The father takes one look at the card and bellows out to his wife, "Hey, Honey. Little Einstein is home. He's finally gotten an *A.* Wouldn't you know it? It's in P.E.!" Unlike the Critical Father he doesn't go into a long harangue about how poorly his son is doing in school. He just delivers a cutting one-liner the boy will never forget. The boy learns to be wary of his dad, even though his father may never hit him or yell at him. He just decks him over and over again with his sarcasm.

The reason the Smart Ass Father uses verbal sarcasm instead of a belt to vent his rage is that he has an inner proscription against anger. When he was young, he learned it was not safe to be angry, so he transformed his rage into one-liners and put-downs. He stabs his son with words. The little flesh wounds the Smart Ass Father gives his son are rarely fatal. But over the years the constant jabs take their toll. It's not uncommon for the boy's flesh wounds to multiply until he becomes "anemic" and suffers from low self-esteem and chronic depression.

Bill, a balding, middle-aged contractor, was the son of a Smart Ass Father. He told me about a shaming incident that took place in his early childhood. He was about four or five years old. His family was staying at his uncle's farmhouse for the Fourth of July holiday. Bill remembers wandering onto the front porch and spotting a bowl of party mix on the picnic table. He scooped up a handful and popped it into his mouth. He spit it out immediately. It was laced with hot pepper. His dad and his uncle came out from their hiding place and started hooting and hollering at the trap they had laid. Bill ran over to his father and tried to hit him to make him stop laughing at him, but his father grabbed him by the head and held him at arm's length. Bill flailed at the air with his tiny arms as the men laughed at his futile attempts to defend his dignity.

Bill has many of the characteristics I have come to expect in a man who has been repeatedly shamed by his father. He has a hard time looking another man in the eye for more than a few seconds. He walks with his chin down, his shoulders slumped, and his chest caved in. He rarely feels proud of himself, no matter how much he accomplishes. The slightest insult or criticism can throw him into a downward spiral of shame and self-disgust. His father's "harmless" jibes and jabs have robbed him of his pride.

Denial is another common trait of men who were raised by a Smart Ass Father. Denial is a thick blanket we use to keep away a cold reality. The fiercer the wind of unpleasant truth blows at the door, the more blankets of denial we pull over ourselves. Eventually, we cover ourselves with so many "security" blankets that we turn into emotional mummies.

The son of the Smart Ass Father characteristically uses denial to try to hide from the fact that his father is being abusive to him. To admit that his father has malicious intent threatens his very survival. A young man named Allen came to me for therapy several years ago. He didn't come to talk about his father, but to work out problems he was having with his fiancée. She had a common complaint, which was that Allen seemed emotionally dead. After listening to Allen make some remarks about his father during the first few sessions, I began to see that his dad fit the general profile of the Smart Ass Father. Allen described him as a skilled trial lawyer who had many admirers in the legal profession, but who was cool, distant, and full of cutting remarks at home.

Although Allen was able to describe his father's unpleasant personality in some detail, he had a hard time feeling any anger toward him. After all, his dad hadn't beaten him or abused him in any obvious way. Besides, Allen would argue, didn't all fathers have their shortcomings?

Allen finally realized how angry he was at his father one evening when his dad invited him and his fiancée out to dinner. It was the first time Allen had seen his dad since beginning therapy, and he was more sensitive than usual to his father's put-downs. Instead of smiling and letting his dad's remarks roll off his back, he felt warm pulses of anger.

He had an even stronger reaction when his dad began telling his girlfriend an embarrassing anecdote about him. When Allen was a young boy just learning to ride a bicycle, he kept catching the wheel of his bike in the groove between the sidewalk and the lawn. His father laughed his infectious laugh and said, "It was like the edge of the sidewalk had a magnet in it, pulling the bike off course. Remember Allen? It was hilarious! I thought it was so hysterical that I took a picture of it. Here, I brought the picture with me." Allen watched incredulously as his father reached into his jacket pocket and pulled out a fifteen-year-old snapshot. There he was, a little boy of five or six, lying in a heap beside his bike, tears streaming down his face. Allen felt a surge of rage as he looked at the picture. He realized that his father had planned in advance to tell his girlfriend this humiliating story, and—skilled prosecuting attorney that he was—came equipped with the evidence. Allen began to realize that his father had belittled him in this calculated manner for as long as he could remember.

The Passive Father

The Passive Father is a man whose emotions barely raise a blip on the screen. He rarely laughs, cries, or gets angry. Because of the extent of his repression he has a diminished sense of personal power and low self-esteem. He's not an angry or punishing father, but he wounds the boy nonetheless by failing to provide a credible model of manhood.

Most Passive Fathers have a simple pattern of anger that goes like this: frustration → repression. The more annoyed he becomes, the more he represses his anger. His internal injunction against anger is so strong that he unilaterally disarms himself. But when he represses his healthy anger, he also surrenders his ability to defend himself against attack, to secure what he wants in life, and to provide a strong role model for his son.

Typically, the Passive Father runs away from challenges. He may have a low-risk job that requires little from him, or he may have a more demanding job that he fails to put much energy into. The boy sees other fathers driving around in their luxury cars while his father pulls up in a cramped Ford Pinto. He hears other fathers talk about their stock mergers and fat bonuses, while his dad has trouble paying the bills.

The Passive Father may make a habit of deferring to those around him. He can be bullied by his boss, bureaucratic officials—even other shoppers in a store. One man remembers a time when he went shopping for school clothes with his meek and mild-mannered father. After going to several stores, they finally found a jacket that was perfect in every way—the right size, the right style, the right color, the right price. His father put the jacket down for a moment while they searched for a pair of slacks to go with it. When the father's back was turned, another shopper wandered over to the rack and picked up the jacket. The boy tugged at his dad's sleeve to alert him to what was going on. The boy watched in dismay as his father remained mute and let the woman walk over to the counter and purchase the jacket. The boy's face felt flushed with shame.

Every time a father yields without good reason to the people around him, he sells a little piece of his soul. Unbeknownst to the father, he barters away a piece of his son's soul as well.

It is not unusual for Passive Fathers to have a volcanic pattern of anger. They are quiet and withdrawn for long periods of time. Then, with little warning on the seismograph, they erupt. But as soon as the eruption subsides the Passive Father is filled with remorse. He apologizes for his irrational behavior and tries to be even more docile in the future. He views anger as a childish fit of self-indulgence that needs to be kept under control. What he doesn't realize is that his son longs for him to display his angry energy, but to do it in a consistent, wise, and judicious manner. The little boy needs to know that if anything threatens him or his family, his father is his first line of defense. And even more important, he needs to have a father who has enough strength and credibility to earn the respect of those around him.

All little boys look to their fathers for a vision of manhood. The son of the Passive Father sees that a man is subservient, cautious, and conciliatory. He grows up believing that a man allows other people to take advantage of him. Although he may hunger for a stronger role model, the boy usually finds himself becoming passive and unassertive like his father. The law of the family jungle seems to be monkey see, monkey do.

The Self-Centered Father

The Self-Centered Father is one who is so preoccupied with his own view of the world and so delighted by his own thought processes that he rarely forms a clear image of his son. The boy enters his consciousness only to the degree that he supports or opposes him. Whenever the Self-Centered Father talks, it's about his own ideas and successes. When he gets involved in outside activities, it's to suit his own tastes and interests. He rarely stretches outside of his comfort zone to see his son's point of view; he's too enthralled with his own reality.

Some Self-Centered Fathers acquired their feelings of grandiosity at an early age by being the favorite child of an adoring parent. They grew up accustomed to adulation and expect it as their birthright. Other Self-Centered Fathers are merely claiming their male prerogative. It is only natural that they sit at the head of the table and be in the driver's seat. It is only natural that their thoughts and opinions be given the most weight in the family. A man's home is his castle.

But none of this fully explains the degree of self-involvement of the most extreme cases of Self-Centered Fathers. Some fathers act as if other people don't exist. Other people's needs and concerns simply fail to register on their psyches. The root cause of their solipsism is their extreme emotional isolation. They've repressed so many of their feelings that they can't detect or respect the feelings of others. They are operating in an emotional void. This is what I call "male narcissism," a narcissism based on an inability to connect with others emotionally.

Typically, the son of a Self-Centered Father has two choices: he can emulate his dad and win his praise, or he can oppose his father and preserve his identity. However, even if a son chooses to follow in the footsteps of his Self-Centered Father, he faces considerable difficulty, because every step will be monitored. I recently talked with a man named Carl who is in his late forties. Carl's father is a wealthy, influential man who, in his mid-seventies, is still a force to be reckoned with. He is an architect and continues to make significant contributions to his field even though he's been officially retired from his firm for ten years.

Unconsciously, Carl made a decision early in life to please his father and follow in his imposing footsteps. He went to the same university as his father and, like his father, studied architecture. However, Carl found himself more fascinated by architectural engineering than by architectural design. His father was annoyed that he insisted on carving out his own niche.

Carl further irritated his father by remaining a bachelor until he was in his mid-thirties. His father had married when he was in his early twenties and was convinced that his two sons should marry equally early. As usual, he had a long list of reasons why his particular course of action had been the correct one. When Carl eventually married at thirty-five, his father showed his disapproval by refusing to come to the wedding.

Carl finally began to comprehend the degree of his father's self-centeredness one weekend when his father consented to visit him and his wife in their new home. His father criticized everything about their life-style that was different from his own. Among other things, he questioned Carl's judgment for heating the house with gas and not oil, for having the daily paper delivered in the morning instead of the afternoon, and for painting the walls of his house muted shades of pastel instead of off-white. His father could tolerate only one view of the world, and that was his own. The final straw came Saturday night when Carl offered his father a feather pillow to sleep on. His father said with derision, "Don't tell me you don't have any foam pillows in the house."

To the Self-Centered Father, there is no such thing as individual preference. There is only his way and the wrong way. Carl told me his reaction to the exchange over the pillow: "I'm supposed to do everything the way my father does it. I've known that for a long time. But how am I supposed to know what kind of damn pillow he sleeps on?"

A son who chooses to oppose rather than appease his Self-Centered Father faces a different set of challenges. Carl's younger brother, Dale, was labeled the black sheep of the family because he resisted his father's preaching. He declined to study any form of architecture and followed his own love of biology. His father was so upset by Dale's career choice that he refused to pay his college tuition. In a sense, Dale had an easier row to hoe than Carl because he was freed from the need to keep earning his father's approval every step of the way. But in exchange for his freedom he was forced to carry the heavy burden of his father's rejection.

The Hostile/Abusive Father

Fathers like mine are what I call Hostile/Abusive Fathers. As I write these words, I can still recall the burning of my hands, my bottom, and my legs from the lashings of his belt. I can still feel the shame of being beaten like an animal. I have no idea how many times my dad whipped me—it could have been twenty times or a hundred—but beatings don't have to happen very often to create deep fear and hatred in a child.

Hostile/Abusive Fathers have a pattern of behavior that goes like this: frustration → anger → attack. They have so little self-control they jump quickly from annoyance to abuse. Their violent outbursts keep the whole family on edge. Some abusive fathers add another factor to the equation: frustration → drinking → anger → attack. For these men it takes a few cans of beer or shots of whiskey to lower their inhibitions and bring out the hostility. But whether alcohol is involved or not, the Hostile/Abusive Father uses his anger as a weapon to control and punish his kids. By bullying his children he feels the power and authority he doesn't feel anywhere else in the world. He can come home from a humiliating encounter with his boss and shore up his bruised ego by lording it over his little boy. Typically, he lays out such strict and arbitrary rules of behavior that his son has no choice but to step over the line. When the boy breaks a rule, his father convinces himself that the boy deserves his abuse.

All too often the son of the Hostile/Abusive Father is the first one, and sometimes the only one, to bear the brunt of his frustration. I remember walking home from elementary school one day feeling happy-go-lucky as I kicked the rocks along the sidewalk. When I got home, I played for a while by myself. After about an hour my father came home and I overheard him complaining to my mother in the next room. I heard him say something about a "god-damn foreman" and I felt my stomach start to clench. He was in one of his moods. I heard my mom's voice followed by silence. Then I heard the dreaded sound of my dad's footsteps. I turned to see my father glaring at me as he whipped his belt out of his belt loops. "You're going to get it," he said. He was breathing heavily. He grabbed me by the arm and started hitting me. "I'm going to teach you if it's the last thing I do," he yelled. I begged him to stop. I screamed out to him, "Why? Why? What did I do?" I had no idea why I was being punished. After a dozen lashings, my brother, Lewis, came into the room and cried out, "Daddy, I did it. I broke Mom's vase." My dad let go of my arm and I tumbled to the floor. I looked up at him in hopes of an apology. He said, "That was for all the times I didn't catch you. It's for general principles." The broken vase had given my father a convenient outlet for his anger at his foreman.

As in my case many boys who are raised by Hostile/Abusive Fathers are more terrorized by their fathers than by anything their fathers are supposed to protect them against. Instead of fighting off the dragons that plague little boys, the father becomes the most terrifying dragon of all. A client told me that when he was a little boy, the last thing he would do each night before turning out the light was to push a chair against his bedroom door. He had an overriding fear that his father was going to barge into his room in the middle of the night and attack him. This little boy didn't have the typical fears of children his age—boogeymen in the closet and strange noises in the dark. He was scared to death of his own father.

Bart, a member of one of my men's groups, is another son of a Hostile/Abusive Father. One night he told the group about the way his father taught him to swim: "Before I knew what was happening, my father was throwing me into the deep end of the pool. I frantically pawed the water, barely able to keep my nose above water. I thrashed my way to the side of the pool and grabbed the edge for support, but my dad stepped on my fingers, mashing them into the concrete. He laughed and ordered me back out into the middle of the pool. I went under water again and again, swallowing mouthfuls of water. I thought I was going to drown."

One of the men tried to break the tension with a lighthearted comment: "Well, Bart, did you learn how to swim?"

"Yeah," Bart replied with a grim expression, "I did learn how to swim. But I also learned how to hate my father's guts."

Invariably, when a father is physically abusive, he is emotionally abusive as well, and the emotional abuse can be even more devastating than the beatings. The pain from a slap on the face or a cuff on the arm lasts a few minutes; the pain from verbal abuse lasts a lifetime. One all-too-common form of emotional abuse is shaming. When a father shames his son, the boy feels inadequate. He feels as though he can never do anything right. He feels that he's a lost cause. Unfortunately, a father doesn't have to go to great lengths to shame his son. A turned-down mouth, a shake of the head, a roll of the eyes, or a sigh of exasperation can cut to the quick. A few choice words of ridicule can demolish a boy's self-esteem: "Jesus Christ, son! I told you to watch the ball!" "Do I need to clean out your ears so you can hear me?" "What's the matter with you, Dummy? Can't you learn?"

Maurice, a member of my Tuesday-night group, had a Hostile/Abusive Father. He remembers a time when he was eleven years old and his father asked him to put away the garden hose. The hose was cold and stiff so he had a hard time coiling it in neat loops. His dad, who had been watching from a short distance away, suddenly blurted out at him, "Gimme that goddamn hose. Jesus Christ! Can't you do anything right? Go in the house with your mother and sister." Maurice walked toward the house like a dog with his tail between his legs. When he got to the door, he heard his dad mutter, "That boy will never amount to a goddamn thing!" Maurice told us that his dad's parting shot burned into his soul like a brand on the back of a steer.

Typically, Hostile/Abusive Fathers add to their sons' distress by not allowing them to express the rage they feel at being mistreated. It's a two-stage form of abuse: first they stir up the boys' anger, then they make them repress it, forcing the rage to live on in their souls. I remember sitting at the dinner table and feeling hurt by a cruel remark from my dad. As I glanced over at him with narrowed eyes, he yelled at me, "Don't you *ever* look at me that way again." His subjugation of me was so complete that I wasn't even allowed to make an angry face.

Many men who grew up with Hostile/Abusive Fathers try to downplay the damage that comes from those early years of torment. They say things like, "It's water under the bridge," or "Hey, what good is it to cry over spilled milk?" or "That was when I was a little boy. It's all behind me now." What they don't realize is that their father's abuse left ugly footprints on their souls. One of the reasons that a little boy is so deeply wounded by his Hostile/Abusive Father is that on some level he is convinced that he deserves the abuse. He has no idea that his father is turning on him to compensate for his own feelings of inadequacy. That's beyond his comprehension. Besides, his father finds some way to justify every ugly word and every blow to the head. A Hostile/Abusive Father has a knack for turning perfectly normal behavior into a cause for abuse: "Why did you leave your bike out in the rain, you idiot?" "You left your goddamn socks in the middle of the floor!" "What do you mean you forgot to walk the dog?" The boy takes his father's tirades to heart and begins to see himself as bad and unloveable. He feels he deserves to be beaten up and abused. Tragically, he inherits his father's feelings of worthlessness.

When a boy's self-esteem is eroded away by his Hostile/Abusive Father, he tries to cover it up with an elaborate defense system. My defense was to become a pleaser and try to stay out of harm's way. A more common form of defense is to become macho/aggressive, just like the dad. Without fully understanding why, the boy becomes a "chip off the old block" and goes through life feeling paradoxically wooden and full of rage—a replica of his father. Over time this rage can turn inward and cause him to abuse himself with drugs or alcohol. Or it can turn outward and cause him to abuse his wife and children. As we have learned, the majority of men who are guilty of domestic violence were themselves victims of child abuse.

Ultimately, being raised by a Hostile/Abusive Father skews a man's entire outlook on life. A deep-seated fear of the father can translate into a basic mistrust of all men, of all authority, or of the world at large. In extreme cases the repressed rage at the father can become the fuel that feeds the burning hatred of the skinhead, the racist, or the murderer. Childhood abuse is not "water under the bridge"—something that is transitory, fluid, and easily forgotten. It's a deep reservoir of pain and anger, threatening anyone who wanders too close to the hastily constructed dam.

The Neglectful Father

The Neglectful Father is a father who fails to give his son the time, attention, and guidance he needs. He may slight his son for any number of reasons, including being divorced, preoccupied with work, self-absorbed, passive, alcoholic, addicted to drugs, obsessed with sports, or chronically depressed.

A majority of fathers fall into this final category. Most of the Dysfunctional Dads I've already described add neglect to their other failings. Although many fathers give their boys bursts of attention every now and then, they fail to give them the reliable, steadfast, patient fathering that young boys require. The rules on the MAN BOX encourage a man to direct his energy away from his family, away from his son.

Another reason many men neglect their children is that they don't have good parenting skills. Society hasn't seen fit to educate men about their fathering role. The assumption is that women will bear primary responsibility for the child rearing. As a result, few fathers learn that young children need what I call "usable love," an observable, concrete form of daily interaction. I like to use the metaphor of gold coins. Every time a father picks up his baby boy and sings to him, hugs him, or reads him a story, it's as if he is taking a gold coin from his pocket and depositing it into his son's tiny pocket. When he tucks his son into bed, gives him a ride on his shoulders, or takes him with him to the store, the little boy's emotional bank account grows. When the boy is a little older and his dad plays ball with him, takes him fishing, or reads to him, he is depositing yet more gold coins. When the boy is a teenager and his dad shows him how to tune a car's engine, install a memory chip in the home computer, or balance a checkbook, he is dispensing still more usable love. Years later when the boy has his own child, he will reach down and discover he has a pocketful of gold coins to hand out to his son or daughter.

A friend of mine can attest to the enduring quality of usable love. One day he was holding his two-year-old boy on his knee, jiggling him up and down. As he was doing this, he found himself reaching out and patting the boy's leg in time with the bounces. Something about this motion seemed very familiar to him, and he realized with a flush that his father used to bounce him on his knees and pat him in the very same way. My friend had reached into his pocket and pulled out a usable form of love.

I don't think many fathers have any idea how much these simple, daily rituals mean to their little boys. From their sons' point of view, fathers are godlike creatures. Unfortunately, most men tend to see themselves from the opposite direction, from the eyes of their own, internalized critical fathers. They focus on their shortcomings, their inadequacies, their confusion. Lost in self-criticism, they fail to see the adoring eyes of their sons.

A middle-aged physician named Garret with curly black hair and rounded shoulders talked about his dad during a recent therapy session. He adored his father, but as the fourth child in a family of eight he had rarely gotten enough time with him. There were always seven other siblings competing for his dad's attention.

One day when Garret was about seven years old, his father took him along with him to the grocery store. Garret was elated. For the first time in a very long time he had his dad all to himself. He clambered into the pickup truck and scooted over close to his dad. On the drive to the store he watched in awe as his father's large hand moved the stick shift. His dad seemed so masterful. Garret said, "That ride remains one of the clearest, dearest memories of my childhood. It meant so much to me to be alone with my dad."

My guess is that Garret's father has no recollection of that ride to the store. To him it had probably been just another errand. His mind may have been filled with dozens of mundane thoughts—a leaky roof, problems at work, the grocery list. He probably had no idea that the little boy sitting next to him was in seventh heaven.

One kind of usable love that is crucial to every little boy is verbal and physical affection. A boy longs to be hugged and touched by his father and to hear him say those all-important three words: "I love you." It's the most direct way for him to be assured of his father's love. Regrettably, many fathers in this culture have been taught that demonstrations of love are "unmanly." During one Wildman Gathering three men stood up one after another and talked about hungering for affection from their fathers. The first man said that the only time he could recall the touch of his father's hand was when he was ten years old and sick in bed with a fever. He said, "I remember my dad opening my door, coming into my room, and sitting on the edge of my bed. I'll never forget what he did next. He rested his hand on my forehead and pushed his fingers through my hair." As the man related this memory, he took off his baseball cap and ran his own fingers through his sandy crew cut. "I'll never forget the coolness of his palm against my hot forehead and the sensation of his fingers running through my hair. I can't recall him ever touching me before or since."

A second, older man stood up. "The only time I remember my dad touching me," he said, "was on the day of my wedding. I was twenty-three years old. When the ceremony was over, my dad reached out and shook my hand. That was thirty years ago. I can still remember the feel of his hand. I remember all the crevices and calluses. The heat of his hand. The breadth of his palm. The pressure as he squeezed my fingers."

The third man stood up. He recalled a night when he was about twenty-five years old when he and his dad were on a camping trip. They were drinking beer around the fire, and the beer had loosened his inhibitions. He felt closer to his dad at that moment than ever before. "I decided to screw up my courage and tell my father how much I cared for him," he told the group. "I looked at him and said, 'I love you, Dad.' I expected him to say, 'I love you, too, son,' but instead he looked down and mumbled, 'Yeah.' He died six months later without ever telling me he loved me."

A particular kind of Neglectful Father can be especially confusing to a little boy, and that's what I call the Good But Too Busy Dad. This is a father who seems to have all the qualities necessary to be a wonderful father—he's emotionally available; he's never rageful or violent; he has a strong, forceful personality—but he's rarely at home. He allows his work to take precedence over his children.

It's doubly hard on a boy when his Good But Too Busy Dad has a noble or prestigious profession. His father may be a university president, a CEO, a congressman, a minister, a physician, or a crusader for human rights. Everywhere the dad goes, he is greeted with accolades. His little boy hears over and over again how lucky he is to have such an illustrious man for a father. But the boy feels as bereft as any orphan or child of divorce.

Typically, the whole family colludes in the father's neglect—even the boy's mother, though she, too, may be struggling with her own feelings of abandonment. She says to her son, "Your father is working late again tonight. You'll have to be very quiet when you get up in the morning." She creates a protective bubble around her husband, allowing him to concentrate on his career with as little guilt or interference as possible. For the most part the boy goes along with the program. When his dad apologizes to him for being too busy or for breaking yet another promise, the boy rushes to his rescue, "That's okay, Dad. I know you have a lot to do." But underneath he feels abandoned. The fact that his father has important business away from the family makes sense to his rational mind, but it fails to register on his soul. He grows up feeling unloved and rejected.

A man named David told me about attending the funeral of his Good But Too Busy Dad that was held in one of the largest Presbyterian churches in New York City. He said that so many people showed up for the funeral that they had to put up loudspeakers for all those who couldn't find seats inside. Dozens of VIPs were there, some of them having flown in from around the country. David felt lost in the crush of mourners. As he looked around him, he realized that his relationship with his father had been diluted by a cast of thousands. He told me, "That moment I felt no more important to my dad than any of the other people who were packed in around me. I felt cheated. My father may have been a great man, but he shared only a fraction of his greatness with me."

It is not unusual for a Good But Too Busy Dad to do an about-face in later years and devote himself wholeheartedly to his son. Retirement, reduced work pressure, a heart attack—something brings him to his senses and makes him realize that his family is vitally important to him. All of a sudden he is calling his son on the phone, writing effusive letters, pressing him for visits. A part of the son relishes this long-overdue attention, but another part of him resents the fact that his dad wasn't there when he needed him most.

THE PAIN OF A FATHER'S NEGLECT

When a boy doesn't get enough consistent, usable love from his father for whatever reason, he develops what Robert Bly calls "a hole in the soul." Deep down he feels inadequate. He doesn't blame his dad for neglecting him; he blames himself for failing to be worthy of his dad's attention. Ultimately, this leads to deep-seated feelings of inferiority.

Only in the past few years have I come to realize that my father's neglect injured me as much or more than his physical abuse. He was never able to show his love and support to me. I recall all those times when I had mastered some new trick or skill and went to him for approval, but his hawklike eyes never registered a flicker of pride. I remember the first rubberband gun I made and how anxious I was to show it to him. As I held it up to him and looked in his face, I yearned to see his proud eyes looking back at me. Instead, he said sternly, "If you hurt anybody with that thing you're going to be in big trouble."

No matter how many times he rejected me, I kept struggling to see his proud eyes. When I was eight years old, I had fast reflexes and could outdraw all the kids on Pearl Street with my six-shooter. But when I whipped out my gun for my dad, there was no applause. When I was fourteen, I took on a paper route and delivered papers every morning for a year, never missing a day. With the money from the paper route I made monthly payments on a motor scooter from Sears. I never missed a payment, but my father never praised me.

I knew that my dad liked football, so I tried out for the high school football team and made the starting lineup on the B-team, even though I had a slight build and weighed less than some of the cheerleaders. The night of our big game, a homecoming game, I played with all my might. I knew my dad was watching because the stadium was right across the street from our house, and he went to all the high school games. That night I caught two long passes and made some key tackles. My heart sang out each time I heard my name announced over the loudspeaker. I was high as a kite as I walked into our living room later that night. Surely my dad would have something to say to me now! I can still see him sitting in his easy chair reading the sports page of the newspaper. He didn't look up. Just once—just this once—I wanted to see my dad's proud eyes. I mustered the courage to ask him if he had been at the game. He said, "Yeah, I went. It was a good game, too." But he wasn't able to say one word about me.

I heard a poignant story about another Neglectful Father during a talk I was giving to a hundred men who were packed into a small hotel meeting room in Seattle. In the middle of my lecture about Neglectful Fathers, a middle-aged man was embarrassed to find himself sobbing out loud. He continued to cry for a few minutes. Then he stood up, took a deep breath, and said that he had a story that illustrated the very point I had been making. He said that his parents got divorced when he was five years old, and his father had packed up his things and moved out of the house. He had been very attached to his dad and was brokenhearted by his absence. In the months that followed he saw his father quite frequently, but then, as is usually the case, his dad's visits began to taper off. By the time he was nine years old, he was seeing his dad only five or six times a year.

During one of those rare visits his dad asked him if he wanted to go trout fishing the following weekend. He was thrilled. His dad said he would pick him up on Saturday morning at seven o'clock. He wanted him to be waiting on the front porch so they could get an early start.

On Friday night the boy set his alarm clock for five-thirty in the morning. He had his mom check it twice to make sure he had set it right. The next morning the alarm went off and he leaped out of bed. He felt like a grown-up as he made his own breakfast and fixed some bologna sandwiches for himself and his dad. He got his fishing pole and tackle box from the garage, grabbed the sack of sandwiches, and was out on the porch by six-thirty. Seven o'clock came and his dad hadn't arrived. He was tingling with anticipation, expecting his dad's car to show up any second. He kept imagining that he heard the sound of the car turning the corner at the end of his block. Eight o'clock and still no dad. At nine o'clock he went into the house and asked his mom what could be keeping him. She said he was probably tied up and would be there any minute. The boy hurriedly went to the bathroom and ran back outside, worried that his dad had come and gone while he had been inside the house.

He kept up his lonely vigil until noon. Finally, he had to accept the fact that his dad had forgotten him. He felt hurt and humiliated, but he was careful to act as if nothing had happened. He put away his fishing gear and went inside, too ashamed to say anything to his mother. When he saw his dad six weeks later, he didn't say a word about the fishing trip to him either. He acted as if the invitation had never been made.

The man told the group that he would never forget that long day on the porch. "That memory will always be with me," he said, "but what surprises me is that I've waited forty years to release the pain."

I saw compelling evidence of how long grief can lie submerged when I gave a talk about fathers and sons later that year at a Rotary Club. When I was done with my talk, a man who must have been in his nineties slowly made his way to the podium. I had talked to this same group of men the previous year and had noticed this ancient man then. I remember thinking at the time that this was probably his last year on earth, but here he was walking toward me. I studied him with admiration. His hand trembled as he leaned hard on his cane. His nose and ears had grown disproportionately large with age, and his yellowing eyes seemed to have retreated deep into their bony sockets. When he got to the table, he looked down and spoke haltingly in a hoarse voice. I had to bend down close to his face to hear him. "Sir," he said, "I just wanted you to know that you were talking right down my alley. I've never understood why my dad didn't want to spend more time with me. I wanted him to play marbles with me and take me fishing like other dads. But he never did much of that at all." He looked up, and I could see that his eyes were moist with tears. He wiped at his eyes with a shaking hand. "You know, I don't think he ever liked me. Thanks for your talk. That was right down my alley." As he turned and slowly made his way toward the door, I had to brush the tears away from my own eyes.

THE ADEQUATE DAD

I have heard so many men tell stories about abusive, passive, and neglectful fathers that I've sometimes wondered if there are any good, or even Adequate Dads out there. Tamera Smith Allred, a journalist from Portland, Oregon, had an experience recently that underscored the dearth of information about good fathers. She was assigned two articles by *This Week Magazine,* a weekly newspaper in the Portland metropolitan area with a circulation of over four hundred thousand.

She was to write an article on mothers for Mother's Day and an article on fathers for Father's Day. She solicited letters from readers for both articles. The notice asking for letters about fathers read, "Tell us about your dad and how he's been a hero in your life." She received fewer than fifty letters about fathers. What was even more surprising was that only three of the letters about fathers were written by men, and those three men described their own parenting efforts, not their dads'. Not a single man volunteered any information about the heroics of his own father. Says Allred, "I had a wealth of information about good mothers. I had to do extra research to flesh out the article on fathers."

Why don't we hear more about good fathers? Part of the problem is that we've dramatically raised our fathering standards in recent decades. In the past a man who supported his family, didn't drink too much, didn't yell at or hit his kids, came home every night, and spent half an hour playing ball with his kids on the weekends was regarded as a "good enough" father. That's about all I expected of myself when my own kids were young. In fact, I remember taking pride in the fact that I didn't abuse them verbally or physically. That alone made me think of myself as an Adequate Dad. It didn't take much to surpass the standards set by my father.

Now we expect so much more of fathers. In addition to financially supporting the family we expect them to assist in childbirth, change diapers, take part in nightly feedings, tend to their children when they're sick, understand their children's feelings, help them with homework, validate them. . . . The list seems to expand every year. When we look back at the fathers of yesterday, we tend to judge them by 1990s standards. Our mothers fare better in this postgame analysis because our mothering standards have always been high, and there has been tremendous social pressure for women to live up to them. In fact, now that so many women are doing double duty outside the home, mothers of years ago may shine with more luster than present-day moms.

But there are a number of Adequate Dads in the world. I am happy to say that my brother, Lewis, is one of them. He has spent a lot of time with his daughters and son. Years ago, when he and I went on our outdoor adventures, he invited his kids along. I remember being in awe of the respect that he showed them and the patience with which he answered their questions.

It's a miracle that he became such a good father. He spent just as much time around an angry, violent, and Neglectful Father as I did. However, there were some important differences between us. Our father raged against me more than he did against Lewis. I was his primary scapegoat. Also, Lewis studied education in college and was required to take some child-development courses. His wife took the same courses, and the two of them had many conversations about child rearing before having children. His children are reaping the benefits.

I learned about another remarkable father at a Wildman Gathering that I held in Texas in April 1991. On that weekend, television commentator Hugh Downs and his crew were filming parts of the Gathering for a *20/20* special on the men's movement. During one of the breaks I went for a walk with Hugh. I was accustomed to cynical and road-weary journalists, so I was delighted to see that he showed a genuine interest in what we were doing. Seventy years old, he had both feet planted firmly on the ground, yet his spirit soared with wonder and fascination. I learned that, in addition to being a journalist, he was a pilot, an avid sailor, and a scuba diver.

As we walked together across the ranch, I wondered what kind of father this successful, self-assured man must have had. When I asked Hugh about his dad, his face lit up. He said that he remembered sitting in his dad's lap as a little boy, talking with him for long periods of time. His dad would listen to him and nod thoughtfully, making him feel both wise and worthy of his attention. He talked about the many times his father had taken him to the symphony and explained the names and sounds of the various instruments. He told me of visits to museums and how his dad had discussed art history with him in a way that made it seem fascinating, even to a little boy. As we got to Hugh's cabin, he said that his father had not only shared a great deal of information with him, he had communicated an overall enthusiasm for life.

Later, as I thought about Hugh Downs and his many accomplishments, I could see how the joy of the father lived on in the son. Hugh's openness to new ideas, his compassion, and his wide-ranging interests are a testimony to how rich life can be for those fortunate men whose fathers were skilled in the art of dispensing usable love.

THE WIND BENEATH OUR WINGS

When I think about healthy, soulful fathering, this line from a popular song pops up in my head: "You were my hero, you were the wind beneath my wings." Little boys need a hero who is more than a two-dimensional character on a comic-book page or a movie screen. They need a real-life, day-to-day hero. They need someone who will hug them and protect them and give them a shining model of manhood. They need someone whose trust and belief in them will buoy them up when they are young eagles just learning to fly. Boys who are lucky enough to have loving, supportive fathers discover that the frantic wing flapping of their boyhood soon gives way to strong, rhythmic beats of their wings. As young men they are able to ride the thermals above the mountains and valleys.

All too many of us had Dysfunctional Dads, and we left the nest without the information and self-confidence we needed to function as powerful, independent men. Instead of soaring and celebrating our manhood, we have to continually flap our wings to prove ourselves worthy. Because of our insecurity we take experiences like sex, which should bring us pleasure and spiritual connection, and turn them into tests of manhood. How many of us have flapped our way through sexual performances trying to prove our manhood to women we hardly know? Without realizing it we fall into that dark, unhappy pattern of "just once more." Just one more sexual conquest and I'll feel complete. Just one more lover and I won't have to prove my virility ever again.

In the workplace we push and compete as though our very lives depend on it. We flap so hard we barely notice the people around us. When we manage to eke out a success, we derive little pleasure from it. Instead of celebrating the accomplishment we push ourselves on to the next task. In the little time we take off from work, we play so hard at sports that we risk a heart attack.

We don't even have any peace of mind during those few moments when our bodies are at rest because we are harangued by the internalized voices of our critical fathers: "You can't relax and enjoy yourself until you have more money stashed away." "A man your age should be doing much better in life." "You're fifty years old and you're still floundering?" "How many times are you going to have to fuck things up before you finally get it right?" "Here you are, married with three kids and you're still masturbating? When are you going to grow up?" "Your car is five years old and showing some wear. What are the neighbors going to say if you don't get a new one?"

As we flap through life, we feel exhausted, impotent, powerless, unworthy. We feel like impostors and live in fear that others will discover how worthless we truly are.

When we finally gain some perspective on our childhood, we begin to understand why our dads didn't teach us to soar: they didn't have the time or peace of mind. If we slow down the frantic beating of our wings long enough to look down, we discover an even more painful truth: we have been so preoccupied proving our self-worth that we have been neglecting our own sons. Because no one was there to show us the way to a dignified, confident masculinity, we cannot buoy up our sons as they fly away from the nest. Grandfathers, fathers, and sons— we fill the sky with the desperate beating of our wings as we search in vain for the rising thermals.

CHAPTER 4

MEN AND THEIR MOTHERS

For the most part I welcome the heightened interest in the father-and-son relationship. Psychologists have long placed too much blame for a child's emotional problems on the mother. As we have just seen, fathers have a profound effect on their sons as well. Coming to terms with this paternal legacy is an essential part of my approach to men's therapy. However, it's important not to go overboard and place *all* the blame on fathers, which has been a tendency within the men's movement. Men need to examine their relationships with their mothers as well. Only when both parents are brought into view is it possible to unravel the complexity of family relationships. Mothers and fathers and sisters and brothers are all involved in a spontaneous interplay—acting, reacting, and interacting in a complicated loop.

Though this chapter focuses on the relationship between mothers and sons, it also brings the father back into the picture. In particular, it explores what happens to the mother-son relationship when the father is emotionally unavailable. Spouses play a vital role for each other. They are supposed to provide each other with companionship, financial support, emotional support, and sexual satisfaction. When a husband fails to satisfy these needs, his wife has to look elsewhere. The most common tendency is for her to turn to her kids. As family therapist Dr. Patricia Love writes in her book, *The Emotional Incest*

Syndrome, "One fact has been confirmed to me over and over again in my work with families: *people instinctively try to satisfy their emotional needs within the family group.*" Instead of turning to adults outside the family the mother relies, unwittingly, on a child. More often than not she calls on her son—Momma's Little Man—to abandon his own needs and become her surrogate spouse. Many, many men in this country have grown up in this precarious position: deprived of the love and support of their fathers and forced to rely on their mothers, who, in turn, were relying on them.

It is common for a boy who grows up in this situation to become a Pleasing Man, a man who gives up a part of himself in order to gain a woman's love. A new client of mine, a thirty-eight-year-old man named George, makes frequent sacrifices to please his wife. He owns his own small business. His wife also owns a business, which she operates out of their home. George's office is five miles from their house. Several times a week his wife calls him and asks him to come home and pinch hit for her while she runs errands. George drops whatever he's doing and rushes to her rescue. He never questions the importance of what he's doing at the moment versus the importance of what she's doing. The mere fact that she has requested his help galvanizes him into action.

Through his work in the men's group George is beginning to see that he is suppressing his own needs not out of *love* for his wife, but out of a deep fear of losing her, a pattern that is a continuation of his need to please his mother. As a boy he had little sense of connection with his father, who was cool and rational. His only sibling, an older brother, spent most of his time shut up in his bedroom reading books. His relationship with his mother was his only vital emotional link.

Typically, a boy who grows up without a strong father figure not only becomes overly reliant on his mother, but his mother becomes overly reliant on him. This creates a central dilemma for him. He can't turn away from his mother, even when she comes to him with inappropriate needs, because he wants and needs her attention. Without a strong relationship with his father his well-being is in her hands. A part of him may even exult in the close relationship with his mother and struggle to retain the privileged position. But there's a stiff price to pay for being Momma's Little Man. For one thing, if there are other children in the family, they will resent the favoritism. Children are always on the lookout for preferential treatment from a parent, and if Johnny always gets a bigger piece of Mom's apple pie, there is going to be trouble in the ranks. And this won't be ordinary sibling rivalry, but a deep rift between brothers and sisters that can last a lifetime. When adult brothers and sisters fail to get along, the conflict can often be traced to unequal treatment by a parent.

Another consequence for a son who is allied with Mom is being resented by Dad. On some level Dad knows that his son is usurping his role in the family, and this makes him intensely jealous. But even though the relationship between his wife and his son feels wrong to him, he doesn't know why. Aren't mothers supposed to love their sons? Aren't they supposed to spend time with them? Like most people, he doesn't know the difference between love and enmeshment. Not knowing whom to blame, he takes his frustration out on his son. It's far easier to punish a child than to confront a spouse. Now Dad is not just a neglectful or passive father—he may become abusive as well.

It took me many years of therapy to realize that one of the main reasons my father picked me out for punishment was that my mother singled me out for praise. My mother saw in me, and perhaps cultivated in me, many of the qualities she found lacking in my father. For example, she would praise me openly for being such a hard worker, a trait not displayed by my father. She enjoyed my companionship and called on me when she was lonely. I had the same name as my father, and when she called out for "Marvin," neither my father nor I would be sure whom she meant. If it turned out to be me, which was often the case, my father was upset. How many slights like this did he have to endure before he began to recognize me for what I was—his rival?

In the following pages I explore a number of different forms of dysfunctional mothering. At the opposite end of the spectrum from the overly involved mothers are the remote mothers who satisfy their needs by turning *away* from their children. They neglect their sons and devote themselves to their jobs, their boyfriends, or their personal interests. Instead of drawing their sons too tightly into their embrace, they push them away, making them feel worthless and abandoned. A boy who is rejected by his mother can feel rejected by the entire world.

A number of other mothering styles fall between these two extremes. As with fathers, few real-life mothers fit neatly into any one category. Most parents have a complex, and sometimes contradictory, blend of traits. It is fairly common for a boy to have a mother who alternates between paying him too much attention and paying him too little attention, depending on her circumstances. Part of the time her son is of vital importance to her; the rest of the time she pushes him to the side. For example, some mothers are totally devoted to their sons when they are infants, but lose interest in them when they grow up. The boys feel privileged for a portion of their lives then experience a fall from grace. Other mothers may parent obsessively for the first few years of a boy's life, then work at an outside job just as obsessively for the following decades. This on-again, off-again behavior is very confusing to a little boy and makes him want to do anything in his power to stay in his mother's good graces.

SEVEN KINDS OF DYSFUNCTIONAL MOMS

The Smothering Mother

The Smothering Mother is a neighborhood classic. This is the mother who polishes her son's tennis shoes, irons his underwear, writes his essays, eavesdrops on his phone conversations, reads his mail, obsesses over his health, and commandeers his social life. Invariably, she is either single or has an unsatisfying relationship with her spouse. There is an emptiness in her life, which she fills up with her son. Although she is unaware of it, her hidden agenda is to keep her son a little boy so he remains dependent on her.

The telltale signs of maternal enmeshment can appear when a boy is still in his infancy. In a healthy parent-child relationship an infant and his mother form a vital link by mirroring each other's actions and moods, an instinctual process called "synchronicity." The mother smiles at her baby boy and he smiles back. He looks at her and she returns his glance. He cries and his mother's face telegraphs her concern. This intimate interplay builds a strong bond between mother and son, a bond that is essential for his well-being.

However, a baby boy also has a strong drive for independence. When he has momentarily experienced enough connection with his mother, his instinct is to turn his attention to something else. There is a whole world out there for him to explore. A Smothering Mother will not tolerate this separation. She may physically turn the baby's head so they maintain eye contact, or she may coo and cluck at him in such an engaging manner that she remains the most interesting thing in the room. Through one ploy or another she doesn't allow the boy to have a mind of his own.

The reason that she requires her son's undivided attention is that she is struggling with a hidden fear of abandonment. She discovers that she feels less anxious when she is locked in a one-on-one relationship with her child. In effect, she uses her son as an antianxiety drug. The relationship soothes her because she knows her son is completely dependent on her. Unlike an adult partner he's not going to divorce her or abandon her for another woman. He is bonded to her for life.

A mother rarely realizes that she is overly involved in her son's life. She cares a great deal for her son and would never consciously harm him. But unwittingly she disempowers him. She fights his fights with his teachers, even when he begs her not to. She fusses over him to such a degree that he fails to develop his own common sense. She does so many things for him that he develops few skills on his own. She believes she is doing all of this out of love, but the message she sends to her son is that he is too weak or immature to fend for himself.

I am currently working with a college student named Jamie who is trying to break away from his Smothering Mother. One of his most difficult tasks is to sort out how his mother has helped him and how she has disempowered him. On the positive side his mother showered him with love and concern. She held him, cuddled him, and read to him. She made him feel special and privileged. But she also overstepped the parent-child boundary, preventing him from having a sphere of his own. For example, she insisted on coming along with him to all his friends' birthday parties, even when he was eleven and twelve years old. The other parents left their kids at the door and picked them up after the party. Jamie's mother stayed to "help out." She was an active volunteer at his school, finding an excuse to be in attendance several days a week. She became the reading tutor, the librarian's helper, and the perennial room mother. Whenever there was a class camping trip, she would bundle up her sleeping bag and go along as a chaperon. Her husband colluded in this overinvolvement—perhaps because his own mother had died when he was a small boy. He had no model for healthy mothering.

Clearly, Jamie's mother cared for him a great deal. But in reality she was suffocating him. She was enveloping him in her feminine world and frustrating his drive for independence. It's not surprising that he remained overly attached to her as a young adult. He was still living at home when he was twenty-two, which he tried to convince himself was for financial reasons. He'd had several casual girlfriends, but never a serious one, until last year. It was the intensity of his mother's rejection of his girlfriend that convinced him he needed therapy. He knew he was going to need outside help to break free of her influence.

The Seductive Mother

The Seductive Mother is an enmeshing mother who turns to her son not just for companionship but for the romantic and sexual stimulation that is missing from her marriage. Her relationship with her son becomes an ongoing flirtation. Most Seductive Mothers stop short of actual incest, but nonetheless there is an undercurrent of sexual tension between mother and son that can cause a host of difficulties for the boy later in life. I remember watching an attractive, forty-year-old mother romp with her teenage son at the beach. She was wearing a revealing bikini more commonly seen on younger women. The two of them kicked water at each other, chased each other up and down the beach, snapped towels at each other's fannies, giggled, and wrestled. This wasn't ordinary horseplay: the sexual tension between them was palpable. Except for their difference in age, the two of them could have been mistaken for lovers. It is likely that the mother was using her son to provide a missing element of romance and sexual intrigue in her life.

Sometimes the sexual undertones between mother and son are even more blatant. I have heard instances of mothers lounging around the house naked in front of their teenage sons, giving their sons sponge baths long after such physical intimacy is appropriate, talking to their sons about their own sex lives, touching their genitals in their son's presence, and kissing their sons passionately on the mouth. Some men found this behavior disturbingly pleasurable and erotic; others found it repulsive. But in either case, their sexuality and their feelings about women were deeply affected. A common repercussion is that the boy grows up feeling sexually inadequate. As a child a part of his unconscious mind believed that his mother's seductive behavior was an invitation for him to satisfy her sexually. Yet he knew he would never be able to fulfill her expectations. He saw the size of his father's genitals and knew he couldn't compare or compete. This feeling of sexual inadequacy follows him into adulthood.

Dale, a man whom I saw briefly in individual therapy, was raised by a Seductive Mother and a Passive Father. His mother's seduction of him started when he was about thirteen or fourteen. One of the signs of her excessive interest was her preoccupation with his developing manhood. She commented frequently on his deepening voice, his hairy legs, and the fuzz on his upper lip. She put her arms around his waist and marveled at the breadth of his shoulders. She would point out his physical attributes to her friends, which made him feel deeply embarrassed. To Dale's intense dismay, she also seemed curious about the size of his genitals. She bought him some briefs one day and insisted that he model them in front of her to see if she had bought "the right size." He felt deeply ashamed as she tugged at the briefs to "examine the fit."

As Dale grew older his mother's fascination with his body turned into a fascination with his love life. She would ask him probing questions about his girlfriends, including questions about his lovemaking techniques. She called him "a stud." She assumed he was having sex years before that was a reality. One night she came into his room while he was sleeping and went through his wallet. When he woke up he found his condoms lined up in a neat row on his dresser.

Dale tried to protect himself from his mother's invasiveness as best he could by refusing to answer her questions and by spending most of his time alone in his room. One night he woke up to find his mother sitting on his bed. She had been drinking. Although she made no move to touch him, he felt so invaded by her presence that he screamed at her to leave his room. This episode remains one of the most haunting memories of his childhood.

Dale is now forty-nine. He has been single except for a brief, two-year marriage in his early twenties. For the past few years he has had a long-distance relationship with a younger woman. The woman lives in a different state, and they see each other only a few times a year. He was satisfied with this arrangement until he realized how badly he wanted a child. However, the thought of actually marrying the woman made him feel so anxious he decided to get some therapy. He sensed that if he didn't resolve his old issues with his mother, he would never be able to be close with a woman.

The Dependent Mother

The Dependent Mother is also overinvolved with her son. What distinguishes her from other enmeshing mothers is that she's always going through an emotional or physical crisis, and she relies on her son to rescue her. Her husband has either left her or proven incapable of meeting her needs, so she becomes overly reliant on her son. Through various means she lets him know that she would be lost without him. She says to him, "I don't know what I would do without you!" The boy experiences a strange mixture of pride and terror in her dependency. He yearns to be important to her, but he knows he's not able to take care of her needs. One of my clients recalled one evening when he was home alone with his mother. He was about seven or eight years old. His mother was panicked for some unknown reason, and she kept asking him to talk to her and hug her. He was terrified that his mother was so frightened, and tried everything in his power to calm her down.

A little boy is not equipped to handle his mother's emotional problems, but he feels compelled to try. One of the hidden costs is that he has to repress his own needs. The son of a Dependent Mother can't express or even *experience* his own needs because he has to be a tower of strength for Mom. Also, he is burdened with a great deal of anxiety. His mother always seems to hover between life and death, emotional health and insanity, or drunkenness and sobriety. He never feels safe. By extension he feels insecure in all his relationships and in the world at large, first as a boy and later as a man.

Manuel, an engineer who has been in therapy with me for two years, grew up taking care of his mother. The phrase that she used for him was "my little man." As he said to me, "And what's a man supposed to do? The answer is obvious: take care of the woman." One of the ways he was supposed to assist his mother was by trying to keep his father from drinking and using drugs. At the tender age of six he was assigned the task of finding out where his father had hidden the booze and pills. While his mother engaged his father in conversation, he was supposed to sneak around and find the latest stash. One of his earliest memories is digging under the leaves in the hedgerows and finding a bottle of pills his father had hidden. In his mind's eye he can still see the writing on the label and the whiteness of the pills as he dumped them out on the ground.

As an adult he has spent a lot of time dwelling on the fact that his mother pitted him against his father. "I don't know how my dad tolerated my interference. He knew I was the one finding all the drugs and alcohol and pouring them out. He knew what was going on. He wasn't stupid. He never caught me pouring anything out, but he knew." When a mother asks her son to join forces with her against his father, the boy not only gains his father's enmity, he can acquire a lifelong burden of guilt.

Like many boys who grew up enmeshed with their mothers, Manuel found that at times he meant everything to his mother, and at other times he meant nothing at all. His mother's mercurial moods determined the role he played in her life. If his father was late getting home from work, it usually meant he had stopped off at a bar and was going to arrive home drunk. His mother then began an anxious vigil, sucking Manuel into the drama. "Your father's late. He's probably drunk by now. What if he has a car accident? My God, what's going to happen to us?" He tried to comfort his mother and reassure her that everything was going to be okay. He would sit in her lap and put his small arms around her. Then, as soon as his father had arrived home safely, his mother's fear would turn into anger and she would pick a fight with her husband. Manuel would be completely ignored. "I got shoved aside," he said. "I had served my purpose. Nothing I had to say or do was of any importance for the rest of the evening. I would lie in bed and listen to them fight for hours and hours and hours. My mother just switched, like you flip a switch. One minute I was in. I was important. I was close. The next minute I was brushed off. She used me, and it makes me very angry to think about it."

It is not surprising that a boy who is raised by a Dependent Mother tends to view all women as dependent. He may remain a bachelor for years because he is wary of the pressure and responsibility of taking care of another adult. Or he may go in the opposite direction and unwittingly select a wife who is sickly, weak, dependent, or depressed—just like his mother. But no matter what kind of woman he marries, he will feel a heavy sense of responsibility for her. If she gets sad or depressed, he will feel it's his job to make her happy. If she gets angry at him, he will do everything in his power to mollify her. It feels perfectly natural to him to transfer his obsessive caretaking behavior from his mother to his wife.

The Martyr Mother

The Martyr Mother is like the Dependent Mother in that she relies on her son to take care of her. But she weaves an even stickier web. The Martyr Mother begins laying her trap by letting her son know that her happiness depends on him. She is totally incapable of satisfying her own needs, and since no one else cares enough to try, it's entirely up to him. But in a thousand subtle ways she lets her son know that he, too, is failing at the job. No matter what he does, she's not satisfied. Then she tops it all off by appearing to let him off the hook. In so many words she tells him: "I've counted on you to make my life worth living, and you've failed me. But that's okay. You go ahead and have a good life, because mine is ruined. I've paid for your happiness with mine. I've sacrificed everything I have so you can enjoy yourself and have nice things. But that's a mother's lot."

Typically, the child hasn't the slightest clue to what's going on in this convoluted relationship. All he knows is that his mother wants something from him that he can't provide and that he feels guilty most of the time. I can still remember how guilty I felt when my mother used to buy me a new pair of jeans at the beginning of each school year. I couldn't help noticing that she was walking around in torn slips and worn-out shoes. She told me she didn't care how she looked as long as I had something to wear. But if I didn't display enough gratitude, she would become highly resentful and start listing all her sacrifices. She made me feel ashamed of the little I had and even more humiliated about all that I desired.

Typically, the son of a Martyr Mother grows up feeling responsible for everyone around him but feeling incapable of meeting their needs. If something goes wrong at work or at home, he feels that he's to blame. He has difficulty accepting favors or gifts from loved ones because any show of affection makes him feel guilty. He's been trained to believe that all love comes with a price tag.

Hal, a handsome man in his early forties, grew up with nine brothers and sisters. He had a Passive Father and a Martyr Mother. As a young boy Hal heard over and over again about all the sacrifices his mother had made in raising so many children. She told him that she had lost her figure from all the pregnancies and that she had to quit college to raise them. He was the youngest of the nine, and, according to his mother, his birth had been the most difficult. His mother told him several times how she had almost died in childbirth with him. She also mentioned that she was so tired when he was a little boy that he was almost the death of her.

Hal recently flew to the West Coast to visit his mother on Mother's Day. He tried to have a good conversation with her, but all she would talk about was her physical ailments. When Hal tried to console her, she told him, "Don't worry about me. My life is over. You go on with your busy life. I managed to get you kids grown up. That's all I ever wanted. There never was any time for anything else."

Hal thought about that conversation all the way home. He began to recall all the similar comments he'd heard from his mother throughout his childhood. He decided to call his mother and tell her how tired he was of feeling guilty around her. He wanted to see if they could find some other way to communicate. When he told her about his feelings of guilt, she immediately started criticizing herself. "I know I've let you down," she said. "I did the best I could, but obviously it wasn't enough. I'll have to live with that the rest of my life. It's hard to hear from your son that you don't measure up."

Hal was exasperated. She had deftly turned his complaint about guilt feelings into yet another reason to feel guilty around her. He couldn't win. "Mother," he broke into her lament, "I didn't call you to make you feel bad or to have you try to make me feel bad. I just wanted to be clear about how I felt. I wanted to tell you how I wanted to relate with you from now on." They talked for ten more minutes. Hal tried to set some new ground rules between them, but his mother insisted on talking about her ruined life. Finally he said, "I need to go now. But I want you to know that I love you."

"I'll pray for you, Son," was her reply.

It was this conversation that made Hal realize how extremely difficult it was to interact with his mother. It's the way their relationship had always been and probably always would be. He gave up trying to improve their relationship and vowed to see her as little as possible.

The Abandoning Mother

The Abandoning Mother is quite different from the mothers I've described so far. Instead of turning to her children to satisfy her unmet needs, she turns to her job, her boyfriends, or to her own personal interests. In extreme cases she deserts her son and leaves him with relatives or foster parents so she can live a free and unencumbered life. More typically, she keeps her children with her but withholds her love and affection. All she can seem to do is feed and clothe her children.

One type of Abandoning Mother is the divorcée who is always going out with new men. She goes out on a date, becomes wrapped up in the excitement of romance, and forgets that it's eleven-thirty Wednesday night and she has children at home all alone. One of my clients remembers the anxious vigil he used to keep at the front window of his house, waiting for his mom to come home from her dates. He'd watch a car pull up in his driveway and witness his mother being kissed and fondled by some strange man. One night he watched as a man lifted his mother on the hood of his car and began to kiss her all over her body. He became sick to his stomach with fear and disgust.

Another type of Abandoning Mother who is becoming increasingly common these days is the woman who puts so much energy into her job that she doesn't have time for her children. She may have the best of intentions and she may care deeply for her son, but she directs most of her energy outside the family. She may work outside the home out of necessity; she may be a single parent or have to work to supplement the family income. But the reason she's gone so much of the time matters little to her son. All he knows is that he misses his momma. Even though he is well cared for by a nanny or a sitter or is placed in an elite day-care center, he still feels a hollowness in his soul.

In an ideal world his father would step in and satisfy his emotional needs, but few boys with abandoning mothers are blessed with nurturing fathers. Their fathers are just as preoccupied with outside activities as their mothers. For a growing number of boys in this country neither parent is primarily focused on the home, the family—or on him.

A third type of abandoning mother is the woman who spends so much time trying to please her husband that she has little energy for her son. In many cases the boy's father or stepfather doesn't relate well with children and prefers to spend time alone with his wife. Grandma or a sitter fills in at home while Mom and Stepdad go off for yet another vacation. One of my clients, Larry, told me that his mother was a virtual slave to his stepfather, bringing him his beer and cigars, sitting next to him on the couch, and flirting with him for hours. His stepdad seemed to have no interest in him at all. Although Larry had a sister to play with, there were times when he felt like a stranger in his own family.

Searching for a sense of belonging, Larry spent a lot of time with the family next door. There were three kids in the family, and their parents seemed to have time not only for their own children but for him as well. They would play Monopoly or other board games every evening. On the day of his birthday, a Saturday, Larry went next door right after lunch. The neighbors gave him a warm welcome and invited him in. He stayed all day. When it was time for dinner, the neighbor mother suggested that Larry spend some time with his own family. After all, it was his birthday. Larry felt that he wasn't welcome there anymore, so he went back to his house in tears, only to discover that neither his mother nor his stepfather had realized he was gone.

The Critical Mother

Just as there are a multitude of Critical Fathers in this world, so are there a multitude of Critical Mothers. But there is a key difference between the two parenting styles. Traditionally, the father's role has been to teach his son physical skills such as hitting a baseball, mowing the lawn, rolling up the garden hose, driving a car, or baiting a hook. It's been his job to make sure his son is competent and masterful. As we have seen, when a father teaches those skills through criticism, his son grows up feeling incompetent, inadequate, and unmanly—the opposite of what the father intended.

A mother's traditional parenting role is somewhat different. Her time-honored responsibility is to be the spiritual leader of the household. It's her job to civilize all the "heathens." She teaches her children good manners and instills sound morals. When the Critical Mother tries to teach those values through criticism, she too fails to produce the desired results.

Here is the way some Critical Mothers talk to their sons:

"Don't treat your brother that way. You ought to be ashamed of yourself."

"Stop touching yourself down there. That's dirty."

"Don't you know how to act at the dinner table? Are you an animal?"

"Clean your room. You are such a slob."

"Sit still! Can't you control yourself?"

"Share that with your sister. You are so selfish!"

The boy appears to be deaf to her criticisms, so the mother repeats them over and over again. What she doesn't realize is that her son is paying very close attention. But he's not listening to her pleas for better behavior: "Clean your room!" Instead, he's registering the criticism that follows: "You're a slob." As the years go by, he absorbs her low opinion of him. He says to himself, "I'm shameful. I'm dirty. I'm an animal. I'm a slob. I'm out of control. I'm selfish." He grows up feeling that there is something inherently wrong with him. It's not his *actions* that are unacceptable to his mother; it's his very being.

In some cases a mother's tendency to criticize her son's character may stem from a lack of understanding of the inherent differences between boys and girls. As a general rule, boys tend to be more physically active, more aggressive, and less cooperative than girls, and these behaviors can show up as early as age one. Later on boys are likely to spend less time playing with one friend and more time roaming the neighborhood in a pack. In adolescence they exhibit a higher level of sexual desire than girls. While we may never know to what degree these behaviors are influenced by gender conditioning, there appear to be some inborn differences between the sexes.

A mother who is not aware of these differences may unwittingly expect her son to behave more like a girl. She may rail against him for his boundless energy, his persistence in climbing on the furniture, or his compulsion to exercise his muscles. She might put him down for failing to treat his friends the same way her daughter treats her friends. After all, her daughter seems to be perfectly content to spend hours with her one "best friend." Why does her son insist on roaming with the herd?

But in some cases the Critical Mother does not just fail to understand the nature of little boys—she doesn't *like* the nature of little boys. This unhappy truth is not lost on her son. Rodger, a thirty-seven-year-old bachelor in one of my groups, told us that both his mother and his two sisters seemed to unite against him simply because he was male. His mother frequently ridiculed him about his dirty room and told him he was a slob, "just like your father." She criticized him for not playing with his sisters, but when he tried to join in their games, his sisters told him to go away. His mother and his sisters would openly criticize him and his friends, and talk about what jerks men were. When he was a teenager, his mother caught him looking at a *Penthouse* magazine, and she said to him, "Don't tell me you're going to grow up to be a sex addict like your Uncle Mark." Rodger grew up feeling unsafe in his own home, partly because he was male.

To get insight into the kind of mother who does not like little boys or grown men, it helps to examine life from her point of view. Like all women she grew up in a patriarchal system, a Good Ol' Boy world where she was often excluded or treated like a second-class citizen. As a young girl her creative and intellectual talents may not have been encouraged. If she had a career, she had to fight for equal pay for equal work. For any number of reasons, she grew up harboring a lot of resentment against men. But society tells her she's not supposed to show her anger. The rules on the WOMAN BOX are quite explicit: "Women are sweet, gentle, patient, receptive, and compliant." But rage will find a way out, whether directly or indirectly, and unfortunately, the safest and most logical target for her repressed anger at men is her son. She becomes a Critical Mother who sees ten things wrong with her son for every one she approves.

The Hostile/Abusive Mother

The witch is a common figure in fairy tales, representing the shadow side of the mother. Typical examples are the witches in "Hansel and Gretel" and "Snow White" who do their damage through seduction, manipulation, persuasion, and trickery. Their evil is disguised behind a comely mask. "Come eat my red apple." "Come have some candy." Once the child falls for the bait, the witch peels off her mask and reveals her malicious intent.

For a few unfortunate men the witch in the fairy tale is an apt metaphor for their mothers. At times their mothers loved and nurtured them; at other times they abused them. The boys' deep need for nurturing kept them within their mothers' grasp.

The Hostile/Abusive Mother is a more extreme version of the Critical Mother. She doesn't just shame her son; she torments him. She doesn't just criticize her son and send him from the room; she lashes out at him with a belt. In some instances her violent behavior arises from physical or sexual abuse she suffered from a male relative or stranger. The rage she feels against men is immense, and she takes it out on her helpless son. One of the most abusive mothers I've ever encountered was sexually abused by her father. She had yet to deal with this tragic event when her son was born. She became hysterical the moment the doctor handed her baby to her and she saw his penis. His maleness triggered an unconscious association with her sexually abusive father. She neglected her son for the first year of his life. She would leave him crying for hours without feeding him or changing his diaper. She eventually abandoned him when he was four years old.

A small number of boys have the misfortune of living with two abusive parents. To the boy it's as if he were living in a cave, and his mother, the "witch," is the keeper of the cave. Her abuse casts a spell over his soul, and he tries to escape to the outside world. But his father, the dragon, lurks just outside. When the boy escapes from the cave, the dragon attacks him and drives him back inside. Even though his mother's spell weakens him, her power doesn't seem as life threatening as the fire-breathing dragon just outside the cave. In fact, the dark energy of the "witch" mother can feel a lot like love to a scared, trapped, naïve little boy with a dragon for a father.

More commonly, a boy with a Hostile/Abusive Mother has a Passive Father. Like Hansel's father in "Hansel and Gretel," the father allows himself to be emasculated by his wife. Unconsciously, the boy fears he is going to suffer the same fate as his dad because his mother has such an aversion to anything masculine.

Jason, a divorced, middle-aged city planner, grew up with a Hostile/Abusive Mother. He came to see me because of a checkered love life. Every time he'd get involved with a woman, he'd have a storybook romance. But it would end abruptly after about six months or a year. He'd wake up one morning and look over at the woman lying next to him with a deep sense of revulsion. He'd call off the affair in a matter of days, claiming he needed more space. Unlike some men, he felt no guilt for ending the relationship, only a tremendous sense of relief.

When we began to explore his childhood, I learned that he was one of those unlucky boys with two abusive parents. His father punished him by hitting his backside with a two-inch-wide cowboy belt. If he talked back to his mother she would wash his mouth out with soap.

When he was about eight years old, his mother punished him so severely for some minor infraction that he told his mother he was going to run away. She promptly handed him a suitcase and told him to start packing. His little brother cried and pleaded with their mother to let him stay. His mother finally agreed, but not until Jason promised to change his behavior. He was eighteen years old before he had the nerve to stand up to her again.

As an adult Jason has a recurring dream that is filled with transparent symbolism. He dreams he is in a giant, underground sewer beneath the city, a bleak landscape representing his childhood. He stumbles around in the dark, smelly sewer looking for an escape. There is no one to lend him a hand in his struggle, just as there was no one to nurture and support him in his family. Eventually he finds a way out—a manhole, which symbolizes his maleness and his sense of internal power. He shoves aside the manhole cover and hauls himself onto the street. Just as he begins to stand up, he sees a gigantic milk truck (his mother) bearing down on him. The truck runs over him, knocking him back down into the sewer.

The past two chapters have described the most common varieties of dysfunctional mothers and fathers I have encountered in my work with men. Once we have labeled and scrutinized these parents, we need to step back and get the larger picture. Families do not operate in a vacuum. They reflect the values and mores of the larger society. As we have seen, one of the reasons there are so many dysfunctional fathers in our culture is that the masculine code trains men to repress their emotions and focus on external success. This makes it difficult for them to give their children the love and validation they need. It can also prevent them from being adequate companions for their wives. Meanwhile, women who do not have enough attention from their husbands often turn to their sons for the missing support, causing the women to become dysfunctional mothers. Male gender conditioning can have a ripple effect throughout the entire family.

The next chapter looks at the problems men have with love relationships. It's what brings the majority of men in for counseling. A man's relationships with his mother and father may be at the root of his emotional problems, but the pain of his failed love relationships is what usually forces him to get help. Many men can dismiss their childhood difficulties as "water under the bridge." But a bitter marriage or divorce creates pain that even the most stoic men cannot ignore.

CHAPTER 5

THE MALE VIEW OF LOVE RELATIONSHIPS

Seven of the ten men in my newly formed Thursday-night therapy group are there because of relationship difficulties. The seven men represent some common scenarios. John is a forty-year-old employee in a small pharmaceutical company. He joined the group because his wife had taken their three kids and moved out of state, claiming he wasn't meeting any of their needs. She told him he was "just one more child to take care of." At first John tried to hide the extent of his pain about the separation, but finally he has acknowledged how devastated he feels. He told us that without his wife he feels like "an astronaut who's been shoved out of the space shuttle without a lifeline. I'm floating around in deep space. I am totally alone." His tenuous connection with his wife had been his only connection to the rest of the world—and, he fears, to reality.

Larry is a middle-aged lawyer. To escape a strained, distant relationship with his wife he threw himself into his work, staying late at the office almost every day. His long work hours made his wife withdraw even more. Although he and his wife are still living together, he fears that the gap between them has grown so large that they won't be able to bridge it. So far she has seemed indifferent to his efforts to revive the relationship. One of his main concerns is that his wife no longer desires him sexually. He is still attracted to her and is hurt by what he sees as the rejection of his masculinity.

Tom, forty-one, a woodworker, has the opposite problem. He has no sexual or romantic feelings for his second wife. This is a familiar problem for him. He has a history of getting into an intense relationship with a woman, then "going dead" after only a year or so. As his love wanes, he finds himself getting involved with another woman, almost against his will. Sooner or later the affair serves the purpose of getting him out of the old relationship and into a new "hot" one. "I'm the kind of guy you read about in the women's magazines," he told us. He's not proud of it. He said he is "tired of hurting women, tired of feeling guilty, and tired of being in and out of relationships like a fucking yo-yo."

Steve, thirty-two, is a dentist. He's in therapy because his marriage of eight years is on the rocks. His wife accuses him of treating her like one of his patients. She complains that at home he is "polite, eager to please, and impersonal." She has fond memories of how spontaneous he used to be when they first met. She recalls a time when they were walking home from the theater and Steve ran through a lawn sprinkler in his suit and tie. She has given Steve the ultimatum that he needs to relate to her on a more emotional level or she is going to find someone new.

Duke is twenty-nine. He lost his sales job at a large discount store because of the recession. A year of unemployment destroyed an already troubled marriage. At his wife's request he moved out of the house and has been rooming with a friend from work who is also separated from his wife. His two girls, ages seven and three, live with their mother. Duke would like to get back with his wife. He admits that as much as 90 percent of their marriage difficulties can be traced to him, and he has even entered therapy to show his willingness to change. All that he asks from his wife is more passionate sex. Except for her lack of interest in sex, he considers her an ideal mate. Unfortunately, his wife shows no interest in getting back with him.

Norman is a thirty-five-year-old schoolteacher. He's recently decided to leave his wife. He doesn't feel sexually attracted to her, and he's tired of being nagged all the time. During the last session of the group he told us that he'd told his three children, ages eight, thirteen, and fourteen, he was planning to file for divorce. They were very upset.

Their reaction was giving him second thoughts about breaking up the marriage. In passing he said to the group, "I'm also a little bit uncomfortable about living by myself." I asked him what was more distressing to him, his kids' reaction or his anxiety about being alone. He said, "I have to be honest with you—it's the fear of being alone. When I think about it, I feel what some people might call panic. Whatever it is, I don't know how to deal with it."

Keith, a fifty-five-year-old journalist, joined the group two months ago because his wife was threatening to leave him. He was desperate to hold on to her so he decided to get some therapy in the hopes of becoming a better partner. A month after joining the group his wife left him and moved in with another man. He was crushed. His wife meant the world to him. He told us she was a caring "mother" who cooked his meals, washed his clothes, looked after his health, and made sure he kept his appointments. She was a live-in therapist who helped interpret his feelings and support his sagging ego. She was his best friend, and for all practical purposes, his only friend. When Keith finished listing her attributes, he threw up his hands in defeat. "Now tell me," he said, "how am I going to replace all that?"

On the surface it appears that each of these men has a different problem with women. Tom, for example, has a history of abandoning women, while Keith is highly devoted to his wife. But these seven men have one thing in common: women appear to be central to their well-being. When they were unable to sustain a long-lasting, satisfying love relationship, they were driven to get therapy. Their misery and fear forced them to go against the masculine code of self-sufficiency and admit they needed help.

There is a common myth that men don't appreciate their girlfriends and wives, and that they don't care enough about love relationships. The truth is that love relationships mean a great deal to men—they just don't know how to nurture and sustain them.

WHY MEN NEED WOMEN

Why are so many men so dependent on women? Perhaps the most obvious answer is sex. Nature has given men a bounty of testosterone, the hormone that creates physical desire. Men have from ten to fifteen times as much of this potent androgen as women, which is one of the reasons they have such a strong sex drive. Most men are willing to go to great lengths to satisfy that drive, especially in their teens, twenties, and thirties when their hormones are at peak levels. Said a friend of mine, "I don't think women realize what a strong force sex is in a man's life. When I was in my twenties, there was really nothing worth doing other than sex. If you had given me a choice between being a celibate millionaire and being poor with lots of sex, there would have been no contest. I would have chosen sex. Sex was all-encompassing for me. It still remains one of the most powerful forces in my life."

But as powerful as the biological sex drive may be, for most men sex is more than the satisfaction of a physical urge—it's also a vital outlet for their emotions. Of the three traditional masculine roles—providing, procreating, and protecting—only one of them, procreating, encourages men to feel. The other two demand stoicism, fortitude, competitiveness, and self-denial. Men are obliged to channel their emotions through one narrow conduit—their sexuality—which makes the feelings they experience during lovemaking all the more intense. Many men tell me that they feel a deep sense of connection with their sexual partners. Most of the time they feel cut off from people. Sex can create an instant connection. For a few passionate moments they feel united with another person body and soul. For many of the thousands of men whom I've talked to, sex can be a spiritual, almost religious experience. It's one of the rare opportunities they have to feel truly alive.

Physical affection is another reason men are dependent on women. Our culture offers men limited opportunities for physical contact. Men tend to hold and cuddle their young children less than women, partly because women are assigned the primary nurturing role. Other problems arise in later years. Men are wary of touching their pubescent daughters for fear of becoming sexually aroused; and they're wary of being too affectionate with their sons because affection between men isn't "manly." Touching adult women friends is also restricted, because any physical contact might be interpreted as a sexual advance. Finally, touching a male friend is risky because it might trigger either man's homophobia. This means that just about the only person a man can touch with any degree of comfort and safety is his wife or girlfriend. Starved for sensory stimulation, men feel as if the kissing, hand-holding, and cuddling they get in their love relationships is a sensory feast.

At an even more fundamental level men depend on women for the satisfaction of their unmet needs for attachment. Many of my male clients had mothers who were needy, distant, invasive, or self-involved and who didn't satisfy their dependency needs. The men found it difficult to *detach* from their mothers when they approached adulthood because, on an unconscious level, they were still struggling to feel connected to them. Without realizing it the men transferred their unmet dependency needs to their female partners. It's as if they yanked the umbilical cord from their mothers and plugged it into their wives. They *attached* themselves to their wives the way a young child clings to its mother.

How does a man know if he has a healthy connection with his female partner or is unwittingly trying to satisfy unmet childhood needs? One indication is how he reacts to the thought of losing her. If a man is *connected* to a woman in an adult manner, he will feel a poignant, grieving loss when he thinks of separation. However, if he's *attached* to his wife the way a child is attached to his mother, he may flare up with abandonment anxiety. The thought of losing her may make him feel he's going to die or go insane. A man with violent tendencies may experience an upwelling of rage at the thought of being abandoned by his wife. He may have fantasies of harming her, even killing her. After all, she seems to be threatening *his* very existence; why shouldn't he threaten hers?

A final reason that men tend to be overly dependent on women is that women offer them the warmth and tenderness of their vulnerable emotions. A man's world can be a cold and sterile place. It is such a relief to have that harsh environment enlivened by the presence of a nurturing, warm, sensuous woman. Being with her can even help him awaken his own sensitivity. Within the relationship he feels free to reveal some of the vulnerability and the whimsy he has had to conceal for so much of his life.

It is a tremendous relief for men to be given this permission to feel. Deep down, many men feel ashamed of their emotional numbness. They consider themselves petty, selfish, and narcissistic—even unable to love. They are troubled by the fact that they can't cry at movies and are unmoved by the horrors they read about in the paper. I recently asked seventy-four men at a Wildman Gathering how many of them felt they were somehow basically defective and incapable of love. All but a few men raised their hands.

A man has a more positive view of himself when he's in a new love relationship. He discovers that he has spontaneous feelings of love, not only for his partner but for those around him. He feels tender and compassionate and joyful. Being in love gives him a brief interlude of emotional wholeness.

WHAT MEN GIVE UP FOR LOVE

Considering all that women offer men—sex, affection, nurturing, and the restoration of their feelings—it's not surprising that men are willing to give up a great deal in exchange. As they settle into a long-term relationship, the first thing they jettison are all those "foolish" masculine pursuits of the past—the poker playing, the ball games, the hunting and fishing, the pool, the beer drinking, the motorcycles and sports cars. Suddenly these seem like juvenile distractions. They were a way to mark time, hide from their pain. Men who are in love will give them up in a heartbeat. They've found salvation instead.

They'll also forsake their male friends. They have no interest in hanging out with the guys when they're in love. The little support they get from men can't compare to the nourishment they draw from their female partners. If need be they'll even give up their creative pursuits. When they're in love, they don't have to work so hard to fill the holes in their soul.

What does it matter that after a few years of marriage a man's world has shrunk to a desk at the office and a home in the suburbs? The woman who presides over that home is a taproot that burrows into the ground, connecting him to a life-giving substance he's been unable to get for himself. Why does he need to roam?

But once romantic love fades away, as it invariably does, men discover to their dismay that they don't have the skills or insights to revive it. They do what they can to hold on to the good feelings, but they find that they're caught up in a complicated, high-stakes game in which nobody has bothered to tell them the rules.

It's painful for me to recall how naïve I was in my first marriage. To me, being a husband meant making money during the day and making love to my wife at night. Both of those things I knew how to do. I took pride in my ability to work hard and love hard. I had our marriage all planned out. I was going to be the super hero who goes to school in the daytime and then valiantly puts in another eight-hour shift at a job. I was going to crawl home at midnight to my little sexpot of a wife who was going to meet me at the door with a plate full of cookies. It was going to be like coming home after school to Mom, except my wife would be wearing nothing but a skimpy little T-shirt, and I was going to pounce on her and make love to her all night long.

My marriage turned out to be exactly like my fantasy for about six weeks. Then the fantasy started to crumble. Even though neither my energy level nor my determination wavered in the slightest, I couldn't earn enough money to meet all our needs. My wife volunteered to get a job to help out, but that wasn't part of my plan. She was supposed to stay home and take care of me and the house. I didn't like the idea of my little honeybear going out into the big world. I didn't like the idea that I couldn't protect her or provide for her. It made me feel less of a man. And I also didn't like the thought of her working with other men. She might find a real hero, someone who made more money than I did and wouldn't let her down.

But the real surprise for me in my marriage was that my wife wanted more from me than money and sex. It wasn't enough for her that I was working as hard as I could sixteen hours a day. It wasn't enough for her that I was an indefatigable lover. It wasn't enough for her that I had given up seeing my buddies, chasing women, playing sports, and going fishing. She wanted something more from me, something that I found impossible to give: intimacy. I was keeping such a tight rein on my feelings that there was no way I could let her get close to me. Unconsciously, I was afraid that if I let her penetrate my defenses, she would flush out some of those forbidden feelings that were threatening to blow me apart. If I was going to keep a safe distance from my feelings, I would have to keep a safe distance from her.

It doesn't take long for a relationship to go awry when a man doesn't know how to be intimate. Misunderstandings multiply. Conflicts become commonplace. A power struggle develops. One of the more devastating consequences of the power struggle from a man's point of view is that the lovemaking starts to be rationed. Many men discover that married sex turns out to be less frequent and less erotic than they could have ever imagined. How can you sleep in the same bed with a woman every single night and have sex only once a week?

Children are another rude awakening. When children come onto the scene, they double a man's financial pressure and add the weighty responsibility of a brand-new role—fatherhood, a job that he knows little about. There were no required parenting courses for boys in school, and, chances are, his own father failed to provide a good role model. I remember looking into my daughter's face when she was a newborn and experiencing not joy but anxiety. Inside I felt just as helpless and dependent as she was. How on earth could I be a father?

In the space of a few short years a man can experience a dramatic reversal in his outlook on marriage. Forget joy, forget happiness, forget the ecstasy of sex. Just find some way to endure another day, another week, another month. The question now becomes: How can I survive this peculiar existence without being horribly wounded? Some men try to survive the ordeal by going on the attack and becoming hostile or violent. Others try to defend themselves by becoming critical or demeaning. But the majority of men protect themselves by withdrawing. They withdraw into the newspaper, the TV, the liquor bottle, the job. The one relationship skill men have in spades is self-protection.

LOSING A SENSE OF SELF

It's only when the relationship ends, as so many do these days, that a man has a chance to take stock of all that he's lost in the bargain. Alone once again, he can't remember what it was that he used to do with himself. What else is there to life besides his job, working in the yard, watching TV, refereeing the kids, and paying the bills? Where are all his old buddies? Does anybody go fishing anymore? Didn't he used to play the guitar?

As men gain more distance on their failed relationships, many of them get the distinct impression that the game of love had been played on a woman's terms and a woman's turf. They were living according to feminine morals and mores. Their wives determined what they ate, what they wore, which friends they saw, how the house was decorated, how often they had sex, how the kids were raised, and where and how they spent most of their time. It's not that their wives hadn't solicited their opinions—it's just that the men hadn't been able to stand up for themselves.

John, the man I mentioned at the beginning of the chapter whose wife left him and moved to another state, has been doing a lot of soul searching in recent weeks. He has come to the conclusion that he had allowed his wife to make virtually all the decisions for him throughout the course of their marriage. He told me, "I bought a house and it was furnished the way she wanted it. I slept in the bed she picked out. Her friends became our friends. I dressed the way she wanted me to. We raised the kids the way she wanted them to be raised." When he tried to analyze why that had happened, he realized it wasn't his wife's fault. "*I* was the problem," he said. "My wife was doing good things. She was just marching through her life and taking care of business. She would check things out with me, but I didn't know what to say. I didn't know how to be honest with her. For some reason I couldn't say to her, 'I don't want a flowered sofa with striped wallpaper behind it.' Now she's gone and I'm stuck with a flowered sofa and a striped wall."

One night he sat on the sofa and tried to figure out why he'd made all those concessions. He realized he'd made some of them to make his wife happy. He'd made others to keep the peace. But he made most of them because he'd lost sight of what he wanted and needed. He'd been more than happy to let her fill in the blanks.

Charles, a friend and colleague of mine, has just ended an intense love affair and is undergoing a similar process of self-examination. Only, in his case, he's trying to make sense of a thirty-year history of failed relationships. "I've lost myself in every relationship I've ever been in," he told me. "In my first marriage I was the 'young man with promise.' In my second marriage, I was the responsible guy who lives in a nice house with a nice lawn at the end of the block. I was like the character in T. S. Eliot's 'The Love Song of J. Alfred Prufrock' who measured his life in coffee spoons." Like many men, Charles believed he had two choices in marriage, either to be a good-time Charlie who drinks beer and hangs out with the guys, or to put on slacks and a sweater and fit into Mr. Roger's Neighborhood.

When his second marriage ended in divorce, Charles felt the need for a major change in his life. He moved out of his nice, big house with the nice, big mortgage into a small cottage in a country town to start a new life that wasn't so measured. Single once again, he began to rebuild his life. He started lifting weights and jogging. He began meditating, something he hadn't done since the 1970s. Life began to feel good to him. He said to me, "When I had time on my hands, there was always something I wanted to do. I felt in control of my life. I didn't have to defer to a woman who was more spiritual than I was or more moral. I began to make my own decisions about what was right for me. Something inside of me was rising to the surface, and I recognized what it was. It was me."

As a part of his rehabilitation, Charles created a morning routine that gave him a lot of pleasure. He would wake up early each morning, do some stretches, meditate, and then sip tea out on the patio as he listened to the birds and gathered his thoughts about the coming day. Then he would wander back inside and make a breakfast out of homemade granola, powdered milk, and water. "It was just a few simple rituals," he told me, "but it did wonders for my health and my state of mind."

At this stage in his recovery Charles met a new woman. He wasn't going out of his way to find one, at least not in the desperate way he'd searched for women in the past, but the attraction to her was strong nonetheless. It wasn't long before she moved in with him. All went well for almost six months. His girlfriend felt like a pleasant addition to an already rich life. Then, little by little, Charles began to surrender his daily routine. At six o'clock in the morning he would be gently easing himself out of bed to begin his rituals when his girlfriend would whisper to him, "Oh, honey, it feels so good to have you lying here next to me." He took that to mean, "Why would you want to get up and do that silly stuff when you could lie here with me? Don't you love me?" So he told himself, "Okay, I'll just do my routine later." But he would rarely do it later. Gradually, his morning activities didn't seem so important to him.

Then his girlfriend started influencing his diet. She was an avid coffee drinker and didn't think much of herb tea. She made a comment to him one day about nice it would be to share a cup of coffee with the man she loved. A few weeks later, for his birthday, she gave him a present of a coffee grinder and a pound of gourmet beans. He began to drink coffee. Next to fall by the wayside was the granola and powdered milk. His girlfriend thought that drinking powdered milk was impractical and rather strange. "It's not that she said anything about it," he told me. "It's just that she'd smirk as I fixed my cereal. It didn't take much. Before long she was buying regular milk, and I was using it. Then she began fixing waffles and eggs—the whole breakfast scene—and I was eating it. It was almost like I had to do things her way to prove to her that I loved her. Or maybe I had to do them to prove to myself that I loved her. I don't know."

These concessions seemed insignificant to Charles at the time. "She was a great woman," he said, "and we had great sex." But after a while all he had left in his life was his relationship with his girlfriend and his work. His sense of self, the core of him, had receded. And when this relationship ended, he had no choice but to start all over again, rebuilding his life from the ground up.

I realize that the view of married life I have gotten from listening to my male friends and to hundreds of my male clients presents only one side of the story. There is an equally valid female point of view, one that I have heard poignantly expressed by many of my female clients. The same man who feels himself under his wife's sway much of the time may still dominate certain aspects of the relationship. For example, he may be making most of the major financial decisions. He may insist that the demands of his job take precedence over hers. He may allow his wife to do the majority of the parenting, cooking, and housecleaning duties while he relaxes in front of the TV.

But while it cannot be denied that many men exercise some measure of domestic entitlement in their marriages, this is not what they really want out of life. It's not what makes them happy. The men who vegetate on the couch and allow their wives to mother them and run the household are not self-actualized people. They may command the best view of the TV set, but they've lost their souls in the bargain.

When I think of the deceptive balance of power in marriage, I often think of my dad. On the surface he appeared to be king of the roost. He made us kids say "Yes, sir," and "No, sir," at every turn. He demanded to be the first person waited on at the dinner table, and he refused to demean himself by helping out around the house. I never saw him lift a broom or wash a dish—not even when my mother got an outside job, which added forty hours of work to her already full schedule. When my mom got off work she went grocery shopping, cooked dinner, and cleaned up the house. When my dad got off work he read the newspaper and watched TV.

But this privileged position didn't empower my father in any meaningful way. In reality, it *disempowered* him and kept him in a state of childlike dependency. When he left my mother and lived by himself in his late sixties, he was unable to take care of even his most elemental needs. He took his clothes to a full-service laundry so they could be washed, ironed, and folded. He ate all three of his daily meals at a fast-food restaurant. He didn't even know how to make coffee. One day I took him a loaf of bread and some peanut butter and jelly so he could at least make himself a sandwich every once in a while. I came back two weeks later to find everything exactly where I had left it. He hadn't touched a thing. The bread was blue with mold.

My father's much-vaunted "male prerogative" was also of little help to him when it came to any significant negotiations with my mother. In virtually all serious conversations, she had the upper hand. What my father wanted to do more than anything else in life was to be a commercial pilot. He had developed a love of flying during World War II, and he was thrilled when he was offered a job with a commercial airlines at the end of the war. But my mother didn't want him to take the job. She didn't like the thought of him being away from home for days at a time and mingling with stewardesses. My dad gave in to her wishes and declined the job for "family reasons." He spent the next thirty years of his life standing beside an assembly line making parts for planes he would never fly.

Recently I asked my mother for her side of the story. She claimed that she didn't do anything drastic to keep my father from being a pilot. She said, "I just rolled my eyes and shook my head and said something about pilots and stewardesses. He could have taken the job if he'd really wanted it." I suspect there's some truth to her version. When I look back on the way my mother and father interacted, it seems all my mother had to do to get her way was to indicate a clear preference. My father would fuss and fume for a few hours, abuse us kids if we happened to be around, then cave in. My guess is that my mother complained about the pilot job only a few times, but that's all it took to get my father to abandon his dream. If so, it took but a few sentences to change his life.

Although it's tempting to blame my mother for the sorry state of my father's life—and in the larger view to blame women for our culture of hollow men—that's not an accurate picture. My father was emotionally damaged long before he met my mother. Like many men, he was so out of touch with his feelings by the time he got married that he couldn't make his needs known, not even in the most trivial matters. He would drive my mother up the wall because he couldn't even tell her whether he wanted a Coke or a Dr Pepper. My mother prevailed simply because she had a better sense of what she wanted from moment to moment. She didn't have any better relationship skills than my father. She wasn't more wise or more worthy. It's just that her gender conditioning allowed her to be more in tune with her feelings and needs, which enabled her to place her agenda on the table. And that made all the difference.

In the first four chapters of the book I focused on two main sources of men's emotional problems: (1) being conditioned to repress their vulnerable emotions, and (2) being raised by neglectful or abusive parents. Most of the discussion about male psychology in recent decades has revolved around the second issue—the pain of growing up in a dysfunctional family. But we are now becoming aware that gender conditioning is a major factor in a man's emotional development as well. Even if a boy has the good fortune to grow up in a healthy family environment, he still will have emotional difficulties if he is raised to adhere to a strict interpretation of the masculine code.

This final chapter in Part I has focused on the third major source of men's difficulties: inadequate relationship skills. Men, like women, are social creatures who depend to a large extent on the love, support, and validation of others for their well-being. Unless they develop good relationship skills, they can't tap into this wellspring. They have disappointing love relationships and struggle with the pain of separation and divorce.

These problems are interrelated. As I mentioned earlier, male gender conditioning and family dysfunction are intertwined. When men are repressed, they make inadequate dads and disappointing husbands. The whole family suffers. Poor relationship skills are also a by-product of the masculine code. A man's gender conditioning makes it hard for him to communicate on an emotional level. He can't open up and let his partner see inside him. He finds it equally difficult to understand

and empathize with her. In short, he doesn't have the ability to sustain an intimate relationship for an extended period of time—a trait psychologists term being "relational."

In Part II of the book, I describe a comprehensive therapy for men called Masculine Relational Therapy, which addresses all three of these primary issues. As you will see, it evolved out of my own circuitous healing journey. Not finding the help that I needed in traditional therapy I had to cast around for alternatives. By combining the techniques that worked best for me with traditional psychotherapy I was able to create a gender-specific therapy for men. At the center of this new therapy is the idea that a group setting is uniquely suited to the emotional needs of men.

In the last chapters of the book you'll read how some courageous men in my therapy groups are turning their lives around. They are resolving their relationship difficulties, creating healthier work habits, reaching out to their children, and finding more joy in their daily lives.

PART II

A NEW THERAPY FOR MEN

CHAPTER 6

MY OWN STRUGGLES WITH THERAPY

The emotional problems discussed in the first half of this book are common among men. Many men have unresolved issues with their parents, disappointing relationships with their partners, and distant relationships with their children. In addition, they fail to take care of their health, are dissatisfied with their jobs, and find too little joy in their everyday lives.

Despite all these difficulties, only a small percentage of men seek psychological help. In most groups of people, twice as many women as men seek psychological counseling. In some groups, the ratio is as high as four women to every one man.[1] It's a catch-22. The very gender conditioning that lies at the heart of their problems prevents men from getting any help resolving them. Big boys don't cry, and grown men don't go to therapy. Torie Clarke, the spokeswoman for George Bush's 1992 election campaign, said it best, "Real men do not get on the couch." And she's right. A man who will drive around in circles for an hour before asking for directions is not likely to go to a therapist

1. Zapper, L. T. and Weinstein, H. M., "Sex Differences and the Impact of Work on Physical and Psychological Health," *American Journal of Psychiatry,* October 1985, 14 Z(10), pp. 1174–78.

and admit he's a lost soul. He is far more likely to turn to a more masculine version of "therapy" such as drinking, work, drugs, sex, or TV—in short, anything to mask his difficulties.

Just last month I heard a tragic story about a man who was unable to ask for the help he so desperately needed. Ralph, one of my long-term clients, told me the sad news that his friend, Doug, had just committed suicide. For the previous few months Doug had been drinking more than usual. Ralph finally worked up the courage to ask him what was wrong. Doug confessed that things weren't going well at home—his wife had filed for divorce. Ralph suggested he see a therapist and had even given him my name and phone number. Doug never called me. Instead, he relied on some "manly wisdom" to get himself through. He'd often told Ralph, "When you get knocked on your ass, you gotta get back in the line and block." But this time Doug hadn't been able to get back in line. At five A.M. on the morning of his daughter's eighth birthday he shot himself in the head.

Each year, approximately twenty-four-thousand men commit suicide, four times the number of women.[2] It is my heartfelt belief that if more men got the kind of psychological help that they need, we could cut that number in half. There would also be fewer battered women, less child abuse, fewer male alcoholics, fewer depressed men, fewer failed businesses, fewer men in prison, fewer divorces, and fewer children living with single parents. The world would be a better place to live.

But in order for this to happen, two fundamental changes must take place. First, more men have to become comfortable seeing a therapist. They have to rid themselves of the notions that getting help for emotional problems is a sign of weakness. Second, more therapists need to practice gender-specific therapy. The masculine code not only makes it harder for men to admit they need help, it makes it more difficult for them to benefit from traditional forms of therapy. Many therapists need to adapt their practices so they are

2. In 1988, for example, 24,078 men committed suicide versus 6,329 women, according to the U.S. Bureau of the Census, *Statistical Abstracts of the United States: 1991* (111th Edition), Washington, D.C., 1991.

better suited for men. These are the issues I'll be exploring in this second half of the book.

MY OWN FEAR OF THERAPY

I can sympathize with all those men who are reluctant to see a therapist. I still recall how desperate I had to be before I was willing to get psychological help. The first time I saw a therapist I was a young man, twenty years old, trying to salvage a failing marriage and a struggling business. Like many men, I saw few options. The only solution I saw to my troubled marriage was divorce, but to leave my wife was to invite feelings of loneliness and abandonment that were far greater than the nagging pain I felt being married to her. The only option I saw for dealing with my work anxieties was to quit my job. But I couldn't quit my job because my work was my primary means of *distracting* myself from my anxiety. Like many men, I was playing a grown-up game of hide and seek. The more I *hid* from my feelings, the more I had to *seek* success in my job. Yet any success that I eked out did not give me any emotional satisfaction. It just forced me to set higher goals. I was living a miserable life but saw no means of escape.

The tension became unbearable one frosty morning in January as I was leaving the house to go to work. It was still dark outside, and I faced an unbroken twelve-hour stretch of painting houses. As I reached for the door handle of my car, my hand seemed to freeze in mid-air. I could not go one step farther. I wanted to die rather than go on with the day. I hated my job, I hated my wife, and I hated my life. But at that moment, what I hated most of all was my job. I hated it! Yet the thought of not going to work threw up a wall of anxiety. If I didn't go to work, what would I do with myself? I couldn't go to work, and I couldn't stay home. I was trapped. Suddenly, waves of fear began to wash over me. My heart pounded until I thought it would explode. I was having a panic attack, but I had no words for it. I thought I was going insane.

I fought down the panic the best I could, forcing myself to breathe, and after two or three terrifying minutes, I was finally able to move. I opened the door, got in the car, and put the key in the ignition. I drove off to work, desperately trying to convince myself that this was just another ordinary day. But whenever I thought about that "episode," panic flooded over me once again.

I wanted to call my wife and tell her what had happened to me, but I was afraid she wouldn't understand. She, too, would think I was crazy. When my anxiety threatened to overwhelm me for the fourth time that day, I knew I had to get some help. Not knowing what else to do I grabbed for the phone book and searched for the name of a therapist. I called the first name in the book and was relieved to get an appointment that very week. I was so desperate that all my negative thoughts and fears about psychiatry flew out the window.

The therapist turned out to be a middle-aged, expressionless man with black half-glasses. His posture was rigid, and he insisted on calling me "Mr. Allen," even though I was just out of my teens. He started the session by asking why I'd come. I didn't feel safe enough to tell him about my panic attack. To fill in the silence I started talking about my work pressures. Every few minutes the psychologist would duck down his chin so he could gaze at me over the top of his glasses. Whenever he peered at me, my heart pounded in my chest. I was convinced he was thinking that there was something horribly wrong with me. The only words I can recall him saying the entire hour were, "Yes" or "Hm" or "Please go on, Mr. Allen." Finally, he said that the time was up. I walked out the door, never to come back again.

Clearly, I thought, therapy wasn't going to work.

A BETRAYAL OF TRUST

Somehow I managed to subdue my panic and get on with life. It's a tactic countless men have mastered: no matter how deeply we're wounded, we get back in the line and tackle. But about a year later my anxiety again threatened to overwhelm me and I was compelled once again to get help. This time I signed up with a prominent therapist in his mid-thirties. From the first appointment he called me "Marvin" and reassured me with a warm smile. I began to look forward to my sessions with him because they gave me momentary relief from my anxiety. He would dissect my dreams, interpret my comments, and help me gain insight into my past. A few pieces of my early history started to make sense to me, but inside I was still a "bundle of nerves."

By the second year of our work together, a warm relationship developed between us that transcended the usual therapist-client relationship. I got to know his lovely wife and children, and he hired me to paint his mansion and beach house. Once, when I needed to borrow some money, he cosigned a note at the bank. I didn't realize that this degree of involvement outside the office was unorthodox, perhaps even unethical. All I knew was that he seemed to like me, and that gave me a great deal of pleasure. He was a pillar of the community, and I still saw myself as a lowly, working-class boy, even though I was starting to earn good money. He was a father figure to me.

My trust in him was shattered later that year at the end of an appointment. I had been braving new waters by describing a few of my sexual fantasies. When the session was just about over, he surprised me by getting up from his chair and sitting next to me on the couch. He'd never done this before. He draped his arm around me, and I sat in stunned silence. He smiled and said words that I'll never forget, "I think what you need, Marvin, is some fatherly closeness." Then, to my astonishment, he leaned over and began to kiss me. As his tongue probed my mouth he leaned the length of his long body against me. I was repulsed. I turned my head to avoid his kisses, but I was afraid to defend myself more aggressively. This man was my hero. I smiled nervously and pushed him away. We talked about inconsequential matters for a few minutes, then it was time for me to go. I rushed out of the office.

I showed up for my next scheduled appointment, hoping that what had happened the previous week had been an aberration. But once again he tried to seduce me. This time I struggled free and left his office without saying a word—to him or to anyone else. I never saw him again.

In the weeks that followed I tried to push down my reaction to his seduction, but it kept coming up. Some of the time I was worried about being homosexual. I hadn't been aroused by his advances, but the mere fact that he had been attracted to me made me doubt my sexuality. What bothered me most about the experience was the betrayal of our relationship. All my life I'd been hungry for a father's love, and until that fatal appointment, it seemed as if he was giving it to me. He had made me feel special, as if I were his chosen client—his favorite one. Yet I didn't feel angry at him for shattering that relationship—just deeply shaken. I had been abused, used, or ignored by most of the men in my life, so this was par for the course.

What I know now is that the success of long-term therapy depends to a large degree on the trust that is built up between therapist and client. To build that trust it is imperative that the therapist draw clear boundaries in the relationship and honor them scrupulously. It wasn't my job to define the terms of the therapeutic contract. I knew nothing about limits and boundaries. It was my therapist's job to keep those healthy parameters. I trusted him to do it and he failed me—first by treating me like a "son-client," and then by making sexual advances. It's not surprising that it was some time before I was willing to look for another therapist.[3]

CONTINUING THE HEALING JOURNEY

Without the comfort and support of therapy I staved off my anxiety by putting even more effort into my work. By now my painting business had grown to one with eighty-five employees, and I was beginning to enjoy the trappings of a middle-class life-style. But I still went home at night to a marriage devoid of passion or intimacy. The only thing that kept my wife and me together was our mutual terror of abandonment and our sense of obligation to the children. When I turned twenty-five, despair once again pushed me into therapy. This

3. I want to emphasize that few therapists sexually abuse their clients. A questionaire was sent to 5,574 randomly selected psychiatrists. 1,442 responded. Six percent acknowledged having sexual relationships with their clients. (From the article "6% of Psychiatrists Admit to Client Sex, Poll Finds," by Daniel Q. Haney, *The Washington Post,* August 31, 1986, p. A9.) Other surveys have found that the vast number of therapists who initiate sex with their clients are male, and "those they prey upon are overwhelmingly female." (From the article "The Ultimate Betrayal" by Erica E. Goode. *U.S. News & World Report,* March 12, 1990, pp. 63–66.

time I deliberately sought out a woman and found a lovely, middle-aged psychologist. She counseled me with warmth and validation, never once betraying my trust during the four years we worked together.

As the therapy deepened and we began to probe my childhood memories, my repressed feelings threatened to emerge, but I didn't feel safe enough to release them. I could only talk around them. My feelings felt dangerous, uncontrollable, alien. I had boxed them in for twenty long years. This lack of exposure to the light of day had transformed them into frightening beasts. To my therapist's credit I had to make more and more of an effort to keep my feelings at bay. My anxiety would mount shortly before my appointment, so I would reflexively arm myself with props. I'd walk into her office with a can of Coke in one hand, a cigar in the other, and a wad of chewing gum in my mouth. All through the session I would chomp on the gum and alternate between sips of Coke and puffs of tobacco. Meanwhile, I would nervously tap my foot. The unconscious purpose of all this activity was to tamp down my feelings. One day she asked me to stop smoking in her office because it was making her sick. From then on I had to work overtime on the Coke and the gum.

I'm sure my therapist was aware of my anxiety—it would have been obvious to a casual bystander—but she chose not to address it directly. A part of me was begging her to notice my underlying distress and confront my denial, but the larger part of me still wanted to keep up my defenses. I didn't want her to see how "sick" I was, that I wasn't doing as well as I was pretending. That frightened part of me wanted to convince her that I was fine. That she didn't need to probe any deeper. I was afraid that if she looked inside my soul she would discover there was something deeply and permanently wrong with me. I was in an intolerable situation. I desperately needed to release my feelings, but I didn't feel safe enough to let them out. Every once in a while a little bit of emotion would leak out around the fissures in my denial, and she would gratefully acknowledge it. But she was never able to mine the mother lode that was buried inside me.

Looking back on my early experiences with therapy I can see that all my therapists misjudged the strength of my masculine defenses. They hadn't been able to create a safe enough environment nor come up with the right techniques to break through my thirty-year history of repression. What I needed was for someone gently but firmly to probe beneath my denial. But I would not have permitted that without first getting massive doses of reassurance: "You are safe with me, Marvin. You can feel any feelings you want to in my office. You can cry, scream, or have a full-scale panic attack. If at the end of the hour you feel unsettled, you can stay longer. Or come back the next day. Or call me at night. I am here to help you feel all of your emotions." Only if I had been fully convinced that my safety was assured and that I was in competent hands would I have been able to open the door to my feelings.

But I didn't get the reassurance I needed from my therapists. In fact, the nonverbal message they gave me, intentionally or not, was that they were just as afraid of my feelings as I was. "We'll sit here and *talk* about your feelings, Marvin, and they will go away. But we won't let you *feel* your feelings—at least not in our presence—because they are too scary, too powerful. You might explode. You might make a mess all over the office, and we can't handle that."

OVERCOMING MY FEAR OF FLYING

Ironically, the person who helped me break through the crust and begin confronting my fear was not a traditional therapist but a retired pilot for Pan Am. In 1977, at the age of thirty-three, I signed up for a fear-of-flying class taught by Captain Slim Cummings. At the time I knew a few other people who claimed to be "white knuckle flyers," but I was the only person I knew who was so terrified of planes he'd never stepped foot in one. I had been plagued by nightmares of plane crashes as long as I could remember. I didn't know why. As I look back on it, I know it had something to do with the fact that my father had been an airplane pilot and I had so little trust in him. But all that I knew at the time was that my phobia was a source of intense embarrassment for me. One of my business suppliers had awarded me a round-trip airplane ticket for two to any place in the world. I had to turn it down. Just the thought of boarding a plane made me panic. In place of the trip around the world I'd had to settle for a new set of golf clubs and reduced self-esteem.

When I walked into the fear-of-flying class that first evening, I felt vulnerable and exposed. There I was openly acknowledging the fact that I had an uncontrollable fear—a most unmanly posture. I sat in the back of the room and looked at the backs of the other members of the class, curious to see what kind of people shared my humiliating weakness. I was surprised to see an equal number of men and women. The back of one man's head looked familiar. When the man turned around, I was stunned to see that it was Peter, a good friend of mine from my Wednesday-night poker group. Peter was a big man, about six-foot-four, lean and muscular. In the two years I had been playing poker with him, he had never let on to me that he had any fears whatsoever. I realized that his fear of flying must be just as bad as mine or he wouldn't be in the class. I began to wonder what secrets were hidden behind the "poker faces" of the other men in my Wednesday group.

As I sat there thinking about my poker buddies, the instructor, Captain Slim Cummings, walked into the room. I liked him immediately. He was a tall, balding man, sixty-one years of age, but still young, vibrant, and powerful. His poise, his soothing voice, his pilot's uniform, and his compassionate eyes inspired great trust. That very first night he managed to reduce my shame. "I know you're all scared to death," he said to us, "and I congratulate you for coming despite your anxiety. You are brave people. There are many people like you who are afraid to fly but are not ready to confront their fears."

Slim's basic philosophy was that there was a courageous self and a frightened self in each one of us. Part of his job was to bolster the courageous self by explaining the basics of airplane aerodynamics and by reassuring us about the safety of jet travel. He knew that the courageous self required a lot of encouragement because this was the part of us that needed to step forward and convince us to get on the plane. But he didn't neglect or deny the fearful self. He was careful to invite our anxiety to come along for the ride as well. His goal was to help us experience and survive our fears, not repress them. "Fear is a *feeling*," he would tell us over and over again. "It won't kill you. You'll think you're going to die when the plane takes off. You'll be scared to death. But in the end you won't die. You will be able to experience your fear and live through it."

The culmination of the classes was a flight on a real plane. Everything led up to this one graduation exercise. As the date of the flight approached, I was still harboring a lot of fear. I felt embarrassed that I hadn't been able to overcome my anxiety. I still thought the goal was to *repress* my feelings, not *express* them. Toward the end of the third session Peter raised his hand and voiced the fear that I had been too ashamed to admit: "What if we're still feeling afraid when it comes time to step on the plane?" he asked.

"It's very likely that you will be afraid," Slim said. "You're going to have to get on the plane despite your fear. The experience of flying will eventually convince you that you can survive it. Are you feeling afraid now?"

"I am," he admitted.

"You don't sound very scared," Slim said.

"But I *am* scared," he replied.

"Show us how scared you feel."

Peter raised his voice a notch, "I'm scared. I'm really scared."

"You still don't seem all that scared, Peter. Say it in a way that lets us know how terrified you really feel."

Peter stood up to his full height and yelled as loud as he could, "I'm scared! I'm scared! I'm scared to death!" He took a big breath and sat down.

"How do you feel, now?" Slim asked.

"It's funny," he said, "but I don't feel all that scared anymore." We all laughed, but I could see the method in Slim's madness. By getting Peter to express his fear, even exaggerate it, he had somehow helped him release it. Peter no longer had to sit there trying to hold in his fear and pretend it didn't exist. It was out in the open.

What surprised me about the exercise was how cathartic it had been for *me*. Suddenly, I, too, felt less afraid. It was almost as if I had been standing up there with him. The fact that it was a man revealing his fear had made it easy for me to identify with him. If my poker-playing buddy could reveal to the whole room that he was frightened, then maybe my own fear was acceptable. Although I had no idea at the time, I had stumbled upon one of the elements I would later incorporate in my approach to men's therapy: it helps men immensely to see other men express their emotions. It challenges all the gender conditioning that says men cannot feel.

At the end of the class Slim led us in a group exercise. He encouraged all of us to scream out how terrified we were of flying. Making a public display of my emotions was a totally new experience for me. All my life I'd struggled to appear calm and in control, no matter how terrified I felt on the inside. Peter's example made it easier for me to let down my barriers. It was such a relief to let my feelings out of me.

As I stood in the midst of a roomful of screaming people, I gained even more admiration for Slim. There he was, standing in front of us, assuring us he could handle all of our fear, all at once. He was convincing us that *he* could handle our anxiety, even if *we* couldn't. This was the first time in my life that someone was telling me that my fear was manageable, that it didn't mean I was going crazy, and that it wasn't going to blow me and the rest of the world apart. It was the breakthrough I'd never had in traditional therapy.

Watching Slim calmly absorb all of our fear was another experience I would call up when I started leading men's groups: a therapist working with men has to reassure them over and over again that their feelings are normal and natural. He or she has to counter all the years of programming that have convinced them that their emotions need to be repressed and managed at all costs. He needs to restore the safety and the permission to feel that have been taken away from them by the abuse or neglect of their parents and the weight of the masculine code.

I remember Slim's parting words at the end of our fourth and final class: "Let's look at it this way: if the plane is going to go down and we're all going to die, I can't think of a more courageous group of people to die with." As he said this, I looked around the room and felt a great love for my fellow fearful flyers. We had exposed our naked fear to each other and found not ostracism but acceptance. In this one special setting we had learned we could be the flawed, frail human beings we really were and still be loved. It was an especially moving experience to see behind the men's masculine façades.

The morning of the flight arrived and as Slim had predicted, my fearful self was still afraid to get on the plane. A part of me truly believed I was going to get on the plane that morning and never return to the earth I loved so much. All the mental preparation in the world wasn't going to eliminate my fear. I was going to have to live through it. I arrived at the terminal thirty minutes ahead of schedule in an effort to summon up some last-minute courage. Peter was already there nervously pacing the floor. We hugged each other and nervously joked about plane crashes while we awaited the big moment.

When our flight number was called, all forty-one members of the class walked down the ramp and boarded the plane. I managed to keep my own fears fairly well under control until the door slammed shut. Then my claustrophobia set in. My fear escalated as the jet engines began to whine. I used the breathing and relaxation techniques that Slim had taught us, but my fear edged its way toward panic. The plane taxied, poised itself at the start of the runway, then roared up to speed. My fear kept pace with the acceleration of the plane. When the jet lifted off the runway and began what seemed like a dangerously steep angle of climb, the full reality of what I was doing finally hit me. This wasn't just another bad dream of being on an exploding airplane. This was real. There was no waking up or getting off.

I tried to control my panic by gripping the armrests. I tried visualization. I tried deep breathing. Nothing helped. Finally, I had no choice but to surrender to my fear. I loosened my grip on the armrests and let my anxiety wash over me like a tidal wave. As I gave in to my fear, I started to cry. To my surprise, after I had cried for no more than a minute or two, the immense pressure bearing down on my chest began to give way and in its place came a warm, relaxed feeling. A few minutes later I was flooded with exhilaration.

For thirty years I had lived in terror of being trapped in an airplane high above the earth. Now, the very thing I'd feared most was happening to me, and I was surviving it. I looked around me at my companions and realized they were having the same experience. We began to congratulate each other and drink champagne. As I looked in awe out the window of the plane, I recalled something Slim had said to us. He had told us that crying was one of the keys that would liberate us from our fear, and I had just found out that he was right.

After that momentous flight I had greater confidence in my ability to face my fears, whatever their cause. Fear is fear, no matter what provokes it. Having survived my greatest phobia, a fear of flying, I now had the courage to look at my other fears as well. I was beginning to sense that all my dark, "unmanageable" feelings—my rage at being abused, my fear of abandonment, my grief at not having been loved and accepted by my parents—would prove to be paper dragons just like my fear of flying. I suddenly had the courage to battle my way through my anxiety and start facing my underlying feelings—not just talk about them, but *feel* them. I had finally learned *through direct experience* that feelings don't kill, that I wasn't the only human being on the planet to struggle with repressed emotions, and that in the right setting—with massive doses of support and encouragement—I would be able to make steady progress toward emotional wholeness. In reality, Slim hadn't just helped me reduce my fear of flying, but my *fear of feeling* as well.

CHAPTER 7

HELPING MEN RELEASE THEIR EMOTIONS

After graduating from Slim's class I continued to work on my personal growth. I found that the work was more productive than it had been in the past because I was now more willing to explore my emotions. As I loosened the grip of repression, I began to get in touch with feelings that had been buried since childhood. As a result, I started to see some spontaneous changes in my daily life. I began to have healthier relationships with women and became less compulsive about my work. I still had a considerable distance to travel, but at least I was on the right road.

The more headway I made in my personal growth, the more interested I became in the whole subject of psychotherapy. I eventually decided to become a therapist myself. I went back to college and finished my undergraduate studies, then began work on a master's degree in counseling and psychology.

In graduate school I was taught a gender-neutral, one-size-fits-all brand of counseling. I was trained to sort clients according to symptoms and syndromes, not gender—which is true for virtually all therapists practicing today. Within each category I was instructed to give men and women similar, if not identical, treatment.

One of the main tools I was to use with my clients was a technique called "empathic listening." Regardless of the sex of my client I was taught to "mirror and empathize, mirror and empathize." This meant I was supposed to paraphrase a client's remarks, then indicate that I understood and empathized with what the person was saying. For example, a client might say to me: "I had a hard time getting out of bed this morning. I had nothing to look forward to." I was supposed to respond with something like: "So you woke up feeling unmotivated. There wasn't anything you wanted to do. Is that right?" If the client indicated I'd heard him correctly, I would add: "That makes sense that you'd feel that way. After all, you've just lost your job. It's hard to get motivated after something like that." If I sensed a client was suppressing an emotion, I was permitted to ask, "Is there anything you might be feeling right now?" But if the client said no, I was supposed to move on. To suggest that a client might be having a particular feeling was committing the sin of "projection." To try to draw out his or her feelings was being "too directive."

This noninvasive style of therapy was drilled into me. In one of my classes the professor divided us into two-person teams, one person playing the role of client and the other the role of therapist. If the "therapist" tried to elicit the other person's emotions, he or she was immediately corrected: "No, you are projecting onto the client." The rule was that the client, not the therapist, led the way.

Ironically, this was the same style of talk therapy that my own therapists had used. But even though it had had only limited effectiveness with me, I was hopeful it would work with others. My assumption was that I had been an especially difficult case and that other people would respond to the technique more quickly. I didn't realize how representative I was of other men.

MEN AND WOMEN IN "TALK THERAPY"

I adhered faithfully to my training for the first few years of my practice. To my delight, I was able to help many of my female clients a great deal, even though I was fresh out of graduate school. At the end of our work together the women would have increased their self-knowledge and would be better equipped to meet their emotional needs in the workplace and at home. It was rewarding work. However, this was not the case with my male clients. Many of the men would quit therapy after a few sessions or make much slower progress. It took some of them six months to reach the level of candor that women were showing by the second or third session.

As I look back on those early years, I can now see that one of the reasons more of my female clients made steady progress is that they had a positive attitude about therapy in general. The negative stigma that had long been attached to psychotherapy had been eroded by their exposure to women's groups, self-help books, and TV talk shows. Instead of viewing themselves as "neurotic" or having some form of shameful personal defect, they saw themselves as basically healthy people who had been wounded in childhood. They regarded therapy as an effective way to recover from those early traumas. One of the underlying reasons they could embrace this healthy attitude was that their gender conditioning allowed them to seek help. In the words of Deborah Tannen, author of the book *You Just Don't Understand,* most women "not only feel comfortable seeking help, but feel honor-bound to seek it, accept it, and display gratitude in exchange."

The women's gender conditioning also made it easier for them to discuss their personal problems with me. Talking with a therapist was not all that different from sharing confidences with a friend, which is something they'd been doing since they were little girls. The feminine code of openness, trust, and sharing had primed them for talk therapy.

The fact that they had been allowed to remain in touch with many of their vulnerable emotions was an additional bonus. Most of my female clients wouldn't just talk about their pain—they would cry about it, which allowed them to work the grief out of their systems. Although all of the women I saw had unchartered emotional territory to explore (which was why they were in therapy) they felt more comfortable traversing the general terrain. Even though they had some repressed anger and grief about the way they were raised, they didn't have to overcome a lifelong prohibition against expressing vulnerable emotions as well.

Some of the women turned out to be such ideal clients that all I had to do was be a supportive listener. They would make great strides just by having me paraphrase their remarks back to them in an empathic manner: "So you felt sad last night when you came home and your husband wasn't there, and he hadn't even left a note. I can understand that." At least some of their difficulty could be traced to the simple fact that they hadn't been listened to by their parents or their partners, and simply having a therapist listen intently to them and understand what they were saying and feeling helped them to heal.

If the women stayed in therapy long enough—and, fortunately, many of them did—they would eventually draw some connections between the pain they were having in the present and the trauma they had experienced in the past, which is one of the goals of psychotherapy. This awareness helped them begin to let go of some of the maladaptive behaviors left over from childhood. Before long they would be making significant changes in their lives. They would be leaving abusive or stultifying relationships, finding better jobs, making new friends. I was heartened by their progress and gained confidence in my ability as a therapist.

I had the opposite experience working with men. Perhaps 10 percent of them made the same kind of progress as the women, but the rest of them were much more emotionally blocked. It didn't help that many of the men were in therapy at the insistence of their female partners. A few of them viewed counseling as a waste of time and money and an invasion of privacy. If anything was wrong with their marriages, they would prefer to work it out in the sanctity of their own homes. These men also had naïve views of relationship dynamics, which further hampered their progress. For example, several men told me that the only thing wrong with their marriages was that their wives had too much time on their hands. If the women would only get a job, go back to school, or have another baby, then everything would be fine. One man blamed popular therapist and author John Bradshaw for his troubles. He said all his problems would end if his wife would "stop going to those damn Bradshaw therapy seminars and coming home with unrealistic expectations about marriage."[1]

1. There has been far too little research on how men respond to traditional therapy. One of the few studies I have found examined the reactions of twenty couples to the therapeutic experience. The men were shown to have significantly lower expectations for therapy than the women. The men also perceived their therapists as less trustworthy and experienced. Campbell, James L., "Marital status and gender similarity in marital therapy," *Journal of Counseling and Development,* Vol. 69(4), 1991, pp. 363–66.

In another study, men were shown to be less verbal than women and harder to reach with traditional talk therapy. Johnson, Ron, "Gender-specific therapy," *Journal of Psychology and Christianity,* Vol. 7(4), 1988, pp. 50–60.

I have a vivid memory of one of these resistant men. He was in his fifties, and he and his wife had come in for marital counseling. As was so often the case, it was his wife who had made the appointment. During their initial visit I listened to their problems and made some introductory remarks about couple communication. At the beginning of their second session I asked them to tell me what had stood out for them from the time before. The woman spoke first: "I remember you said I should tell my husband what I'm feeling and tell him what I want from him in specific terms. And you said not to pressure him for an answer because he needed time to think." Pleased that she had gotten so much out of the session, I turned to her husband and asked what he had recalled. He thought for a moment, looked up at the ceiling and down at the floor, and said, "Hmmmmm." Finally he looked me in the eye and said, "Well, what I remember most was that your socks didn't match."

His wife continued to drag him to my office for the next couple of months, but his attitude changed very little. Like all too many of the men that I saw, he had virtually no interest or motivation to be in counseling.

Some men did come to see me out of their own volition. But many of them were at the end of their psychological rope. Whereas many of my female clients came to me because they were mildly depressed, stressed, or "feeling stuck," these men would show up in the throes of despair. A few were so depressed they were suicidal. However, despite the fact that they were in desperate straits and were paying me good money to help them, they still found it hard to discuss their difficulties. I saw one man for an entire year before he felt safe enough to tell me about the pivotal event of his childhood, which is that he had accidentally drowned his younger sister in an innocent game of teenage horseplay. After confiding in me he told me it had been twenty years since he had discussed the drowning with another living soul.

Like this client, many men are used to viewing whatever causes them pain or embarrassment as a private matter. Perhaps after a few drinks or in a close relationship with a woman they might reveal some of their fears. But they rarely discuss their problems when they're sober. And to expose their vulnerability to another man would be to invite ridicule, attack, or at the very least, unwanted sympathy. When men came to me for talk therapy, they were entering alien territory.

Regrettably, getting my male clients to talk freely about their problems turned out to be only the first of many hurdles. An even greater obstacle was getting them to express their emotions. In order to heal, people can't just talk about their feelings, they have to experience them. They can't just complain about their pain and loneliness; they have to cry and grieve and work it out of their systems. In the words of therapist John Gray, "What you can feel, you can heal."

But most of my male clients had repressed their feelings for so long, they didn't feel safe releasing them. They were like rodeo riders sitting on the back of a wild bronco trying to keep it inside the chute. If the gate to the chute opened, God knows what kind of a ride they might have. Their instinct was to lock the gate and guard it by controlling everything and everyone around them. Unfortunately, I represented an especially potent threat to these men because therapists have a nasty habit of tinkering with the lock on the gate. Therefore, to keep their renegade feelings under control, my male clients had to find some way to control me.

They would do this in a variety of creative ways. Some would bring up inconsequential matters for weeks on end, boring both of us to tears. Others would talk about their real difficulties, but only in superficial or rational terms. If I tried to deepen the discussion by asking how they felt about an incident, they would continue to talk about the incident, not their feelings. And still others would "forget" their appointments or arrive late. One way or another they would turn therapy into a symbolic arm-wrestling match, leveraging against my moves as if I were a treacherous opponent. There would be little sense of movement or discovery in our work together.

SEARCHING FOR NEW TECHNIQUES FOR MEN

When I look back on my early efforts with men, I remind myself of a fishing guide who has caught only one fish in a particular hole but who persists in taking hundreds of paying fishermen to that very spot. I was using therapy techniques that had had only limited success with me in the hopes that my male clients would have better luck. My hopes were not realized. Finally my frustration rose so high that I began to cast around for alternatives.

In the back of my mind I was looking for something that would translate what I had learned in Slim's class into a more traditional therapeutic approach. Slim's class had been designed to help a group of people deal with a specific phobia, a fear of flying. It reduced their shame about having the phobia and encouraged them to express their fears. I needed to find similar techniques to help men release their full range of repressed emotions. And those techniques needed to be integrated into traditional therapy.

I explored various schools of thought, including encounter groups, bioenergetics, body work, and Gestalt therapy. Even though I saw merit in much of what I learned, no one therapy seemed to be what I was looking for. Out of necessity I began to piece together my own approach. I'd gather an insight here, a technique there, and brazenly try them out on my male clients. If they proved helpful with a number of men, I'd add them to my increasingly eclectic bag of tricks.

As part of this search I took part in an experimental men's group led by Dan Jones and John Lee, two acquaintances of mine who were nontraditional therapists and early leaders in the men's movement. We met weekly in an old house in the suburbs of Austin. The stated purpose of the group was to help men release their emotions. Dan and John used a wide variety of techniques. Working on us one at a time they cajoled, teased, pushed, and pulled each of us into our feelings. If we remained blocked, they would deliberately provoke us. For example, they might ask us to hold up our hands, palms facing outward, and then they would push against them. As they pushed our hands, they would taunt us: "You can't defend yourself. You're too weak and helpless." The goal was to call forth long-buried feelings. In essence, what they were doing was pitting our bodies against our brains. Our brains were telling us, "Don't cry. Don't yell. Don't get angry. Stay rational." Meanwhile, our bodies were begging us to release decades of stored-up emotion. Eventually the body would overwhelm the brain and trigger the release of feelings.

These feeling-release techniques broke all the rules I'd learned in graduate school. Their purpose was not only to stir up our feelings but to amplify them. They were surprisingly effective. During the six months I participated in the group, I saw more feelings expressed by men than I had seen in my entire life.

Watching men reveal their inner selves gave me some of the same feelings I had experienced in Slim's class, only they went much deeper. The men were like me in so many ways. Most of them had been hurt or neglected by their fathers. They, too, had spent much of their childhood trying to prove they weren't wimps or sissies. They'd felt the pressure to achieve in sports. They had either been in the military or they had known what it was like to have the draft hanging over their heads. They'd had buddies killed in the war. As adults they'd been burdened by never-ending financial responsibilities and had suffered the pain of failed relationships.

As these men opened up and shared their feelings, they were mirroring my experience as a man. I felt understood and validated by them in a way I had never experienced with women. I also felt safe with these men, which was a new experience for me. They weren't trying to compete with me or hurt me. They were there to support me in my efforts to heal. This experience was one of the catalysts that led to my later decision to counsel men in groups.

MY RAGE AT MY FATHER

Almost all my rage work in the class focused on my rage at my "ghost father," the father of my childhood who still haunted me in adulthood. At first I had trouble expressing much anger. I'd go through the motions of being angry—dutifully yelling and hitting the pillow with the bat—but I felt disconnected from my body. I looked angry enough on the outside, but inside I felt numb. Gradually my body began to overwhelm my masculine armor. By the fourth or fifth session I would shudder involuntarily as I approached the bat. At the end of two months my rage was coming up in earnest, and I was shaken by its intensity. All told, I unleashed a dozen or more violent explosions of rage at my father.

Then, session by session, my anger began to subside. I'd hit the pillow with the bat, but there was less energy in my body. By the end of six months I felt as though I had worked most of my rage out of my system.

In the midst of this work, what I now call my "rage stage," I had a dream about my father that is a landmark in my long journey of healing. For much of my life, whenever my dad came to me in a dream, it would be instantly transformed into a nightmare. My father would scream at me, hit me, or threaten me while I cringed in fear. I usually woke up from those nightmares in a cold sweat.

One dream that I had in the midst of my rage work was dramatically different. In this dream my father put his fist up to my face and started yelling at me for something I'd done wrong. I cowered as he bared his teeth in anger, just as in dozens of other dreams. But this dream had a new ending. I endured my father's abuse for a few moments, then my fear abruptly switched to rage. Without warning, I doubled up my fist and smashed my dad in the face. I hit him so hard he flew back against a wall. I watched in amazement as he slowly melted into a puddle on the floor. As his angry face melted into a liquid pool, I felt liberated and powerful. Finally, I had summoned up the power to defend myself against my ghost father.

I woke up the next morning feeling lighthearted and energized. I realized that the work I'd been doing in class had filtered all the way down to my unconscious, empowering me on a fundamental level. I no longer felt like an adolescent boy being pushed around by my unconscious fears. I felt like a man. And to my relief, from that day on, whenever my father came to visit me in my dreams he was a lot more respectful.

COMBINING ANGER-RELEASE TECHNIQUES WITH TALK THERAPY

At first I was reluctant to use feeling-release techniques with my own clients. Although the techniques had proven therapeutic for me, they weren't "therapy"; they hadn't been integrated into a comprehensive system. They were just tools to release pent-up feelings. They needed the underpinning of traditional therapy to be fully effective, and I had no model for combining the two contradictory approaches. Furthermore, some of the methods that had been used in the class were too confrontational for my purposes. Being physically provoked or taunted didn't create the feelings of safety that I believed most men would need in order to release their feelings.

Of all the techniques that Lee and Jones had used, the bat and the pillow seemed the most appropriate. It allowed a man to unlock the gate to his emotions by himself and at his own pace. No one needed to provoke him or physically push him to get the process started. Just swinging the bat was enough to jump start his anger. It was also a highly effective technique, capable of eliciting a great deal of rage.

I bought a red bat and an oversized pillow and brought them to my office. I kept them stored away in the closet for several weeks. It wasn't until I began working with a man named Andrew that I decided to bring them out. Andrew was a computer salesman. He was tall and stocky with a thick head of blond, curly hair, and vivid blue eyes. He was in his late thirties. I still remember the words that he used to describe his problem to me: "I need to clear the air around an indiscretion by my wife." It took me a few moments to realize that what he really meant was that his wife was having an affair.

Andrew was a highly verbal man and unlike many of my male clients needed little prompting to talk about his problems. But that's all he did—talk. He wasn't able to express any emotions. "I'm not sure where to start," he said, "but I'll give it a try. I've been married for ten years to a wonderful woman. She's five years older than me. I fell in love with her during our first date. My feelings for her remain strong, but I'm having my doubts about her love for me. You see, Louise is still seeing her ex-husband. Lately, they've resumed having sex." He took a deep breath and his gaze flitted to the crêpe myrtle blossoms outside my office window. He shifted his gaze back to me. For a fraction of a second his eyes were unguarded. "I called the guy and told him I wanted it to stop and that his involvement with my wife was hurting our marriage. I also told Louise I wanted it to stop. But neither of them is willing to end this thing. I'm confused about what to do. I suppose I could get angry and play the jealous husband, but I'm not sure what that would get me. There's no sense in getting obnoxious about this." Throughout this monologue Andrew's eyes were the only clue that he had any repressed emotions. As he was talking, his gaze would flit around the room.

In stark contrast to Andrew's stoicism I found myself feeling pissed off at his wife and her ex-husband. I was carrying the feelings he couldn't express. But all I said to him was, "I think it would be helpful to explore the feelings you might be having about the affair."

"To be perfectly honest," he said, "I don't know what I'm feeling. I know I've been upset. I can't concentrate at work. I've had trouble sleeping. And when I get home and Louise isn't there, my imagination works overtime. I have vivid images of the two of them making love. If she is home, I find it hard to talk to her. It's so hard to fathom. I can't understand why she's acting like this. Especially after I found out about it. I asked her if she still loved her ex-husband, and she didn't say yes but she didn't say no either." He sighed. "People can sure make a mess out of their lives, can't they?"

Andrew began to muse out loud that maybe he was to blame for the affair because he had worked so much during recent years. Maybe his wife had felt neglected and had been forced to look elsewhere for affection. He ruminated over his culpability until the session was over. As we were scheduling the following appointment, I suggested we might spend the next session exploring his feelings a little more deeply. As I said this, his body tensed up and he avoided my eyes.

I was mildly surprised to see Andrew show up for his second session. All week long I'd been expecting him to call up and cancel. But there he was, quietly reading a magazine in the waiting room, neatly dressed as before in slacks, a vest, a tie, and dress shoes. He walked into my office, sat down, crossed his legs, took off his glasses, and immediately started to talk in his mild, educated manner, tapping his glasses into his hand for emphasis as if to make up for the flatness of his voice. "Well, I approached Louise about this thing and told her I was getting tired of waiting for her answer," he said. "She told me she wasn't willing to end it just like that. She said there were too many feelings involved. I felt like saying, 'What about my feelings?' but I didn't. I just said it must be hard on her and I would try to understand." His eyes scanned the room, searching for a safe place to light.

Andrew took a deep breath and began to talk about how difficult it must be for his wife to be in love with two men. He tried to imagine how torn she must feel making love with both him and another man. As I listened to him sympathize with Louise's plight, my own tension level began to mount. Finally I couldn't stand it anymore and I interrupted him. "Andrew, wait a second. You're talking about your wife, and I want to hear about you. What are *you* feeling right now?"

"I don't know. I guess I feel a lot of things but I don't seem to focus on any one of them for more than a second or two."

As I watched him struggle to contain his feelings, I suddenly had a vision of how I must have appeared to my own therapist years ago, desperately trying to hold myself together with a cigar, a can of Coke, and a stick of gum. I knew I had to free Andrew from his straitjacket. "Are you willing to take a risk?" I asked him.

"I don't know," he said. "What kind of risk? If it will help resolve this situation, I guess I'm willing to try. What do you want me to do, threaten her with divorce?"

"No. Nothing like that. It's just that I have a hunch you've been feeling a lot of rage toward your wife and her lover and you've been holding it inside," I said, confronting him ever so gently. I tried to silence the voice of my college professor who was warning me about projecting my feelings on to the client.

"Of course," Andrew said, "I've been upset at them. But what good would it do to dredge all that stuff up? The two of them have been acting like adolescents. Why should I stoop to their level?" Andrew put on his glasses and then took them off again. His jaw clamped down and his eyes narrowed.

I got out of my chair and retrieved the pillow and the bat from out of the closet. Feeling tentative I put them down on the floor in front of him.

"Now, Andrew, this is the risk. I want you to get down on your knees in front of the pillow, pick up the bat, and allow your anger to come to the surface."

Andrew was willing to try. He took off his glasses, loosened his tie, and knelt on the floor. He grabbed the bat with both hands and rested it on the pillow. Then he nervously straightened the creases of his pants. "I'm supposed to hit the pillow with this bat?" he asked, his voice betraying his discomfort.

"I know it feels a little embarrassing to do this," I said, "but sometimes it's okay to feel embarrassed. It's only a feeling. Now, what I want you to do is take a deep breath and try to relax. I don't want you to think. What I want you to do is imagine that there's some rage inside of you that wants to come out. It may be there and it may not be there, but for the moment we'll pretend that it is. Is that okay with you?"

Andrew nodded.

"Now, when you're ready, I want you to hit the pillow as hard as you can. I want you to make a lot of noise. I want you to open your throat and let the sounds come out."

Andrew started squeezing the bat as tight as he could, so tight the bat started to shake. Then he began twisting his hands back and forth around the handle. His whole body began to vibrate as he twisted the bat. The bat handle squeaked as he wrung his hands for what seemed like an eternity. I watched in fascination, mesmerized by the fight that was going on inside him—his body crying out for release, his mind refusing to relinquish control. Then, abruptly, Andrew whipped the bat above his head and slammed it violently into the pillow. *Wham!* Then—*wham!*—he hit it again. And again. And again. Yet with all that physical energy he remained mute. I had learned in my own bouts with the bat and pillow that making noise was an essential part of the technique. Clenching your teeth while you're venting your rage is like flooring the gas pedal as you slam on the brakes.

"Yell at your wife's ex-husband," I urged him. "Tell him how angry you are."

That's all it took. As soon as Andrew started allowing the anger to come up through his belly and out of his throat, he came unglued. All at once he let loose with a torrent of profanity: "You goddamn mo-therfucking son-of-a-bitch! I could kill you! I could beat your fucking head in! Beat that fucking Ivy League smile off your face, you smug asshole! She's not your wife anymore. She's mine!" He was like a man possessed. His rage was so strong he could barely confine it to the pillow. He stood up and started whacking the pillow from a standing position. He kicked the pillow until it slammed up against the wall. Then he picked it up and smashed it to the floor over and over again. Saliva sprayed from his mouth as he screamed out his hatred of his wife's lover.

When at last he started to wind down, I was vastly relieved, but also a little scared. I felt as if I had let a genie out of a bottle. However, drawing on what I had learned from my own anger work, I knew it was essential to continue to elicit his feelings. I fought against my fear and urged Andrew on, "What about Louise?" I demanded. "Are you mad at Louise?"

This started him all over again. He beat the pillow again with the bat and then with his fists. He threw it against the wall. He screamed at his wife, "You little bitch. How could you! You goddamn fucking whore! You're my wife, goddamnit, not his. You bitch gold digger!" I watched in amazement, wondering how anyone could expend so much energy without stopping.

At last Andrew collapsed in a heap on the pillow. Between gasps, he whispered, "You bitch. How could you do this to me? I love you so much." His rage was gone, and he began to sob deeply into the pillow.

When all his rage and his grief were finally spent, I touched Andrew on the shoulder and asked how he felt. He got up and slumped into his chair and looked straight in my eyes. "I feel totally exhausted. And I feel embarrassed that you saw me do that. Jesus Christ, where did all that anger come from? It was like the room disappeared." For the first time words failed him, and he sat limply in the chair.

I was silent as well. Although I tried not to show it, I was almost as stunned as he was. I knew that he had some rage inside him, but I was amazed by the sheer volume of it. I was also awestruck by how well the bat-and-pillow technique had worked. If I had relied on standard talk therapy, it would have taken him months, perhaps years, to get in touch with all of that rage. All the while I would have been reduced to mirroring back to him all his verbal defenses, a game that could go on for years.

THE HEALING POWER OF RAGE WORK

In the succeeding months, I used the bat-and-pillow technique with most of my clients. Although my female clients profited from the rage work as well, it was the men who seemed to benefit the most. Their feelings were not only buried under the normal layers of childhood repression but under a lifetime of gender conditioning.

Gradually I became more skilled with using the bat and the pillow. I began to sense when the time was ripe to introduce them to a client, and I learned what to say and do to help men overcome their fear of releasing their rage. As I honed the technique, I gained an even deeper appreciation for the healing power of rage work. I was learning that there is a world of difference between randomly venting one's rage and releasing rage in a controlled, therapeutic environment. When a man rages at an employee, a loved one, an animal, or his property, he is causing emotional or physical damage. He senses the harm that he's doing and short-circuits his rage. Soon after his rage subsides, he is filled with remorse and punishes himself through self-criticism or some form of self-abuse. He has gained nothing. Sadly, the fit of rage hasn't diminished his reservoir of pent-up emotions—it may even have increased it. Furthermore, he hasn't gotten any insight into where his rage comes from. He is likely to believe that the triggering event—the child who forgot to do a chore or the dog who chewed on the rug—was the sole reason for his outburst. All he has done is reinforce a destructive cycle of rage and shame.

Provoking rage in a man with violent tendencies in an unsafe setting not only fails to reduce his pent-up emotions, it can lead to tragedy. There is a primitive game called Chest and Ribs that is played by some teenage boys in my area. Two young men stand toe-to-toe and exchange punches to the chest until one of them relents. Not long ago two boys were playing the game when one of them lost his temper and slugged the other boy in the face. They got into a fist fight. One of them ran home, got a gun, and killed the other boy. When two men with pent-up rage provoke each other, the end result can be murder.[2]

Releasing rage using the bat and the pillow in a therapy setting is a totally different experience. First of all, the man's anger is directed at an inanimate object, not another person. Second, the therapist is there to make sure that the exercise remains safe. No one is going to get hurt and no property is going to be destroyed. Third, the therapist plays an essential role by encouraging the client to release the full extent of his anger. All his life the client has been taught to hold in his feelings. He's been punished for his anger and conditioned to believe that it's unmanly to lose control. The therapist counters those messages by affirming his right to his feelings and by praising him for releasing them in an appropriate manner. Ideally, the client will continue to beat the pillow until he works through his rage and can tap into his underlying feelings—grief, sadness, and helplessness. Once this occurs the therapist is there to console, validate, affirm, and draw vital connections between those feelings of vulnerability and the pain he has endured earlier in life. When the client completes the work, he has had a cathartic experience that can dramatically hasten his healing process.

2. Chuck Lindell, "Family Is Stunned by Man's Death over Game," *Austin American Statesman* (September 21, 1992), p. B1.

Jack: Helping Men Who Can't Grieve

The more successful I was at helping men release their rage, the more I thought about grief. Although it is vital that men release their repressed rage, grief is the real key to freeing the masculine heart. All people, men and women alike, need to have some way to come to terms with their losses. One of the most fundamental losses that we all have to grieve is that we were raised by imperfect parents in an imperfect society. Our emotional wholeness was taken away from us by the neglect or abuse of our caregivers. We can never fully erase that reality. We can only grieve for it. We may sustain a host of emotional injuries in later years as well, such as failed love relationships, the deaths of family and friends, disappointments with our children, missed opportunities, and ordeals at work. These, too, can be healed through grief.

The grief process is a mysterious, natural, wondrous reaction. No one can say for sure why it heals. We can only describe what we observe. When we grieve deeply—deeply enough to weep—we experience a complex mix of emotions that can include despair, confusion, fear, loss, and helplessness. We resist those feelings because they are so intense and make us feel so vulnerable. But if we overcome our resistance and continue to grieve, our feelings merge into something entirely different—an overwhelming sense of self-compassion. All of a sudden, we feel as if we truly understand the beauty of our original wholeness and can appreciate fully the pain of what we've endured. It's as if a window has been opened to our very souls. These precious moments soften our defenses and allow us to feel a deep love for ourselves and for all of humanity.

But men, unlike women, are not allowed to grieve in this culture. When I look back over my childhood, I can only recall one time when I saw a grown man cry. My male teachers never cried, my scoutmasters never cried, my uncles never cried, the Lone Ranger never cried, Humphrey Bogart never cried, John Wayne never cried. None of my heroes cried. It's one of those unwritten rules: men do not grieve. The only exception I can recall from my entire childhood involved my grandfather, and it happened just once. I was eight years old and we were all having dinner at my grandparents' house. My grandfather, who was seventy years old at the time, commented on how cute we kids looked in our new Easter clothes. I was startled to see a tear in his eye. He turned to my father and said in a voice thick with emotion, "Son, I wish I could have bought you a new suit for Easter when you were a little boy."

I never saw my dad cry, not even at his father's funeral. In fact, looking back on it, I have only one clue that he experienced any grief over his father's death. He had quit smoking several months before my grandfather died, and on the way home from the funeral, he reached in his pocket for a Camel. He smoked from that day on.

Many men can recall a particular event from their childhood that drilled home the message that "big boys don't cry." My friend and associate, Allen Mauer, remembers a time when he and a group of friends were riding their bikes. One of his friends fell off his bike and broke his leg. His leg hurt so badly he started to cry. The other boys backed away from him because they didn't know how to handle his tears. For a long time after that they called him a sissy.

The intensity of the taboo against crying varies from household to household and from community to community. Once I was counseling a tough-looking Hispanic man with a tattoo on each arm. He had come in for counseling because his wife had just filed for divorce. I watched him struggle to hold back his tears. I urged him to release his feelings. I assured him that it was natural to cry when your wife and children leave you, that crying would be a perfectly natural way to work grief out of his system. He shook his head in disbelief and told me that the men in his east Texas community would cut off his thumbs if they knew he'd been crying. I smiled at his obvious exaggeration. He shook his head emphatically and said he was deadly serious. In his community crying in front of other people was not only shameful, it could result in mutilation.

As I focused my efforts on finding some way to help men grieve, I realized that it was far easier to induce rage than sorrow. It doesn't take much to make a guy mad. If you push against him hard enough, he'll get pissed off. But it is much harder to trigger a man's grief. My stoic male clients were able to talk about the most heart-wrenching events of their lives without shedding a tear. Many of the men I saw had to go through rage work for six months to a year before they could break down and cry. And to my growing frustration, a significant number of men seemed unable to cry under any circumstances at all.

Jack, an engineer in his mid-fifties, was one of those highly resistant men. Like so many men, he sought counseling because his wife had left him. After talking about the separation for a few sessions, he began to reveal other problems. He told me his productivity at work was diminishing and that he was terrified of being fired. He was even more troubled by the fact that his twenty-five-year-old son, his only child, was siding with his ex-wife in the marital struggle and didn't want to speak to him. Jack felt abandoned by both his wife and his son. He felt as if his entire life was collapsing around him.

On the surface Jack seemed ready to do some intensive work. He told me, "If I have to dredge up my whole childhood and bring in the ghosts of my mother and dad every week, I'll do it. Whatever it takes I'm going to do it. I'm tired of being scared all the time and pretending I'm in control."

It took several months, however, before Jack felt safe enough to allow any feelings to rise to the surface. Finally he was able to use the bat to release some of the rage that came from being raised by an alcoholic father and a scared, needy mother who spent more time worrying about her husband than taking care of her son.

As his rage dissipated, I could see that his grief was trying to surface. He said he wanted to cry, but the tears just wouldn't come. One afternoon he was talking about the shame he felt for being the son of an alcoholic, and I saw his eyes gather water. He said, "I think I could almost cry, but I'm afraid somebody might see me." He pointed to my French doors that had no blinds or drapes on them. Although the door opened onto a seldom-used corridor, he didn't like the thought that someone might walk by and see him cry.

That week I went out and bought blinds for the doors and had them installed before Jack's next session. When he came in for his appointment, he thanked me for the blinds, and we again worked on his feelings about his dad. But despite the added privacy, he continued to hold in his grief. He told me he'd only cried once in forty-five years, and that was the day his wife had left him. "It's real hard to cry in front of another man," he said, "even if you are my therapist."

To fight against his resistance, he volunteered to do some more work with the bat and the pillow, but this didn't work either. The tears just wouldn't flow. "I can't do this," he told me, handing me the bat. "I can't cry in front of anybody. I'm too embarrassed. It's too personal." He shook his head.

We talked about his embarrassment, and I asked him if anyone had ever shamed him for crying. He thought for a moment and said, "I just remembered something. When I was a little boy, my mother told me that my face looked ugly when I cried. She even showed me a picture that had been taken while I was crying to show me how ugly I looked. I still feel too ashamed to cry."

Shaming is the most common way that young boys learn not to cry. Shamed by their older siblings, by their parents, by the kids at school, boys lose the healing power of grief. I told Jack how sorry I was that his mother had shamed him for crying. But I also said that he wouldn't fully resolve the traumatic events of his childhood unless he found some way to release his pain.

Jack took my words to heart, and the next session he was finally able to reveal his vulnerability. I saw the tears start to come as he talked about being a young boy and seeing his drunken father babbling incoherently out on the front porch. I encouraged him to stay with that feeling. Before the tears could actually fall, however, he got out of his chair, sat on the floor, and turned his back to me. He cried silently without letting me see his face.

When he finished, he said, "Marvin, that was ten times harder than using the bat." However, because he had cried once and nothing harmful had happened to him—I hadn't laughed at him or shamed him, and he hadn't started to cry uncontrollably—he was able to cry again during later sessions. With each expression of grief, he was able to reach out a little more to that scared, ashamed, angry little boy inside of him. He reached another milestone the day when he was able to sob without turning away from me. Eventually, through letting out more and more of his stored-up tears, he was able to achieve that longed-for feeling of release.

EXPERIENCING ANGER AND GRIEF—
THE KEY TO MEN'S HEALING

Since Freud, it has been generally accepted that a part of the mysterious process of psychological healing involves understanding what happened to you as a child and then *expressing* the feelings that you were not allowed to feel at the time. The inability to express your feelings fully at the time of the trauma allowed the injury to remain a live issue in your psyche. You can heal those wounds later in life by allowing yourself to release your stored-up emotions. Most forms of psychotherapy rely on this process.

However, men are at a distinct disadvantage when they try to heal through traditional forms of psychotherapy because their gender conditioning has trained them to keep their emotions bottled up. They need a great deal of support and encouragement to overcome this programming, more than they may receive in traditional therapy. They also need a tool to help them begin releasing their emotions, something more direct than conversation. An anger-release technique such as the bat and pillow helps them break through their inhibitions.

I was gratified to see these theories borne out in my practice. Those men who were able to cry deeply enough and to use the bat and the pillow often enough began to heal much more rapidly. Within a matter of months they felt more energetic. They experienced spontaneous feelings of happiness and joy. Hostile/abusive men had less of a tendency to rage inappropriately, and passive men displayed a new assertiveness. All of the men began to make better choices in their lives because now they could rely on their emotions as well as their intellect to chart a true course.

This was not a miracle cure. The men had to summon up a great deal of courage and put forth a lot of effort. They had to deal with past issues that most people would just as soon cover up. The full course of therapy took at least two years, sometimes more. But most men felt a significant improvement in their outlook on life by the end of the first twelve months. All of them felt that the investment of time and money was worthwhile.

MY ROLE AS A THERAPIST

As time went on I got a clearer sense of my role in the recovery process. My primary job was to help the men feel safe enough to begin exploring their emotions. To provide that element of safety it was important that I not be a distant, rational authority figure looking down on them from afar, which is the old therapeutic model. They wouldn't reveal their vulnerability unless they saw me as a caring, concerned individual. I discovered one way to do this was to talk about some of my own history with repression. The men were comforted to know I had traversed the same ground. I also assured them that I could handle any emotion they cared to express. I wasn't going to be frightened by the intensity of their rage, and I wasn't going to be embarrassed if they cried. I had seen it all before and I welcomed all of their emotions. Finally, I let them know that I would stick with them throughout the healing process, no matter how many years it took. They needed to know that I would be there to help them deal with the aftermath. One way that I demonstrated my availability was to give them my home phone number, something many therapists won't do for fear of compromising the therapeutic relationship. In my practice I found it a help, not a hindrance.

Despite all my efforts, I was only able to *reduce* a man's fears, not eliminate them. In order to proceed with therapy, he had to rely on his own courage. He had to bolster his courageous self so he could take his fearful self on the ride. After he'd cried and beaten the pillow a number of times, he would learn for himself that his fears of releasing his feelings were groundless. There was no way I could fully convince him of that ahead of time. Exploring this uncharted terrain was a true test of courage.

At this point in the evolution of my approach to men's therapy I had one of the key components: an effective way to help men release their emotions. What I was to learn next was the healing power of a men's group. To my surprise everything that I was doing with men in individual sessions would become even more effective when used in a group setting. Working with men in groups would also allow me to focus on an almost universal male difficulty: inadequate relationship skills.

CHAPTER 8

THE HEALING POWER OF A MEN'S GROUP

Gradually, my emphasis began to shift from working with men individually to working with men in groups. I had already had two experiences that had convinced me of the effectiveness of group work. The first had been Slim's fear-of-flying class. Slim had taught me how much easier it is to deal with your fears when you know they are shared by others. The second experience had been the anger-release class lead by John Lee and Dan Jones. In that all-male group I had felt understood and accepted as never before. The camaraderie and support between the members had been almost as therapeutic for me as the anger-release techniques themselves.

A third experience with groups proved just as influential. To add to my training I spent a year under the supervision of Carl Kirsch, a noted psychiatrist in the Austin area. I later joined one of his co-ed groups for therapists. In that group Kirsch placed special emphasis on the interaction between group members. In some therapy groups "cross-talk," or conversations between group members, is discouraged. Virtually all of the dialogue is a one-on-one discussion between the therapist and an individual group member. Kirsch encouraged group interaction, using it as a way to highlight our hidden patterns of relating. For example, by watching me interact with the others Kirsch was able to point out to me that I was projecting anger more often than I realized, and that I had a strong desire to please. I began to see how both of those tendencies were frustrating my love relationships. He didn't teach us better relationship skills directly, but I found the insights valuable nonetheless.

In the group I spent as much time observing the way Kirsch ran the sessions as I did concentrating on my own issues. I noticed that he spent an inordinate amount of time working with the men. We males seemed to have more trouble listening to other group members. We were more isolated and less communicative. We also were more reluctant to reveal our emotions. I remember thinking to myself, if male therapists have this much trouble relating to others, what about the man on the street? This experience reinforced my belief that a therapy designed for men has to include the actual teaching of relationship skills. Insight isn't enough. Men need instruction and practice.

Within a year my ideas about men's therapy had evolved to the point that I felt comfortable leading my own group. My overall goal was to integrate my formal training with the feeling-release techniques of Jones and Lee and the relationship insights I had picked up from Kirsch. My task was to blend all that I had learned into an effective, comprehensive therapy for men.

I can still remember the initial session of my first men's group. Ten nervous men sat with their arms crossed, trying not to catch each other's eyes—which is difficult to do when you're sitting in a circle. They were reluctant to share much personal information. I found myself wondering if what I had hoped to accomplish was possible.

I was relieved to discover that this breaking-in phase lasted only a couple of weeks. Once a sense of trust was established, the men began to open up just as much as they did in private sessions. In subsequent groups I learned to take advantage of those first awkward sessions by talking about basic aspects of emotional health. With only men present I could focus on problems that were of special significance to males.

One problem I could explore at length was the difference between thoughts and feelings. Because of a lifetime of gender conditioning even a bright and articulate man can confuse the two. When one of the men would make a comment like: "I feel I'm going to get a raise at work," I would suggest that he *thinks* he will get a raise, but what he *feels* is probably something more like anticipation, excitement, or maybe even entitlement. After hearing dozens of comments like this the men became skilled at knowing the difference between thoughts and feelings.

I got an appreciation for how well the men in one particular group had mastered this lesson when I introduced a new member to the ranks. Terry, the newcomer, was a young single man and a recovering alcoholic. At the beginning of each session I asked the men to give what I call a "check-in," which is a two-minute report about the previous week followed by a concise statement about what he is feeling at the moment. When it was Terry's turn, he went into great detail about his recovery program. It was an intellectual report that revealed little emotion. He chatted on for five minutes, oblivious to the time. He concluded by attempting to describe his feelings. "What I'm feeling," he said with a confident smile, "is that this is going to be a really good group and I'm going to get a lot out of it."

"I'm glad you've had some positive thoughts about the group, Terry," I said, "but what are you *feeling* right now?"

He looked at me and said, "What?"

"What are you *feeling* right now?"

He thought for a moment and said, "Well, I don't know. I guess I'm feeling . . . consolidated." There was the sound of muffled laughter from a few veterans.

"The reason the guys are laughing," I explained, "is that *consolidated* sounds like something that would happen to IBM, not a person. I was thinking more in terms of, 'Are you scared or nervous to be joining the group? Are you excited?' "

Terry looked around the circle at the other men and had a brief laugh at himself. "I guess I'm a little nervous. I tend to talk too much when I'm nervous."

Terry was a quick learner. After a couple of sessions he was able to make a clear distinction between his thoughts and his feelings and describe his feelings with considerable accuracy. Some men had a harder time identifying their emotions. They could tell they were having a feeling rather than a thought, but they were only aware of a vague sensation of frustration. To help the men get more insight into the emotion I would explain that there are only four basic "feeling groups": mad, sad, glad, and afraid. Most feelings are a variation on one of those primary emotions. Being able to identify the correct feeling group was all they really needed to do. The subtleties could come later.

But some men would have trouble even identifying which of the four primary emotions they were feeling. When that happened, I would suggest they do a logical analysis. Did it make sense to feel angry in that particular situation? Did it make sense to feel sad? Joyful? Fearful? Using their highly developed rational minds they could begin to explore the unknown terrain of their emotions.

Another way I made use of those initial weeks was to help the men recognize when they were having an emotional reaction in the group. Many times a man would experience an emotion during the session without being aware of it. For example, a man might say, "I can't feel a damn thing. I'm numb," but it would be clear to me and to the other men that he was feeling angry right then and there about the fact that he was numb. I might say to him, "It could be you're having a feeling right now. There's a lot of energy in your voice." The other men would confirm what I had observed. With the help of this feedback the men would eventually become more in tune with their emotions.

THE ADVANTAGES OF DOING RAGE WORK IN A GROUP

As the comfort level in a given group increased and the men showed a willingness to explore deeper issues, I found an opportunity to introduce the bat and the pillow and station them in the middle of the circle. It took a lot of courage for the first man in a group to use the bat. But once the ice was broken, most of the other men followed suit within the next couple of sessions. It seemed that using the bat and pillow in a group setting actually facilitated the flow of emotions. After one man had raged at his father, it wasn't unusual for there to be another man waiting for a turn at the bat.

The group setting also helped remove some of the cultural prohibitions against showing strong emotions. A key part of rage-release therapy is getting validated for expressing rage in an appropriate manner. When the therapist says "good job" once the exercise is over, it encourages the man to release more of his emotions at a later date. It counters the negative messages about "losing control." I discovered that this affirmation has even more power when it comes from both the therapist and the other men in the group. The men sitting around in the circle are the same kind of guys a man runs into at work, at church, and on the golf course. When they say "well done" to a man after a session with the bat, they are not only commending his efforts, but they are also challenging the male taboo against showing intense feelings. They are helping rewrite the masculine code.

Another unexpected bonus of using the bat and pillow in a group setting was that the men observing the exercise got to practice weathering someone else's rage. Many men not only have difficulty expressing their own strong feelings, but they also find it hard to be around the anger or rage of others. When someone gets mad at them, they have a tendency to either withdraw or overreact. When a man observes a number of sessions with the bat and the pillow, he becomes more tolerant of other people's anger. This is a learning experience that can't be duplicated in individual therapy.

Not surprisingly, the men who had the most difficulty witnessing the rage work were the ones who had been physically abused by their fathers. Watching a man display violent behavior triggered childhood memories that sent them into a state of near shock. They would tense up and almost forget to breathe. To counter their fears I gave them a lot of reassurance: "It may be uncomfortable to watch another man do this work, but it's not unsafe. No one's going to hurt you." But no matter what I said, some men wouldn't be able to relax until they had watched five or six episodes of rage work and discovered they could actually live through them. This repeated exposure in a safe setting made it easier for them to tolerate anger outside the group. It erased the old tape that said that rage always leads to destruction.

A LABORATORY FOR RELATIONSHIPS

What pleased me most of all about working with men in groups was the opportunity it gave men to learn new relationship skills. Learning how to relate to others in a healthy manner is of vital importance in a man's emotional recovery. He needs to become skilled at getting his needs met in relationships. This is the only way to break out of his isolation and get the support and validation he so desperately needs. When he is able to form an intimate and lasting love relationship and feel deeply connected to family members and friends, he nurtures his soul and is able to put the rest of his life in perspective. His work life no longer takes precedence over everything else because he is finding deep satisfaction in his relationships. Some men have to have a near-fatal accident, a life-threatening disease, or a heart attack to understand the importance of relationships. The men in my therapy sessions come to the same awareness by taking part in the group.

The development of new relationship skills is a two-stage process. First, men need to identify their self-defeating patterns of relating. As I had observed in Carl Kirsch's group, interacting in a group is an ideal way to gather this information. The therapist and the other members serve as mirrors, reflecting back, and sometimes even magnifying, your hidden personality traits. This gives you the insights you need to start altering the way you treat other people. This feedback is especially important for men. Men are masters at hiding their feelings from everyone, even themselves. They have disguised their emotions for so long, even *they* have lost sight of their true feelings. They need other people to point out to them all the ways they are frustrating their desire for intimacy and connection.

After a year of weekly sessions the men in my groups become highly skilled at detecting each other's hidden patterns. This gives each man an invaluable collection of data. He learns whether he has a tendency to ingratiate himself to others, belittle himself, intellectualize, pontificate, criticize, withdraw—all those traits he'd rather not know about himself, but that interfere with his ability to form close and lasting relationships.

Once men have identified their self-defeating habits, they can go on to the second stage of the process and learn how to develop healthier ones. Once again a therapy group is an ideal setting for this work. It's difficult, if not impossible, to practice new ways of relating on family members and friends. As much as they profess to want you to change, they are likely to be unsettled by any alteration in your behavior. If you change, then *they* have to change, and that would be threatening. But the very purpose of a therapy group is to help you grow and develop. The other members reinforce you for breaking out of old habits and encourage you to adopt new ones. A therapy group is an ideal laboratory for developing relationship skills.

However, it takes a few months for a new group of men to become comfortable enough with each other to start this process. In the beginning they are reluctant to give each other honest feedback. Their gender conditioning makes it difficult for them to express how they feel, whether to someone inside or outside the group. It requires a familiarity with their emotions many men don't have. They need to go through several months of "remedial education" about feelings in general before they are able to identify them and express them. Also, during the initial sessions most men are afraid to break the supportive, caring, safe atmosphere of the group "family." The underlying belief is that if they keep their feelings hidden from each other, the group will remain safe. If they start expressing their true feelings, all hell might break loose. Far better to endure a little pent-up frustration. Far better to be bored and disinterested. After all, most of them have made a lifelong habit of deadening their relationships in order to secure a little safety.

To help the men overcome these inhibitions, I spend a lot of time encouraging a new group to be more forthcoming with each other. I start out each session by asking them to be honest during the coming hour. If they feel bored or disinterested in what someone is saying, I urge them to confront that person in a respectful manner. That person needs to know how he is perceived by others. He won't be able to change any self-defeating traits unless he is aware of them. I give them examples of how to give feedback in a constructive, nonthreatening manner: "John, excuse me, but I'm feeling lost right now. I can't connect with what you're saying," or, "You seem to be talking about thoughts, not feelings. How do you *feel* about this?" or, "I sense some underlying anger. Are you feeling angry about what I said?"

During the session I pay a lot of attention to my own reactions. When I feel bored or impatient or confused by what someone is saying, I look around the room and check out the body language of the other men. Invariably, I see other men yawning, staring off into the distance, or staring at their fingernails. I wait until the person has finished speaking and then ask the other men for their reactions. How had they felt when the person was talking? Had they felt connected with what he was saying? Had they felt bored? Had they felt angry or frustrated?

Ever so slowly the men become more forthcoming about their own reactions and more willing to comment about what they see happening between other group members. When one person volunteers his reaction about another man's behavior—perhaps he is bored by a long intellectual digression or angry about a cutting remark—I stop and analyze what is happening. I want to make sure that the man receiving the feedback hears and accepts what is being said, and I want to support the man doing the commenting. For the most part this is a tedious process, but it is a necessary exercise for men who have been emotionally blocked for years. Without this kind of support they will rarely explore their true feelings.

The process of dissecting these interchanges between the men is a lot like a skull session the morning after a football game where the coach points to a blackboard covered with *X*'s and *O*'s and says things like, "Johnson, when Haager pulled out of his position to block their blitzing linebacker, you should have covered his ass if somebody came through that hole. Then, when Haager moved to his left, you should have come around to his right real quick. Now, let's go over this play one more time to make sure you've got it." By analyzing the play moment by moment, the coach drills key concepts into his team. Our instant replay in the therapy group is equally detailed. But once the men see that the debriefing helps them learn how to connect with others on an emotional level, they are willing to endure the tedium. This is the very quality so woefully lacking in their relationships outside the group.

An exchange during a recent session between Martin, an attorney, and Jeff, an electrical engineer, will give you a sense of how we do this blow-by-blow analysis. Martin was talking at great length about his recent separation from his wife. But instead of talking about his grief he was going on and on about the fact that his wife had purchased a new set of radial tires on his credit card. In manly fashion he was belaboring all the details about what kind of tires she had purchased and what they had cost. He was up in his head and going nowhere. This is a classic example of what Deborah Tannen calls "report talk," as opposed to "rapport talk." Tannen implies that men have an inherent tendency to talk this way, but the men in the group were learning it was more a product of their gender conditioning than their genes. And, more important, they were learning that staying on an intellectual plane was keeping them isolated from other people.

Finally, Jeff got so frustrated with Martin's long digression that he bravely volunteered his reaction: "Martin, wait a minute. You said you were upset because your wife left you, but then you started talking about tires. How do you *feel* about the fact that you go home at night to an empty house?"

Martin paused and went limp, "I don't think I'm feeling anything right now." He had reacted to Jeff's confrontation by cutting off all his feelings.

No one talked for a moment, so I broke the silence by asking Jeff how he felt about confronting Martin.

He said, "I'm worried that you will all think I'm rude. I'm always the first one to make a comment. I'm also worried that Martin might be a little pissed off at me." As a rule, Jeff is more aware of his reactions than the other men in the group, and he's more willing to express them.

I asked the other men if they thought Jeff had been rude for interrupting Martin. Most of them said no. They, too, had felt bored by Martin's digression, but they hadn't had the nerve to speak up. However, one man, Peter, said he felt a little put out by Jeff's interruption. He thought that Martin would have gotten around to talking about his feelings eventually. He added that if he'd been Martin, he might have been pissed off at Jeff.

To check on Peter's perception, I asked Martin once again how he had felt about being confronted by Jeff.

"I think Jeff was right," he said. "Maybe I was rambling on about nothing. I guess I needed someone to shut me up."

"I didn't ask you what you *thought,* Martin," I said. "I'm interested in knowing how you *felt* about being interrupted."

"I don't know. I guess I just went numb."

I persisted. "Peter was worried you might have felt attacked by Jeff. Did you feel attacked?"

Martin furrowed his brow for a moment then said, "Well, maybe I did feel a little heat when he cut me off. Yeah, I did feel a little under attack."

I asked Martin if he was willing to tell that to Jeff directly.

Martin took a deep breath and nodded. "Jeff," he said, "I did feel criticized. And I also lost any interest in talking. I just wanted to forget the whole thing."

I turned to Jeff and asked him how *he* was feeling about what Martin had just said.

"I feel uncomfortable," he said. "I don't like the thought that Martin thinks I'm attacking him. That's not what I intended. We're supposed to speak up in here when we're feeling something, even if it's negative—*especially* if it's negative. We're supposed to call each other on our stuff. If I feel bored or disconnected when you're talking, then something's wrong and it's my job to let you know. I'm in this group to learn to be honest, not to try to make everyone happy like I've always done. I've got to know if it's okay with you if I bring up whatever I'm feeling."

"It's okay with me," said Martin. "I may not like it all the time, but it won't be the first time I didn't like something. I'm here to learn, too. You need to tell me if I'm boring you. Christ! I was angry at you and I didn't even know it. If this is what it takes for me to feel, then let's get on with it—as long as I can be angry at you and it won't shut you down."

Jeff replied, "Well, you might shut me down, but don't let that stop you. I'll open back up later, and then I'll let you know how I'm feeling."

Especially in the early months of a group it takes all this painstaking, sometimes awkward analysis for the men to know what they are actually feeling in the moment and to accept feedback from others. It takes a great deal of effort to penetrate their defenses. It is especially hard for them to detect vulnerable emotions like sadness, grief, and embarrassment because they go so strongly against their gender conditioning. But after months of scrutiny the men begin to recognize more and more of their feelings as they are happening. In essence they are going through a kind of emotional rehabilitation. They are like stroke victims learning how to talk or accident victims struggling to walk again. Eventually they will be in touch with their emotions without going through all of this tedious work. They'll know right away whether they are feeling mad, sad, glad, or afraid, and they will feel more comfortable revealing their feelings to others. When this happens, they will be well on their way to emotional wholeness.

LEARNING HOW TO DEVELOP FRIENDSHIPS

Few men have lasting friendships with other men. It is common for a man to have only one intimate relationship, the one with his female partner, and to keep other people at arm's length. He has business contacts and acquaintances, but few close, continuing friendships. In his book, *The Seasons of a Man's Life,* D. J. Levinson observed that most American men do not have an intimate male friend after they leave college.[1] When a man learns how to relate to others in an open, caring manner, he has the skills he needs to begin making friends.

I recently had an opportunity to watch a friendship develop between two men in my Tuesday-night group—Patrick, a designer, and Jeff, the same electrical engineer who had confronted Martin. At first their attempts to deepen their relationship failed because they were unwilling to be honest with each other. In true manly fashion they kept their reactions to themselves, frustrating their desire to get closer.

Patrick was the first one to indicate an interest in a closer friendship. At the end of a group session he mentioned to Jeff that it would be nice for the two of them to have lunch together. Jeff agreed and called Patrick later that week to invite him to lunch. Patrick wasn't in, so Jeff left a message with his secretary. For some reason Patrick didn't call back for a week, which made Jeff feel angry and rejected, although he said nothing about it. Finally, two weeks after Jeff had left the phone message, Patrick called him to apologize for not getting back to him earlier. The two men checked their calendars and agreed to have lunch that week.

They met each other for lunch at a health food restaurant. Nothing clicked between them, so neither of them made any further attempt to see each other outside the group. About a month after the lunch the issue of male friendship came up in the group, and Jeff felt the need to talk about what had happened between him and Patrick. It was such a familiar pattern in his life. Looking at me, not Patrick, he said that he had felt rejected because Patrick had been so slow to respond to his invitation for lunch. He went on to say that during lunch he had felt that Patrick was dodging any kind of meaningful conversation by changing the subject to safe "manly" topics like business or sports.

1. Levinson, D. J. et al. *The Seasons of a Man's Life* (New York: Knopf, 1978).

A silence fell over the group. Sensing an opportunity to deepen the level of intimacy I said, "Jeff, what I would like you to do is start over from the beginning, but talk directly to Patrick."

Slowly, Jeff turned around to look at Patrick, his face flushed with emotion. "Patrick, I felt hurt when you didn't return my call," he said. "When I call somebody to do something, I expect them to respond back to me in some kind of timely manner. For a week I kept thinking, Why in the hell did you say you wanted to have lunch with me if you really didn't want to do it? That kind of behavior is okay with men who aren't in the group, but I thought we were supposed to be more honest with each other in here."

Patrick looked chastened. "I'm sorry," he said. "I should have called sooner. I was busy, but I should have called anyway. I'm sorry."

"That's not all that bothered me," Jeff said. "At lunch I kept trying to talk about something that mattered to me and you kept changing the subject. I feel like all we did was chit-chat for an hour over bean sprouts and tofu. It wasn't what I'd expected. I felt disappointed. I don't have a close male friend, and I was hoping you and I could really talk."

Patrick's expression changed from guilt to anger. "Well, since you brought it up, let's get things out in the open. Frankly, I don't remember dodging any subject. In fact, I don't remember even talking that much. Yeah, you wanted to talk about stuff that was important to you, but only to *you.* I didn't feel you had any interest in me at all. I was just a sounding board. It was one of those conversations where I'm asking all the questions and the other guy hogs the spotlight."

Jeff said, "That's not the way I remember it."

Patrick persisted. "I remember thinking, 'I'm just an excuse for this guy to hear himself talk. This is not going to work out.' I felt invisible. When lunch was over, I decided that if you ever called me to do anything again, I'd make up some excuse."

Jeff responded, "I'm sorry. I didn't see it that way at all."

At this point, Ben, one of the other men in the group, ventured his opinion. "I hate to say this Jeff, but you seem to do most of the talking in here, too."

Jeff looked surprised. "What do you mean? I don't talk more than anybody else in here." He looked around the room and saw several guys nodding their heads, supporting Ben's observation.

Jeff looked humbled. "I'm sorry. I didn't realize I talked all that much. My wife says I don't listen to her, either. Maybe she's right." He sighed. "Patrick, I want you to know I really do want to get to know you better."

"Well, let's do lunch," said Patrick.

When the laughter died down, I asked Jeff and Patrick if it had ever crossed their minds during lunch to be honest about what they'd been feeling. They both laughed. "Men don't do that," said Jeff. "It's too threatening. You keep it all in." Without the structure and safety of the group, it is unlikely these two men would have ever developed the skills to connect with each other. It would have been just another failed attempt at friendship, each man retreating into his shell, building an even thicker protective wall around himself. Because they were learning to be honest and direct, they've become close friends. They have lunch with each other once a week. Last summer they went for a four-day fishing trip in Alaska, the highlight of the year for both men.

LEARNING TO SURVIVE RAGE

As the men in a given group become ever more comfortable with each other, there is occasionally an outburst of rage between them. Men who have spent their entire lives stuffing their anger rarely know how to control it when it comes spewing out. One of these rare outbursts took place not long ago between Jerry and Brian, two men who happened to be sitting right next to each other.

We'd been talking about Jerry's passive/aggressive tendency. He had a habit of putting down other men in the group, then pretending he'd been joking. The men had been commenting on this pattern for several weeks. That evening Jerry had fallen into this habit and had made a snide remark about Brian. Brian turned to him and said, "You're being passive/aggressive again, and that offends me."

Jerry replied in a threatening tone of voice, "I don't like the way you said that."

Brian bristled, "Well, that's the way it came out. I truly am offended."

"Well, fuck you, then," Jerry retorted.

"Well, fuck you back."

Then, to everyone's surprise, Jerry raised himself up on his pillow, moved menacingly close to Brian, stuck his chest out, and yelled right into his face, "Hey, FUCK YOU!" His face was red and his jaws and fists were tightly clinched.

I could feel the fear tightening my belly and shortening my breath. The rest of the men looked equally shocked. "Okay. Okay, guys," I said. "Let's stop right there. Let's all take a deep breath and figure out what's going on."

One of the other men said, "Hey, I know what just happened. Two guys were just about to beat the shit out of each other and it scared the hell out of me."

The men laughed and got a much-needed moment of relief, but some of them were obviously shaken. Several of the men thought that Jerry was going to get violent with Brian. One man said that in those few seconds of rage his faith in the group had been shaken. "We're supposed to be more civil than that," he insisted.

I reminded everyone that, although it might feel uncomfortable to watch a group member fly into a rage, it wasn't unsafe. I would intercede before anyone got hurt. As the men began to breathe more normally, I asked them to close their eyes and try to remember a time from their childhood when they had been frightened by rage. A couple of men described painful events from the past. We discussed those situations, contrasting them with what had just taken place. Upon questioning, the men acknowledged that in reality they had been far more vulnerable as children than they were in the group, but their reaction to the flare-up between Brian and Jerry had been intense nonetheless. A part of their unconscious mind was still reacting as if they were defenseless children.

Once Brian and Jerry had cooled down, I asked Brian how he had felt about bearing the brunt of Jerry's rage. He said he had been angry at Jerry, but he had also felt a great deal of fear. I asked if he could recall having that same mix of feelings as a young boy. He recalled a time when his older brother had run after him with a bat. We contrasted the limited power he had had twenty years ago with the resources and support he had available to him in the group.

After working with Brian I turned my attention to Jerry. I asked him if he had been aware of how strongly the rest of us had reacted to his outburst. He said he hadn't been. To give him some insight into how others perceived him, I asked the men to tell him directly how they had felt. One man said to him, "Jerry, I was so scared I couldn't breathe." Another said, "You made me want to leave the room." Mark, one of the newer members, said he hadn't been so scared in years. That brief moment of rage had brought back memories of being abused by his alcoholic father. Jerry was truly surprised by how upset everyone had been. He kept asking, "Was I really that angry?" and the other men kept saying "Yes, you were really that angry." He finally began to accept that he had been filled with rage. I asked him if he had been aware of a window of opportunity when he might have stopped his anger from spiraling out of control. He said he didn't think so. It had all happened too fast. Toward the end of the session, he was beginning to ask himself a critical question: Could it be that he had been frightening his wife and his kids with his anger for years?

We devoted the rest of that session and the one that followed to debriefing that one, ten-second blowup between Jerry and Brian. I reminded the men that no violence had occurred. Nobody had gotten hurt. I said that an outburst like that might happen again, but that I would make sure it would be safe for everyone.

We also talked a lot about trust. Some of the men saw Jerry's behavior as a violation of the group trust. I said that in reality it indicated that Jerry's trust in the group had risen so high that he could lower his defenses and reveal some of his old, self-defeating patterns. I told the men that when they felt safe enough, they would probably trot out some of their old habits, too. Even though it might seem unpleasant, even threatening, to see each other act in self-destructive ways, it was an important part of the work they needed to do in the group.

HOW A GROUP CHANGES OVER TIME

After a group of men has been meeting together for about a year, they become what I call an "aged" group and begin to show a dramatic improvement in their relationship skills. There are times when I sit back and marvel at the way they interact with each other. Gone are most of the narcissistic traits. Instead, the men show a genuine concern—even love—for each other. They listen carefully to each other, empathize with each other, and validate each other's feelings. They communicate on a much more emotional level. With increasing frequency I hear comments like, "That threatens me," or "I feel so helpless," or "I felt angry when you said that"—phrases you rarely hear from men.

For much of their lives these men have been shamed or criticized for showing their true feelings. In the group their feelings are not only accepted, they are applauded. After all those years of hiding and holding it in they find they can reveal their inner selves. In fact, they learn that it is only by *sharing* their emotions that they can truly be welcomed into the group. A man who remains detached and rational is viewed as an outsider by the rest of the men. The only way to get initiated into this exclusive men's club is to be free and honest with your emotions.

What is even more important to the men than the changes happening in the group, however, is the way they are transforming their relationships with family and friends. The next two chapters illustrate how the men use their newfound skills to realign their most fundamental relationships—their relationships with their parents and partners. Their work in the group has given them the tools that they need to make peace with their parents and create lasting intimacy with their wives and lovers.

WILDMAN GATHERINGS— AN ADJUNCT TO THERAPY

After working with men's groups for several years I began experimenting with a larger forum—weekend retreats where I could introduce as many as 150 men to the ideas I was exploring in the groups. The idea for these weekends came from a workshop featuring Robert Bly that a friend of mine named Scott Lockhart and I orchestrated in the spring of 1989. I knew of Robert Bly's reputation as a poet and leader in the men's movement, and I was looking forward to the opportunity to meet him. Scott and I found a location for the workshop and began promoting "a weekend with Robert Bly." Our plan was to have Bly work with men and women on Saturday and with men only on Sunday.

We called Sunday's workshop "A Gathering of Men." Political commentator Bill Moyers arranged to film the event for PBS television.

The Sunday workshop drew one hundred men. Bly moved many of the men to tears with his poetry and his astute observations about masculinity. In the discussion that followed, some of the men volunteered truths about their lives that had been hidden for a lifetime. There was a male energy in the room that felt like the power of one of my men's groups multiplied by ten. The charged atmosphere encouraged men to be emotionally revealing.

During the Sunday session Bly talked about the "Wildman," a term he used to describe the part of a man's soul that is wild, natural, instinctive, and filled with energy. He contrasted this with the "soft male," a passive man who is overly influenced by feminine values. I was captivated by Bly's image of the Wildman. It seemed to awaken in me a core energy that had been sleeping too long.

Before the Gathering of Men was over, I decided to design my own weekend retreat for men based partly on Bly's ideas, but mostly on the principles that I was developing in my men's groups. I believed that if I could create the right blend of safety, self-discovery exercises, rituals, and new information, the experience could prove enlightening for men. I drove Bly to the airport at the end of that weekend and told him about my plan to create a Wildman weekend. He gave me some pointers, his blessings, and his phone number. I used that number on a couple of occasions, and he was kind enough to give me suggestions and moral support as I was putting together the first Wildman Gathering.

In the fall of 1989, six months after the workshop with Bly, I held the first Gathering at my family ranch in the Texas hill country. I invited my friend John Lee to be coleader. We created a central meeting area under the natural canopy of an old grove of oak trees. That first Friday night I cooked up some Texas chili and cornbread for sixty pioneers from all over the United States who had shown up for this event. After dinner the men followed a row of torches into the grove where they sat on bales of hay that encircled a large fire pit.

The first thing I asked the men was whether or not they were scared to be there. Every hand went up. We discussed that fear, and the men realized it made sense to be afraid given the competitiveness, lack of trust, and fear of homosexuality that was prevalent in so many men. This led into a larger discussion of male gender conditioning and the hidden oppression of men. We talked about a culture that had long failed to respond to the outer needs of women and the inner needs of men.

Just as at Bly's workshop, the combined energy of so many men seemed to intensify their emotional reactions. This was especially true Saturday morning as the men explored their relationships with their fathers. I was surprised by how many of them had been deeply wounded by their dads. The men told stories about neglect, physical abuse, verbal abuse, and sexual abuse. They had found a safe place to let down their guard and let out the feelings they'd held in for so long.

Throughout the weekend the men lived in the moment—they never knew what was coming next. They listened to lectures, shared their stories in small groups, took part in Native American rituals, swam in the pond, took walks in the woods, sat together in a sweat lodge, and beat drums around the fire. They had to be flexible and vulnerable to participate in these unconventional activities. As they lowered their masculine defenses, many of them wept with grief or joy for the first time in decades. As is true in my therapy groups, the expression of deep emotion by one man created a chain reaction that allowed other men to release their emotions as well.

A number of men from my therapy groups attended that first Gathering, and a few of them tapped into deeper emotions than ever before. One of them, Grant, had been in therapy for three months. Until that weekend he had been unable to connect with any feelings about his abusive father. He participated in an exercise called "The Father Quest" in which men confront their ghost fathers, and he wept openly for the first time since boyhood.

Even though I was very busy throughout that first Gathering and distracted by my multiple roles as promoter, leader, and cook, I was deeply touched by what I was experiencing. To my surprise I also experienced some inner healing of my own. Listening to so many men talk honestly about their struggles resonated deep within me. I left the Gathering feeling exhausted but inspired.

To date I have conducted thirty-four Wildman Gatherings for approximately twenty-five hundred men. John Lee continued to be my coleader for the first year. When John left to pursue other activities, I invited my colleagues Allen Maurer and Dick Prosapio to join me. The three of us have been a team ever since.

Now that the Wildman Gatherings have become a regular fixture in my life, I have gained more perspective about how they fit into the larger context of men's therapy. I have learned that one function of the Gatherings is to help men overcome their resistance to therapy. It's easier for many men to commit to one weekend of self-exploration than to sign up for a longer course of counseling. Somewhere in the course of the weekend many of them decide they want to make a more serious commitment to personal growth. A number of men have joined my therapy groups or signed up with other therapists after attending a Wildman Gathering.

The Gatherings have also proven beneficial for men already in therapy. The experience deepens their insights and allows them to tap into more of their emotions. Some of the men in my groups have gone to as many as five separate Gatherings and have explored new emotional terrain with each one.

Finally, the Gatherings give me a forum in which to explore the subject of masculinity with a large group of men more powerfully than I can in a single lecture. The intensive three-day exposure to lectures and rituals and self-discovery exercises affects most men very deeply. They leave the retreat on Sunday night highly aware of the way they've been conditioned to fulfill traditional masculine roles, and they feel more freedom to break out of the narrow confines of the MAN BOX. I've come to regard the Gatherings as a mass intervention against the masculine code.

However, although the Wildman Gatherings can be dramatic and effective, they are not a *replacement* for therapy—they're an *adjunct* to therapy. Nothing can take the place of the months and years of slow steady work that the men do in the smaller therapy groups. That's where the real healing takes place. The Wildman Gatherings are what I call "breakthrough" therapy, an event that can produce new insights and a burst of personal growth. But in order to consolidate that growth and make continual progress, most men need the ongoing support and structure of a therapy group.

CHAPTER 9

HEALING LOVE RELATIONSHIPS

Years ago when I did couples counseling, I was painfully aware of the uneven playing field between men and women. The women seemed to find it much easier to identify their problems and express their feelings. As a result, much of what I learned about the relationship came from the woman's point of view. Her husband did this. He wouldn't do that. He had a hard time doing this. When I turned to the husband to ask him about *his* concerns, he'd act as if it were a trick question. "What do you mean 'What are my concerns'?" He found it difficult to articulate what he saw wrong with the marriage. He knew he was unhappy, but he had a hard time explaining why.

However, when a man has spent a year or more in a men's therapy group, he finds it much easier to present his issues. The fundamental change is that he is more in touch with his emotions. He doesn't have to rely on his wife to have his feelings for him; he has a wealth of feelings all his own. He is coming alive, and along with this quickening he is becoming aware of all the things *he* would like to change in the marriage. Perhaps he wants more freedom to pursue his interests, a more relaxed life-style, more authority in daily decision making, a less stressful work life, or more passionate lovemaking. For the first time, he has his own agenda, and he's ready to place it on the table. The fact that he is less dependent on his wife for emotional support strengthens his bargaining position. He's discovering that he can feel valued, supported, and connected to other human beings simply by coming to the group. Now if his marriage fails, he can think of at least one or two people he can rely on to help him survive the ordeal. Having a support system outside the marriage makes him less willing to sacrifice what's important to him in order to please his wife.

At the same time that he is defining what he wants in the relationship, he is acquiring some much-needed communication skills, among them the ability to identify and label his feelings. He can now tell his partner, "I'm feeling angry," or "I'm feeling depressed," instead of being hostile or hiding behind the newspaper. His partner no longer has to guess what he's thinking or try to interpret his moods.

Another important change is that he can express his anger more appropriately. He no longer has to cut it off out of fear of losing control. His pool of rage no longer feels like such a threat to himself or others. He is less likely to be passive or abusive or passive/aggressive. He can use his healthy anger to defend himself and assert his needs in a straightforward manner. This gives him more power in the relationship.

He also grows more tolerant of his wife's healthy anger. When she is mad at him, he is less likely to fear that she doesn't love him or plans to leave him or wants to hurt him. He realizes she's just communicating information. He doesn't have to withdraw or go on the attack. He can listen to what she has to say.

Finally, through his work in the group he gains some familiarity with grief. Being able to grieve allows him to work through the pain of his childhood and the pain of prior relationships and become more open to the possibility of love in the present. It allows him to put a seal on the past and be more available to his partner in the here and now.

What he is really doing in all of his work in the group is developing his capacity for *intimacy*, and he suddenly realizes that *this* is what he wants in his marriage. He is no longer preoccupied with the traditional symbols of masculine privilege—the cooked meals, the clean house, the well-behaved kids, the ironed shirts. He now wants many of the same things his wife wants out of the relationship—indeed, what *all* people want—to be validated, known, and accepted. He yearns to see his wife "I" to "I," and he has many of the skills to bring it about. All of a sudden, the playing field is a lot more level.

PRACTICING RELATIONSHIP SKILLS

When I'm learning a new skill, I always do better if I get some hands-on practice. It doesn't matter whether I'm learning to do public speaking, use a spreadsheet on my computer, or execute an eskimo roll in a kayak. Whatever it is, I need to practice it several times before I "get it." I've found that most men need some type of hands-on training to master the skills required for intimacy. They need more than insights. They need more than the will to change. They need more than a book on relationship skills. They need a safe place to practice the new behaviors before they get it. A men's therapy group is just such a place.

We devote a good portion of each session to the honing of relationship skills. Recently, for example, we helped one of the men learn how to defuse an argument. Frank, a man who has been in the group for almost a year, announced to us that he was moving back in with his wife after being separated for six months. He was uneasy about the move. Despite the progress he was making in the group, he was afraid he would fall into some of the old traps. I asked him to explain what he meant. He said he'd never been able to "hold his own" in an argument with his wife. She always seemed to get the better of him. He said, "She overwhelms me with her information and her animation. She talks so fast, and she remembers every wrong thing I've done in the past. She just pushes me around in all these conversations. It's not like she's trying to nail me to the cross. I just can't defend myself. After a while I lose it. I hear what she's saying, but I can't respond anymore. I hate it!"

I said that it was common for men to retreat into themselves when they can't make any headway in an argument. Their feelings of powerlessness turn into rage, and they don't know what to do with the rage. Some men lash out at their wives, but most men shut themselves down to protect themselves and their partners. They throw a breaker to keep the circuits from overloading. In order to keep the lines of communication open, they have to become more skilled at relating. This increases their sense of personal power, reduces their rage, and allows them to stay in the conversation.

I asked Frank if he was willing to do a role-playing exercise to help develop some new skills. He said that he was. I asked the group who wanted to play Frank's wife. Harvey raised his hand. "Your wife sounds a lot like mine, Frank," he said. "I think I've got that part down."

I asked Frank and Harvey to sit across from each other. Then I asked Frank to pretend that Harvey was his wife and start a conversation with her about something he wanted to do, something that might lead to an argument.

Frank thought of a current issue. "Honey, I've decided to go to the coast for the weekend to see my brother," he said to his "wife."

I asked Frank to give Harvey some clues about how his wife might react. Frank said that she would want to come along on the trip, and that she would resent the fact that she hadn't been invited. She'd also be anxious about spending the weekend alone.

That's all the information Harvey needed to get into the role. He said to Frank, "The trip sounds like a lot of fun. When do we leave?"

Frank replied, "I want to go by myself. Just get away for a couple of days. I need some space to breathe."

His "wife" sighed, "That's what you always say. What do you mean you need more space? You're always gone somewhere. You're always at work or out in the garage. You're never with me. I get lonely when you're out gallivanting around."

"What do you mean, 'gallivanting around'?" Frank demanded. "I'm just talking about needing some space. I haven't gone anywhere for two months. And being at work isn't 'being gone.' Work is work. Do you want me to stop going to work?"

His "wife" jumped on him with her contradictory view. "I'm not talking just about work! You are always going off somewhere. What about the time five weeks ago when you did this. And two weeks ago when you did that? And the time you spent with the guys last week? You're gone all the time. You're never around here."

To my surprise, Frank didn't respond. He seemed to be folding in on himself. He looked at me and said, "I can't believe it. I just went into that same place I go when I'm arguing with my wife. I went into my shell."

I asked Frank to start the conversation all over again, but not to go on the defensive. Just stick with the facts. He managed to stay neutral for about three sentences, then he went back to defending himself. "I wish you'd see how seldom I do anything for myself. I work all the time. You just don't understand."

Frank was clearly frustrated. He wasn't gaining any ground. I stopped the exercise and suggested he try a different approach. "This time," I said, "ask your wife about her feelings. When she says she's lonely, ask her how she feels when she gets lonely."

Frank dutifully followed my lead. "How do you feel when I leave?"

Harvey said, "I feel lonely about an hour after you leave. I sit around the house and I don't know what to do with myself. And I'm wondering what you're doing."

Frank didn't know how to respond. I suggested to him, "Ask her if she's feeling anything other than loneliness. Stick with her feelings. When you stay on a feeling level and *you're* asking the questions, then *you* control the conversation. You're directing it."

Frank said, "Do you feel anything other than loneliness when I'm gone?"

Harvey responded, "Sometimes I feel scared. Especially at night. There have been a lot of rapes and murders around here lately. I don't feel safe."

Frank forgot my instructions to stay with the feelings and went on the attack instead, "How could you be scared? I installed bars on the windows. I signed up for a security system. We got a dog. . . ."

I interrupted him and reminded him he was on the wrong track again. I told him to keep asking her more questions about her feelings.

He took a deep breath and continued, "When you're home alone at night, what frightens you? Are you frightened by noises?"

Harvey replied, "Yes. I hear the house creak. Or a branch scrapes against the house. I know I'm an adult and those things shouldn't scare me, but they do."

I said to Frank, "Now tell her you understand how she feels. Give her some validation. It's the same thing you do for the men in the group every week. Show her that you've been listening to her and that what she's saying makes sense to you."

"Until now, I don't think I really understood how you felt when I went away," he said. "No wonder you don't like me to leave. I'm sorry you have to go through that. But I don't think you understand how I feel, either. . . ."

"Hold it," I said. "Hold it! You're one sentence too early. It's okay to talk about your own feelings, but not until she knows you really understand hers. Stay with her feelings a moment longer."

Frank let his breath out with a sigh and forced himself to stay with his wife's agenda. "So, I understand how scared and lonely you've been feeling. I hope we can find some way to keep you from going through all that."

Harvey said, "Thank you. You know, I feel you really heard me and understood me. That feels really good. It makes me feel that you really care about me."

Frank continued to support her without being coached: "I don't want you to be afraid. I didn't realize that's how you felt. I was only thinking of my needs."

As Frank said this, I could sense a real connection growing between him and his "wife." Although this was only a role-playing exercise, a feeling of closeness was developing. The other men felt it too. I looked around and saw that they were giving Frank and Harvey their full attention.

I said to Frank that the time was right to introduce his own agenda.

He said, "I do care for you and I want to learn to understand you even better. I want you to understand me too. Sometimes I can't express myself as well as you, but I have needs too. One of my needs is to just get away by myself. It's not that I don't like you. I just need to recharge my batteries. You know how you get scared and restless when I'm gone? Well, that's pretty much how I feel when I don't get away. I feel extremely restless. I feel closed in. I feel trapped. I just need some space."

Harvey said, "I think I understand. We have some of the same feelings. You feel restless when you stay. I feel restless when you go."

I said to Frank, "Now see if you can come up with a win-win situation. Something that will give you both what you want."

Frank thought for a moment and said, "Maybe I could go away next weekend, and you could have a friend come stay with you. Or you and a friend could go away somewhere together. And next weekend we'll do something together. Whatever you want."

His "wife" said, "Maybe that would work out. It's a good idea."

With the situation resolved, Frank turned to me and said, "My God! That was so much better."

"Did you feel any power in the conversation?" I asked.

"Yeah, I sure did. And, I didn't feel I had to defend myself. It was a thousand times better."

Then Frank did something that surprised me. He stood up, grabbed the bat, and beat the pillow four or five times. "Damnit! Why couldn't I do this before!"

I've seen other men act this way once they "get it." They've been frustrated by their powerlessness in their relationships for years. They've tried so many different approaches. They've exploded with rage. They've criticized. They've sulked. They've tried to defend themselves. None of those tactics did any good. Once they discover a technique that does finally work, they feel angry at themselves that it took so long to figure it out.

I told Frank not to be hard on himself. Although the exercise he just finished may have seemed simple, in reality it was the culmination of almost a year of work. Any man on the street can be walked through the mechanics of the exercise. With a coach by your side it doesn't take long to learn how to cut off your defensiveness and ask questions on a feeling level. But in order for a man to really hear his partner and empathize with what she's saying, he first has to be in touch with his own emotions. And for many men, that takes months and years of work. Frank would not have been able to get into the spirit of the exercise if he had remained blocked off from his own feelings.

Richard and the Grapefruits

Men usually have to go through an exercise such as this one a number of times before the skills really sink in. The approach is so different from their normal style of interaction. Then, when they work up the courage to try the new move out on their wives, it's almost as if they have to start all over again. It's much harder to stick with the drill without the support of the group. But even though they may make a lot of mistakes at first, at least they are aware when they're falling back into the old ruts. When they screw up, they come back to the group and say with regret, "Well, I did it again. . . ." With the men's support, they get back on the right track.

Richard, a fifty-year-old Baptist minister, recently relied on the group to keep from playing a caretaking role with his ex-wife. The primary problem in his marriage was that he catered to his wife's needs all the time, a role he had perfected as a small boy trying to take care of his dependent mother and alcoholic father. Now, three years after his divorce, his compulsion to please his ex-wife is still very much in evidence. His work in the group is helping him see that his effort to stay in her good graces is based more on habit and fear than on love. Unlike Frank his task isn't to try to empathize with his wife's feelings—it's to pay more attention to his own.

Not long ago Richard had a stressful encounter with his ex-wife that he was able to turn around the next day after talking about it in the group. His ex-wife called from Seattle early one morning to ask if he would send a box of organic grapefruits to a new boyfriend of hers who lived in the Puget Sound area. "Well, okay," he told her. "There's been a hard freeze here that has wiped out a lot of the harvest, and I don't know if I can locate an organic grower, but I'll do my best." He was falling into his old role of being Mommy and Daddy's "rescuer." He spent an hour on the phone trying to locate the grapefruits, to no avail.

The group met that evening, and he complained to the men how frustrating it was to spend so much time finding organic grapefruits for his ex-wife. He went on for five minutes about how much trouble it had caused him. "So why did you do it?" asked one of the men. "You don't have any obligation to her. Why didn't you say no?"

Richard realized that once again he had been operating on automatic pilot. "Oh, shit," he said. "I did it again, didn't I?" Several of the men nodded their heads. We spent ten minutes helping Richard rehearse a phone conversation with his ex-wife telling her he was unwilling to do the favor. He called her that very night. His heart hammered in his chest as he picked up the phone and dialed her number. "This is Richard. I've decided I don't want to get those grapefruits for you. It's not something I really want to do." To his surprise his ex-wife accepted his decision with only a sigh of resignation. Richard felt elated as he hung up the phone. Saying no to her had been far easier than he had ever imagined. All he had to do was figure out how he really felt and work up the courage to tell her. Later he told the group that turning down her request was only a "small thing," but in reality it was one of only a handful of times when he had been able to say no to her.

Walter and the Airport

Eventually the men who stay in therapy long enough get to the point where they can interact with their partners in a healthy manner much of the time. Walter, a man in Richard's group who has had long-standing problems with anger, is now able to stop himself from flying into an impotent rage virtually all of the time. He doesn't have to blow up at his wife and apologize later; he can act more appropriately the first time around. The trick for him has been to pay more attention to his feelings on a moment-by-moment basis. This way he can express them before they build up and mushroom out of control.

Walter told the men in his group about a recent encounter with his wife that in the past would have ended in a fight. He flew into the Dallas airport expecting to see his wife waiting for him at the gate, but she wasn't there. Before being in therapy he would have tried to pretend that it didn't matter to him. It's "unmanly" to care whether or not your wife meets you at the gate. He would have tried to ignore his sadness. Now he allowed himself to feel. As he looked around at the crowd of people waiting to greet the other travelers, he felt disappointed. He'd been gone for five days and was looking forward to seeing his wife. He waited a few minutes, then went to the baggage-claim area to pick up his luggage. Fifteen minutes went by, and his wife still wasn't there. Now he realized he was angry. Didn't she care enough to fit him into her busy schedule? More time passed, and he was surprised to see his anger turn into another, less-familiar emotion—a feeling of abandonment. "I was one of the few guys from my flight left standing there," he told the group. "Baggage from another flight was being unloaded. I felt like a kid getting off the bus from summer camp and being the only one not picked up by his parents." Before therapy he would not have been aware of feeling vulnerable; he would have covered it over with rage. More time passed. Now it was an hour after the plane had landed, and his feelings of anger and abandonment were mixed with anxiety. His wife was often late, but not *this* late. Maybe something had happened to her.

He was about to call his wife's office to see what was wrong when she waltzed up to him. "Where have you been?" he asked her. "I've been worried!" Instead of being hostile or giving her the cold shoulder, which is what he would have done in the past, he told her about all the feelings he'd been having in the past hour, feelings of disappointment, anger, abandonment, and anxiety. "After an hour I was convinced you were either in the hospital or you didn't love me. One of the two."

His wife, taken aback by his honesty, apologized for being late. "I'm sorry," she said. "I was held up at the office, then I got caught in traffic." He was able to accept her apology, and minutes later they were catching up on all that had happened in the previous week. The many months that Walter had spent in the group learning to detect and express his emotions had kept him from spoiling his homecoming.

When Walter revealed his feelings to his wife, he was using the first part of a two-step process that I stress when I coach men in relationship skills: (1) Say how you feel, and (2) State what you want. In other words, let your partner know how you're feeling, then tell her what you want or need: "I'm angry that you accepted the dinner invitation without talking to me first. I'd appreciate it if you'd ask me first before you accept." It's a simple concept, but it takes some men a year or more of therapy before they are even *aware* of their feelings. To have the confidence and skills required to express them requires yet more work.

When Walter finished talking about the airport scene, we discussed how he handled it. He decided he'd done a good job of telling his wife how he felt, but he hadn't gone on to step two: he hadn't made it clear to her how he wanted to be treated in the future. "I should have said something like, 'If you say you're going to pick me up, please be on time. If you're delayed, call me so I won't have to worry. It's important to me.' " He vowed to state his wishes in words the next time he was in a similar situation.

Postgame analysis like this takes up a good portion of our weekly sessions. A man reports on an interaction with a girlfriend or partner, we review the way he responded, then, if necessary, strategize a new and better approach. Sometimes we come up with the actual words for him to use the next time around. Some men are so grateful for the help that they get out a pen and write down the dialogue word for word. Then we run through the script a couple of times so they have a chance to practice it. They've learned that in order to have a respectable opening-night performance at home, it helps to have a dress rehearsal in the group.

Practicing relationship skills in this manner invariably feels artificial and contrived to the men. I tell them it's "rehearsed love." But with enough practice they will eventually have a spontaneous, intimate interplay between themselves and their partners. When men begin to see the payoff, they welcome the opportunity to gain new skills.

Recently we had great success in helping one of the men deal with his wife's tendency to be a backseat driver. He told us that whenever he got behind the wheel of the car, she would tell him how to drive. She would warn him about every road hazard and second-guess his every move. Before long he got so angry that he would lash out at her, and they would ride out the rest of the trip in silence. It happened virtually every time they got in the car. He decided he didn't want to go through that tired routine anymore. He was sick of it. With our help he figured out a new approach. He decided that the next time she started harping on his driving, he would say these words: "When you criticize the way I drive it makes me feel inadequate. It makes me feel you don't trust me. I've proven that I'm a good driver time and time again. I've never gotten into a serious accident. I've never gotten us lost for more than a few minutes. I want you to show more faith in my driving ability." Here again was that two-step approach: Say how you feel. State what you want.

He told us next week that he delivered his speech the moment his wife started criticizing him. To his delight she not only listened to him, she even admitted he was a good driver and apologized for having so little trust. As a result of this conversation the two of them were able to enjoy the entire trip. He told us, "It was like we'd been driving down an old, rutted highway for twenty years and suddenly there appeared a neon sign pointing to a brand-new freeway. This stuff really works."

In these small ways, the men in the group are beginning to carve out a sense of identity *within the context of a relationship.* They are discovering they don't have to withdraw or go numb or be abusive or leave the relationship in order to have a sense of self. By developing their relationship skills they can stay in the marriage and redefine its boundaries. They can find freedom and a sense of identity within marriage.

WHAT WOMEN HAVE TO LOSE AND GAIN

Unfortunately, some wives do not support their husbands in their struggles to change old patterns of relating. The women may have begged them to get into therapy, but they're not thrilled with the results. I remember a difficult stretch in my own therapy when I broke down in tears in front of the woman I was living with. "Are you all right, Marvin?" she asked, backing away from me. "Is there anything I can do?" I watched in amazement as she backed her way clear across the room. "Is there someone I should call?" she asked anxiously. She acted as if I were having a nervous breakdown. She had *thought* that she wanted me to be more vulnerable, but as soon as I started crying, she withdrew in fear.

To help men gain more support from their partners, I advise them to give their partners a lot of reassurance. They need to explain to their wives that just because they happen to cry once or twice doesn't mean they're falling apart. Just because they're weak one moment doesn't mean they can't be strong when they need to be. Just because they're learning to feel doesn't mean they're becoming feminine. Just because they assert themselves more effectively doesn't mean they're becoming abusive. Just because they're deepening their friendships with other men doesn't mean they're becoming gay. Just because they're gaining more personal power doesn't mean they're going to leave them for someone else. Above all I tell them to reassure their partners over and over again that they love them—not just automatically, but with feeling.

Despite all these reassurances, some of the men in my groups haven't been able to hold their marriages together. There wasn't enough goodwill in their relationships to weather the transition. One of my long-term clients, Victor, thirty-one, separated from his wife of nine years about a year ago. In the beginning she was the one to insist he get therapy. She said she was tired of "living with a boy instead of a man." After Victor had been in therapy for only two short months, she started complaining to him that therapy wasn't helping him. She told him he was a hopeless case and was never going to change.

Victor, like many other men, had to be in therapy for nearly a year before he was able to make any visible progress. Changing lifelong patterns of behavior is a time-consuming process. But eventually he was able to show some of his anger in the group. As he grew comfortable with his anger, he acquired a greater sense of personal power. To his wife's dismay, one way he manifested this power was by drawing some much-needed boundaries at home. Whenever she began to criticize him, he would show his anger. His newfound assertiveness made her withdraw into a resentful sulk. After a couple of months of Victor's new behavior she suggested they separate for six months until he "got his act together." Victor countered by suggesting that maybe *she* should sign up for therapy too so she could adjust to his more forceful role. She refused. They separated by mutual agreement, and Victor grew stronger and more confident of himself with each passing month. Then, in an ironic twist, his wife called him up to say she wanted to get back together with him. She had only one condition: he had to stop going to the group. She couldn't handle the new and improved Victor. Victor refused to accept her terms. He realized he was getting more support from the men in the group than he had ever gotten from her.

There's no denying that women can experience some losses when their male partners go into therapy. First of all, the women may have to give up the notion that they mean everything to their men. They will still be very important to them, but they may no longer be the *only* important person in their lives. This can fan a woman's abandonment anxiety. Just as a woman who earns a good income has more freedom to leave an unhappy relationship, so does a man with a network of friends.

Another outcome of the men's work in the group is that their wives may have to give up some of their dominion in the home. When men are able to assert their wishes and needs, the domestic arena is no longer just a woman's arena. This is true for parenting issues as well. An emotionally healthy man is likely to become a more involved father. He will be more of a help with the kids, but he will also have some of his own ideas about parenting. The woman's mothering role will have to make room for the man's expanding fathering role. Women can no longer be the gatekeepers controlling all the family relationships.

Some women also have to relinquish the fantasy of having a mate who is an all-powerful, uncomplaining, stoic father figure. Men who have gone through therapy are rarely willing or able to play that role.

They are not super heroes. They are mere human beings, human beings who happen to be male. Last but not least, some women have to give up their tendency to blame all their unhappiness on the men in their lives: "If only he'd open up." "If only he'd learn to communicate." "If only he'd get a life." "If only he wasn't so depressed." "If only he wasn't so angry." They have to accept the fact that their partners have indeed changed. They have become better communicators. They're more open. They're more lively. They have less of a tendency to rage. This forces the women to examine some of their own weaknesses. It's not uncommon for a woman whose husband is in therapy to discover that she could use some counseling herself.

But even though women may experience some losses when men start to change the way they think, feel, and behave, they have a great deal to gain. They now have partners who are able to listen to them and empathize with their feelings. They have partners who are more worthy of their respect and admiration. They have partners who are willing to satisfy more of their needs because more of their own needs are being addressed. They have partners who are no longer overly dependent on them for emotional support. They have partners who have become active parents and positive role models for their children. Women who are able to support their partners' work to reclaim their emotional wholeness are very often rewarded with deep and lasting intimacy.

CHAPTER 10

MAKING PEACE
WITH ONE'S PARENTS

Creating better love relationships is only part of the work the men do in the groups. Exploring childhood issues is just as important. As in individual therapy, the men in a group gain insight into how they were raised, and they release any pent-up emotions they may feel toward their ghost parents. Once those feelings have lost some of their intensity, I encourage the men to go one step farther and examine their current relationships with their flesh-and-blood parents.

Not surprisingly many men balk at the notion of taking a close look at the way they relate to their mothers and fathers. They have less motivation to improve parental relationships than they do love relationships. What's there to gain? Besides, they sense it would be very hard to change the way they interact with their parents. Those patterns are deeply embedded. Why not focus their energy on how they treat their wives, lovers, and children and let the old folks be?

I explain that when they interact with their parents as confident, emotionally healthy adults, they rewrite much of their childhood programming. They drown out the internalized parental messages that have been telling them they're unlovable, undeserving, inadequate, or inferior. They also offer much-needed support to their "inner child," that part of the subconscious mind that still lives with the trauma of childhood. Their ability to interact with their parents in a healthy manner empowers them on a fundamental level.

Furthermore, although few men are aware of it, the parent-child relationship is at the heart of all their other relationships. Their early experiences with their parents became the template they used to create their relationships with their partners, colleagues, children, and friends. They repeat the same underlying patterns of behavior with virtually everyone. When a man realigns his relationship with his parents, he changes that template and begins to have better relationships with all the significant people in his life.

When men understand the importance of dealing more honestly with their parents, they often have an unrealistic fear of hurting them. I explain to them that talking more openly with their parents does not mean haranguing them, accusing them, or abusing them. I also make it clear that any rage or hostility they may still harbor toward their parents needs to be dealt with in the group using safe and structured exercises. Only when their feelings have lost their intensity is it appropriate for them to set up an audience with their parents. When they go to them, they need to be free of the desire to shame them, blame them, or hurt them. The goal is to set the record straight and let go of the past.

WORKING ON PARENTAL ISSUES IN A GROUP

I have discovered that men reap some benefits when they work on a relationship with a parent in a group setting. First of all, as I described in the last two chapters, being in a group allows them to greatly improve their relationship skills. Their newfound ability to communicate on an emotional level is a tremendous asset when they confront their parents. All of those months of practice in the group allow them to speak to their parents with more honesty and authority. Second, men gain added insights into their childhood by listening to other men talk about their early histories. For example, it's not uncommon for one man's revelations about his father's neglect to help other men see that they too were neglected by their fathers. This insight helps them understand their chronic feelings of sadness or depression and gives them a better sense of the issues they want to bring up with their fathers. Third, being in a group gives men more motivation to resolve parental issues because they get to see other men go through the process. For instance, we might spend portions of four or five sessions helping one man become more assertive with his father. Yet all the other men benefit as well because they get to watch the process evolve. When they confront their own fathers, they can draw on what they learned in those sessions. Finally, when a man is having difficulty dealing with a parent, he can turn to the group for support. The men bolster his confidence, give him valuable suggestions, and participate in role-playing exercises to help him rehearse what he wants to say.

Louis: Establishing Closer Ties with an Abandoning Mother

The story of how Louis made peace with his mother is a good example of all that men have to gain when they create a more rewarding relationship with a parent. Louis was twenty-seven years old when he first joined the group. Like many men, he was struggling with low self-esteem and depression. He referred to himself as a "born fuck-up." Of all the issues that were troubling him, what upset him most was his inability to create a lasting love relationship. He'd lived with several women since his stint in the army, but they'd been short-term, disappointing relationships.

Louis was able to trace many of his relationship difficulties to the fact that he was raised by an Abandoning Mother. His mother became widowed when Louis was three years old. His older brother was six. On more than one occasion, Louis remembers her saying to the two of them, "I will not let you kids interfere with my social life." His mother was an attractive redhead and true to her words she spent a lot of time away from the house. She worked full-time during the day and filled her evening hours with social events. Louis not only lost his father, he lost his mother as well. On many occasions he and his sister came home from school to an empty house. They had to do their chores, make dinner, do their homework, watch TV, and then go to bed all by themselves. They lay awake waiting to hear the sound of their mother's car pulling into the driveway.

When his mother was at home, life was little better. It seemed to Louis that she was either criticizing him or his brother or hiding from them in her bedroom. A part of him felt ashamed for taking up her time and even for occupying space in the house. Out of default he spent most of his time with his brother. "My brother and I should have been natural allies," he said. "But we weren't able to do that. There was always an angry competitiveness between us." The two of them fought so viciously that Louis still bears physical scars from their battles.

Abandoned by his father, rejected by his mother, and at war with his brother, Louis tried to minimize his pain by retreating into his room or taking long, solitary walks. Withdrawing from the world gave him a sense of power and identity. Mr. Spock on *Star Trek* became his adolescent hero, and like the celebrated alien, he vowed not to feel anything. Logic was his weapon against the world.

When Louis turned eighteen and moved away from home, his relationship with his mother went through a significant change. Once his mother was freed from the daily pressures of raising children, she became less resentful of his presence. She even encouraged him to do his laundry at her house and to join her each week for Sunday dinner. Obligingly, Louis went to his mother's house quite regularly over the next five years. But even though he was seeing his mother several times a month, they continued to relate on superficial terms. His mother didn't seem capable of intimacy, and Louis still felt cool toward her because of the way she'd treated him years ago.

Unable to express his anger at his mother more directly, Louis took out his resentment by milking her for all he could. Among other things, he let her buy new tires for his car, loan him money for the down payment on a house, and cover his bounced checks. On some primal level he felt justified for taking advantage of her. He felt she owed him something for having deprived him of so much in his early years.

When Louis reached his late twenties, he had a change of heart and began to feel guilty about taking so much from his mother without giving anything back in return. Yet at the same time, he harbored so much anger toward her he had no desire to try to improve the relationship. He decided his only alternative was to stop seeing her altogether. Out of sight, out of mind.

But the psyche doesn't work that way. Although Louis had stopped seeing his mother, he unwittingly transferred his unresolved issues with her to his girlfriends. He was attracted to these women, but he wouldn't allow himself to get close to them. About six months or a year into a relationship he would begin to feel protective of his space. He'd become dissatisfied with the woman sexually and emotionally and find some reason to end the relationship. Symbolically, he was still retreating into his boyhood room to avoid being hurt.

As the facts of his early years became more clear to Louis, his self-image began to improve. He saw that neither his father nor his mother had been able to give him the attention or the love he needed to develop a strong sense of self. He wasn't a "born fuck-up"; he was simply a man who hadn't received the love and attention from his parents that he deserved.

In the group Louis spent much of his time talking about his abandonment issues, his low self-esteem, and his resentment toward his mother and father. However, he was unable to release any feelings. He spent the first couple of months watching other men work with the bat and the pillow. Finally, he was able to drop his Mr. Spock persona and take turns with the bat. After each rage session he seemed to feel measurably better. It was also very therapeutic for him to gain the approval and support of the other men for showing his feelings. He realized it was okay with them if he was mad at his parents. For the first time in his life he felt permission to explore his full range of emotions.

Going to a Wildman Gathering turned out to be another milestone in his recovery. He stood in front of the circle of eighty men and read a poem he had written about his childhood. The poem was filled with dark images about how it felt to be a boy wandering through life alone. In the poem he said he felt as if he had spent his whole life feeling cold and hungry and looking in the windows of restaurants and seeing people eating, talking, and laughing. He felt too unworthy to join them. He felt destined to wander down the dark streets alone. Louis sobbed as he read the poem—a much-needed catharsis triggered by revealing his pain to so many supportive listeners. This was the first time in his life that he had been able to grieve about the pain and loneliness of his early years.

In the weeks that followed, Louis felt a spontaneous urge to go on to the next stage of the healing process, which is to forgive and forget. For the first time in three years he wanted to see his mother again. He no longer felt angry at her, and he no longer wanted to hurt or punish her. What he wanted to do was to show her some of the love for her that had been buried beneath his grief and resentment. We devoted most of a session to helping him decide how he was going to approach his mother. He decided that the first time he visited her, he wanted to keep the conversation casual. Just seeing her again would be enough of a strain.

The first meeting between Louis and his mother went as planned. As usual his mother maintained her distance by steering the conversation toward neutral topics like retirement plans, politics, and the economy. Louis followed her cue.

During the group the following week Louis said he was ready to try to deepen their relationship. One of the men in the group volunteered a strategy. He suggested that the next time they got together, he should ask his mother some questions about her childhood. He had used that approach with his own father and found that it had been a nonthreatening way to create some intimacy between them. Louis thought it was a good suggestion. It seemed like a respectful way to ease into a closer relationship.

Louis visited his mother that next Sunday, and he gently challenged the family's taboo against intimacy by asking her about her earliest childhood memories. His mother was taken aback, but after a moment's hesitation she began talking about what it was like to have her own mother die when she was only three years old. She talked about being raised by her grandmother, only to have the grandmother die when she was ten. A new feeling of closeness began to develop between mother and son. Louis noticed that his mother was settling back in her chair and was making more eye contact with him. He further increased their intimacy by telling her that the two of them had something in common. He said that all the significant women in her life had either died or abandoned her, and all the significant men in his life had either died or abandoned him. His father had died. His grandfather had died before he was born. An uncle had recently died. His mother said, "Yeah, you've not had much of a male role model, and I've not had much of a female role model." She paused for a moment and added, "Because of that, I've always felt that I was not a very good mother to you and your brother. I never knew quite how to do it." Louis wasn't sure how to respond. He didn't want to defend his mother because that would have been dishonest. In many ways, she *hadn't* been a good mother to him. He chose to say nothing. The two of them just sat quietly for a moment.

A few days after the visit Louis felt a surge of forgiveness well up in him, and he called his mother on the phone. He said to her, "That was a good visit. I felt close to you. I was hoping we could continue talking like that." His mother replied that she had enjoyed the visit as well. But then, true to form, she abruptly changed the topic and asked him if he had seen a missing library book lying about her house.

When Louis described the phone conversation to the men in the group, he said he could accept the fact that she was still uncomfortable with intimacy. "It would have been unrealistic to expect any more from her," he said. "It just felt good going on record with my feelings. It was something I had to do."

Step by step, week by week, Louis was able to feel more comfortable around his mother, and she was able to feel more comfortable around him. Because he had been able to resolve much of his anger and grief, he experienced a resurgence of love for her. If he had tried to "get on with life" without going into therapy or working on his relationship with his mother, it is likely he would have remained estranged from her or resumed a distant, disappointing relationship. Louis, like other men, had to take a few steps backwards and deal with the pain of the past before he could create a more rewarding present and future.

Daniel—Breaking Free from a Dependent Mother

Of all the men I've worked with, a client of mine named Daniel encountered the most resistance in his attempts to create a healthier relationship with his mother. Daniel is forty years old, short and wiry. He is a talented graphic artist. As a child he was expected to fill the emptiness in his mother's life. Unlike Louis's mother, his mother didn't distance herself from him—she was a Dependent Mother who clung to him like a leech. She divorced when he was three years old and expected Daniel, her only child, to fill the hole in her life. In essence, she offered him an unspoken contract: "If you'll take care of my needs, I'll take care of yours." In exchange for her love and protection, something that is every child's birthright, she expected him to be her lifelong friend and companion. As young as seven or eight years of age he had to listen to her complain about men, comfort her when she came home from work, and cuddle up with her at night as they watched TV. As a teenager he was expected to be her chauffeur and social companion.

Every Friday night they would either go to the movies together or go out to a restaurant to eat. He was playing the role of her "date."

As a child Daniel saw little wrong with being his mother's main source of support. "It seemed like a fair deal," he explained to the group one night. "She needed me and I needed her. It made sense." Like most of us, he regarded his childhood situation as the norm. When Daniel eventually left home and married, he continued to honor the terms of the unspoken contract with his mother. He settled in the same town as his mother and spoke with her every day, either by phone or in person. Whenever something was amiss in his mother's life—her car wouldn't start, she had a medical problem, the kitchen sink was clogged, she had questions about her taxes, she couldn't sleep, she was bored, she was anxious—she expected him to dash over and remedy the situation. A lot of the time Daniel would comply. He'd been trained to believe that this was his duty as an only son. It took him by complete surprise that his wife resented all these rescue missions. He tried to explain to her that his mother had no one else to rely on. How could he abandon her?

His wife's unhappiness with the mother-son alliance began to build, and soon Daniel was trapped between two powerful women. He did his best to meet both of their needs, but his wife refused to be placated. Fifteen years into the marriage she threatened him with divorce. Daniel dearly loved his wife and his children, so at her insistence he signed up for therapy. When he joined my Wednesday-night men's group, he finally had a chance to begin examining the fine print of the mother-son agreement. After six months of therapy, he realized that the alliance was not a healthy one. His primary allegiance was to his wife and kids, not to his mother.

He also began to see his mother in a new light, primarily by listening to the other men's comments. They pointed out to him that his mother didn't sound like the frail, helpless woman he was making her out to be. She sounded like a woman who was wielding tremendous power over him. He realized that the men were right. They also helped him see that his mother had been reneging on her side of the deal all his life. In reality *her* needs had always come first. Although she had met all his physical needs, she had denied his deeper need to be a little boy being taken care of by his mother. With the men's encouragement he began venting his anger at his ghost mother. By the end of his first year in therapy he was discovering a reservoir of rage he'd been holding in since boyhood.

As energy began to flow through him once again, Daniel realized he could no longer play the central role in his mother's life. She was destroying his marriage and suffocating his spirit. She was going to have to find some other person or some other activity to fill the hole in her life.

The hardest thing Daniel ever did in his life was working up the courage to talk to his mother about how he wanted to change their relationship. He told the men that his mother had a way with words, and every time he tried to say or do anything she didn't like, she would find some way to talk him out of it. He was afraid that he wouldn't be able to stand up to her. On a deeper level he also had the irrational fear that if he stopped seeing his mother so often, she would get sick or die. "What if she holes up in the house and stops eating?" he asked us. "What if she kills herself?" On a still deeper level he harbored the childlike fear common to all of us that if he angered or disappointed his mother, she would abandon *him,* which a part of his unconscious mind equated with death.

To help cope with his mother's resistance and his own internal resistance, Daniel turned to the group for support. I suggested to him that the two qualities we all need in order to hold on to our personal growth are *persistence* and *reassurance.* We need to *persist* in getting our needs met despite the reaction of the people around us, and at the same time, *reassure* them that we have no plans to hurt or abandon them.

To help Daniel rehearse the pivotal conversation with his mother, we did a role-playing exercise. Stewart, one of the group members, volunteered to play the part of Daniel's mother. He did a remarkable job. He pleaded. He cried. He wheedled. He attacked. Despite these evasive maneuvers, Daniel managed to persist in his demand for more autonomy at the same time that he reassured his "mother" that he was not planning to abandon her.

Immediately after the session Daniel called his mother and made a date to see her. He said he wanted to talk about something important, but he didn't want to give any details over the phone. When he went into his mother's house the next evening, she immediately started showering him with affection. Something in his phone call must have alerted her to danger. Daniel felt himself being swept away by her proclamations of love. However, before he reached the point of no return, he steeled himself and interrupted her. "Mother, stop," he said. "This is exactly what I've come to talk about. I've come to tell you that I can't continue this kind of relationship with you. I've always loved you and appreciated you for all that you've done for me, but I can't go on like this."

"Like what, honey?" his mother asked. "Go on like what? We're mother and son. We love each other. We always have. We have a wonderful relationship. You and I have endured great hardships together. We're a terrific team."

Daniel took a deep breath and launched into his speech. "I can't be the most important person in your life, Mom. I have a wife and two kids. I have a job. I want to spend time with you, but I can't be the only person in your life. You need to turn to other people, not just me. It's too much. Your life is empty without me. You need to make some friends, find something you want to do. I have a full life. You need to have a full life. I don't want to abandon you. I still want to visit with you. In fact, I'd like to see you once a week. This will give us time to talk, and I will be able to help you with some chores." As he had rehearsed in the group, Daniel was careful to state his objections and define exactly how much time he was willing to spend with her. His practice session in the group enabled him to deliver the message without backing down.

Daniel's mother burst into tears, which came as no surprise since he'd predicted she would be highly emotional. Between sobs she complained about her loneliness. She reminded Daniel that he was her only son. "I rely on you totally, Daniel. I'm your mother. We can work anything out if we do it together. I just can't understand why you want to create space between us. What have I ever done to hurt you?"

Daniel assured his mother that he wasn't abandoning her. He just wanted to scale down the amount of time he spent with her. He wasn't her husband. He wasn't her therapist. He wasn't her doctor. He wasn't her plumber. He was her son, a grown man with a life of his own. Daniel listened to his mother's desperate ploys for half an hour, then realized she was beyond reason. The only way he was going to be able to create *any* space between them was to disengage from her entirely. He turned away from her and walked out the door. It took every ounce of his strength to keep walking to his car as his mother leaned against the front door, sobbing and calling out for him.

The next day, when Daniel had time to recover from the visit, he called his mother and told her he didn't want to see her or talk to her for six months. He wanted her to know he was serious about changing the nature of their relationship. When she began to argue with him, he hung up the phone. She called back immediately, as he knew she would, so he had his wife answer the phone and tell her he wasn't available. His mother called so often in the next few days that Daniel had to stop answering the phone altogether. Either his wife would answer the phone or they would turn on the answering machine.

When his mother realized that Daniel wouldn't talk to her on the phone, she began paying him impromptu visits. She was so persistent in her attempts to see Daniel that he had to give up answering the door. He felt under siege. Finally, after a month, his mother stopped calling on the phone or coming to his house, but now she started writing postcards.

Daniel's mother's attempts to contact him became less frequent but increasingly desperate. Once she called in the middle of the night and told his wife she was ill and needed Daniel to go to the pharmacy immediately and pick up some medicine for her. It was a matter of life and death. His wife said she would be glad to pick up the medicine, but Daniel's mother refused the offer. She would get the drugs herself, "even if it meant going out in the rain in the middle of the night with pneumonia." A week later she called and left a message on the answering machine saying that since she didn't have anyone in town who cared about her, she was going to move to another city. When Daniel heard the message, he asked his wife to call the house. There was no answer for the next three days.

During the next group session Daniel filled us in on the drama and asked for help in dealing with the situation. He had remained firm up until this point, but now he was worried about what his mother might do. The group helped Daniel consider all his options and promised their support no matter what decision he made. Daniel decided to call his relatives to see if they'd heard from his mother. He called an aunt and found out that his mother was alive and well, staying with one of her friends. A few weeks later he learned from his aunt that his mother had set up an appointment with a therapist to deal with her anxiety and depression. The crisis was over. Six months later he was stunned when his mother married a retired investment banker.

With the support of the group Daniel was able to uncover his lifelong anger at his mother, define what kind of relationship he wanted with her, inform his mother of the changes he wanted to make in a firm and respectful manner, reassure her about his intentions, and weather her overreaction. It had been a difficult struggle, but he finally succeeded in liberating himself from an unhealthy, enmeshed relationship with his mother.

Arnold—Gaining a Sense of Power in the Father-Son Relationship

In helping a number of men realign their relationships with their parents I have noticed that different anxieties arise around the relationship with the mother and the father. For example, when a man thinks about creating a healthier relationship with his mother, he commonly worries about compromising an important bond between them. Even if his mother neglected him or abused him in some manner, he still feels an allegiance to her. She carried him in her womb. She gave birth to him. She nurtured him as an infant. She took care of his bodily needs. He doesn't want to jeopardize that primal link.

However, when a man thinks about creating a better relationship with his father, he is less likely to be worried about compromising their bond. Many men don't have close ties with their fathers. Typically, their fathers were only marginally involved in their upbringing and remain emotionally distant in later years. In fact, some men feel so little connection with their fathers it's almost as if they were strangers. Who is this man? How is he going to react to what I have to say? Will he be hurt? Angry? They can predict how their mothers are going to react and can even guess the actual words they will say. But many men have told me they have no idea how to approach their fathers.

Another difference I've noticed is that men tend to feel more powerless when they think about confronting their fathers. They see themselves as little boys standing up to grown men. As young boys they felt in awe of their fathers, and they haven't had enough direct dealings with them in adulthood to update their perspective. A part of them still feels small and insignificant in their father's presence.

Arnold was one of those men who felt powerless in relation to his father. He was thirty-four when he joined the group, but he confessed he hadn't held any job for longer than a year. He would either quit or get fired. He made up the shortfall in his expenses by borrowing money from his mother who had remarried a wealthy businessman. When Arnold described himself to the men in his group at the start of his first session, he said he felt insecure and anxious much of the time and that he had trouble with love relationships. One of the men joked that he should feel right at home in the group.

As the weeks went by, we began to get a picture of how often Arnold had relied on his father to bail him out of trouble. Every time he had financial problems, his dad managed to bail him out. When he finally graduated from college, his dad used his influence to get him job after job. Arnold managed to quit or get fired from each one. No matter what he did, his dad was always there to pick up the pieces. One of the men pointed out to Arnold that his father had cast himself in the role of "the rescuer." "Your father doesn't seem to pay much attention to you unless you get into trouble," he said. "Whenever you succeed at something, he's never around." Arnold had never seen his relationship with his father in this light. "You're right," he said. "That's just what he does."

After that insight Arnold began to see the hidden agenda behind his father's apparent generosity and helpfulness: Arnold must fail in order to receive his father's bounty. As the terms of this unspoken agreement became clearer to him, some of the anger he had long experienced as self-loathing began to be directed toward his ghost father.

A less direct way that Arnold worked on becoming more forceful with his father was by learning to become more assertive in the group. He had the same tendency to undercut himself in the group as he did with his father. For example, whenever he ventured an opinion, he qualified it with some self-deprecating remark: "This probably doesn't mean very much," or "I'm probably wrong," or "This is probably way off base." The men drew his attention to this habit and helped him see that it was reducing his inner authority. It took him months to be able to state his views in a straightforward manner, but with a great deal of effort he was able to relate on equal terms with the other men in the group.

After almost a year in the group Arnold began expressing some interest in having a heart-to-heart talk with his father. Although his dad was now an older man in his sixties, he was still wary of confronting him. There was a fundamental inequality in the relationship. In his eyes his dad was a sixty-five-year-old man, and he was a thirty-five-year-old boy. The little boy in him kept finding excuses for postponing the meeting.

One day Arnold called me to say that his dad was coming to San Antonio on business, and he wondered if I would be willing to see them together. I agreed. The next day Arnold came into my office with his father. His father made a strong first impression on me. Despite his years he had a mustache and a full, thick head of dark hair that was set off by a handsome blue suit and a colorful tie. Although he was crippled with arthritis and used a cane, he walked with his chest out and his head held high. It was clear who carried the pride in the family. He looked me straight in the eye and firmly shook my hand. We settled into three overstuffed chairs and faced each other.

After some small talk Arnold's dad said he was glad to come to the session to help his son. He said he was willing to do anything he could to help him—even bring out all the skeletons in the closet. He turned to his son and said, "You know that, don't you, Arnold? You know I'd do anything in my power to help you."

Arnold looked down at his knees and squirmed in his chair, looking very much like a twelve-year-old boy. The fact that he was wearing jeans, tennis shoes, and a T-shirt underscored the image. "Yeah, Dad, I know that. You're always trying to help me. And I know you do it because you love me. I've always appreciated that. It's just that, I don't know . . . if I say anything critical about you, I feel like I'm being so ungrateful." He looked over to me and said, "I don't know how to do this."

"Mr. McGill," I said, "Arnold has wanted to have a talk with you for some time, but he's been afraid to do it."

Arnold's father looked surprised. "Why would you be afraid to talk to me, Arnold? I've never harmed you, have I?"

"No," Arnold replied. "I mean, not really. It's just that I'm so afraid of letting you down. It seems like everything I do gets screwed up somehow." I sensed that he was beginning to connect with some anger and I prayed that he would do it appropriately. He looked his father in the eyes and said, "I'm tired of being a screwup. I'm tired of feeling like I always have to please you. I'm tired of not being able to live up to the superman you've always been. I'm tired of you always protecting me, correcting me, giving me advice—always protecting me from myself. I want to be okay the way I am. Even coming over here to the office you were telling me where to turn and how to drive, and you've never even been to San Antonio before! I'm the one who lives here!" Tears began to fill his eyes. "You don't think I can do anything. You're not proud of me, Dad. You've never been proud of me. That's all I ever wanted was for you to be proud of me."

Tears welled up in the old man's eyes too. "Son, I've always been proud of you. Maybe I didn't tell you enough."

"No, Dad. I don't remember you ever telling me you were proud of me."

Mr. McGill sat straight in his chair. "Son, I *am* proud of you. I've always been proud of you. I'm sorry I didn't tell you how proud I was. I thought you knew. I'm so sorry, Son."

Arnold said, "That's okay, Dad. I love you so much." At exactly the same moment Arnold and his father opened their arms toward each other. Arnold got out of his chair and put his arms around his father's neck. They held each other and cried as they each said, "I love you."

I was deeply affected by what I was seeing. This moment was the result of a year's worth of hard work on Arnold's part, and it was worth every bit of his effort.

After a few moments Arnold sat back down and wiped his eyes on his sleeve. I asked them to breathe deeply and stay with their feelings for a moment. Knowing that there was more to Arnold's agenda I suggested he go on.

"I know you do it for my own good, Dad," Arnold said, "but I want you to stop taking care of me. Let me take care of myself. If I get in a hole, let me dig my way out of it. Believe in me. Believe that I'm capable and competent enough to handle things on my own. And when I'm driving, stop treating me like a fifteen-year-old. Treat me like a man, and I'll do my best to act like one." Arnold had never spoken so calmly and directly to his dad in his entire life. They were speaking man to man. Mr. McGill promised he would stop undermining Arnold's efforts to stand on his own two feet.

When Arnold and his father left my office, I found myself thinking of a line from Robert Bly's book, *Iron John.* It goes like this: "Children visit the King, but adults make a place where the King can visit them." Arnold had devoted a lot of his effort in the group to constructing that place. On the surface having an honest conversation with his father may seem like an easy thing to do, but it's something he hadn't been able to accomplish in all his adult years.

Arnold worked on his relationship with his father all the next year. There were times when he regressed and allowed his father to make decisions for him or relieve him of some of his responsibilities. He would talk about these failures in the group. The men encouraged him by reminding him of all the ways he had changed. They told him he was acting more confidently in the group. He had kept his current job for over a year. He was no longer borrowing money from his mother. Even if he had some setbacks, he was able to hold his own against his father most of the time. Arnold drew on the group's confidence in him to continue the hard work of changing a thirty-year pattern of behavior.

FORGIVING MY FATHER

In simple terms, realigning a relationship with a parent can be thought of as a four-step process, each step beginning with the letter *R*: (1) *R*emember the pain of childhood; (2) *R*elease feelings about the past; (3) *R*esolve the blame of the parent; and (4) *R*edefine the relationship in the present. Understandably, many people try to skip steps one and two. They want to go directly to the "forgive and forget" stages without experiencing the pain of the past. They want to avoid the pain and awkwardness of having to feel the injuries of childhood as an adult. But in our inward-looking age increasing numbers of people are having the opposite problem. They are more than willing to feel all the angst of childhood, but they find it difficult to advance to steps three and four. They get stuck in the "feeling and healing" stage and never go on to live more fully in the present. The country seems to be full of "adult children" who don't want to grow up.

Regrettably, I had a somewhat similar problem. Although I was able to release most of my rage at my father in therapy, I found it difficult to let go of my resentment. I felt bitter toward my father much of the time. I was holding onto a grudge. This kept me distant and aloof. I was willing to do everything that is required of an eldest son, but I felt little or no emotional connection with my father.

Ironically, what allowed me to make peace with my father was a bitter exchange I had with my son. The encounter took place several years ago. My father, my son, and I had agreed to appear on *The Oprah Winfrey Show* to talk about the father-son relationship. At the time of the taping my father was sixty-nine, I was forty-four, and my son, Chesley, was eighteen. During the show I talked candidly about my father's abuse and neglect, and I was surprised to see how openly my father acknowledged his failings. He had mellowed dramatically in recent years and was beginning to see how much harm he had done to me and my siblings. When Oprah asked him to explain why he'd been so abusive, he simply said he'd been frustrated with his life and had taken it out on me. He said he was sorry for what he'd done and wished he'd been a better father. I was surprised that he didn't attempt to defend himself or diminish my charges.

Despite the fact that my father was apologizing to me in front of millions of people, his admission of guilt had only a minor effect on me. I was gratified to hear him validate my experience of childhood, but his apology just didn't sink in. There was a brief time out for a commercial break, and when the show resumed, Oprah turned to Chesley and asked him if I'd been a good father to him. I was curious about his reply. Although I had neglected Chesley in his early years because of my divorce and my obsession with work and women, I'd never hit him or verbally abused him. And after all the progress I'd made in therapy, I'd become a much better father to him. In recent years I had stayed up until two in the morning on several occasions listening to him talk about his problems with girlfriends. I'd taught him to fish and ski the way I wish *I'd* been taught—not through shaming and criticism, but through patient modeling and affirmation. I wasn't a perfect father, but I fully believed I was a "good-enough" father.

I was taken aback when Chesley said to Oprah quite matter-of-factly, "No, my dad wasn't all that good a father. He often neglected me." My heart sank. Chesley went on to acknowledge that I had shown some improvement in the past few years (some improvement?!) and he was grateful for it. But it was evident in his voice that he still felt angry and hurt. He said he felt that many of my visits with him in the early years had been obligatory. He recounted a time when he had seen his name on my calendar, making him feel like just another business appointment. He complained about all the times his mother had had to drive him to see me because I had been too busy to pick him up. As he itemized his complaints, I felt both angry and betrayed.

When the show was over, neither Chesley nor I said anything to each other about his remarks about me, but there was a great deal of tension between us. We got into an argument about which limousine to take back to the hotel. I wanted to take the first one in line because I was worried about my father's health. He'd had a stroke a few months earlier and tired easily. Chesley wanted to wait for the same driver who'd taken us to the show. He thought it was presumptuous of us to take a different one. He thought the show producers might be upset. I won the argument. We sat in cold silence as we rode back to the hotel. I settled my father into his room and hoped to have some time to myself to unwind. But Chesley was standing there waiting for me. We glared at each other. In the lush, carpeted hallway we began a bitter argument.

"Why didn't you listen to me about the limo driver? You never listen to me," Chesley said.

"I always listen to you," I said, "but you never give me credit for it. And didn't I just sit there in that studio and listen to you tell millions of people that I wasn't a good father? Don't you think I heard that?" The heat was rising inside me. "Listen, goddamnit. Your mother is the one who moved you halfway across the state of Texas. It wasn't me."

"Well, if you'd loved me, you would have come to see me more often, anyway. We're only talking three hundred miles. You cared more about money and women than you did about me."

For a brief moment I was able to acknowledge this painful truth, and I felt my son's pain. He was right. I hadn't been there for him when he needed me. The anger drained out of me. I told Chesley I was sorry. Sorry for all the hurtful things I had just said to him and sorry for all the years I had shoved him aside. He cried and said he was sorry too. "I love you, Dad," he said. "When you were there, you were a great dad." We hugged, and I promised him I would always, always be there for him in the future.

When I was alone in my hotel room that night, my mind kept going back to that encounter with Chesley. I realized he'd been angry at me for something that had ended ten years ago. Then I had a sudden glimpse of how my dad must feel, having to cope with my never-ending resentment. He was almost seventy years old. He was white haired, docile, and repentant. But I was still dwelling on abuse that had ended *forty years* earlier. He hadn't yelled at me or hit me since I left home at age sixteen. He was being as nice to me as he knew how. Why was I holding on to my resentment? My father could no more go back in time and change the way he'd treated me when I was a child than I could go back and erase what I'd done to Chesley. When was it time to forgive and forget? Why couldn't I accept the fact that my father was now an old man sitting in his wheelchair with glazed eyes and a vacant expression? He was not the same man who had beaten me and yelled at me when I was a boy. Back then he had been trapped in a marriage he hated, he'd been working at a job that he hated, and he'd been encumbered with three children who demanded more from him than he knew how to give. When would I be able to see him and relate to him as he was in the present?

As is true for most people who are struggling to grow and change, this one insight, no matter how profound it felt, failed to turn my life around. The next morning I found myself dutifully wheeling my father around in his wheelchair and getting him in and out of airplanes. But I didn't feel much emotional connection with him. I still felt distant and removed. My resentment may have diminished, but no good feelings had rushed in to fill the void.

It wasn't until six months later, when my father was in a nursing home recovering from a broken hip, that I was able to take another step toward reconciliation. Once again I was playing the role of the dutiful, distant son. I would visit him in the nursing home and make small talk with him. He was an avid sports fan, so we would talk about the Oilers, the Cowboys, the Astros, and the Rangers. I would ask him how he was doing, and he would complain about his pain or comment on some small bit of progress, like the time he'd managed to shuffle fifty feet down the corridor before he'd had to collapse in his wheelchair. I would console him or congratulate him, bullshit about sports, make sure he had enough money for Cokes, and then announce it was time for me to go. There was only a tenuous link between us. I was unable to experience him as a thinking, feeling human being.

I had an insight one night as I was driving home from visiting him that finally turned things around. I realized I was not only incapable of treating my father as a feeling person, but I was also incapable of being a feeling person in his presence. When I was with him, I was just as numb as he was. My old childhood defenses were taking over. I was just as cut off from my feelings as I had been as a small child sitting at the dinner table trying to survive his violent temper. What would happen, I dared to ask myself, if I allowed myself to be emotional the next time I visited him? What would it be like to open up to him and try to connect? I was always telling the men in my groups that if you don't feel, you're not alive. And there I was relating to my father like a dead man.

Before my next visit I sat in my car in the nursing home parking lot and made a conscious effort to try to visualize my father as he was in the present. First, I thought about all he'd been through in recent years. I thought about how he'd left my mother ten years earlier and run off with a younger woman. I thought about the spark that had come to his eyes when he'd been living with this new woman. I thought about how vengefully my mother had sued him for divorce, stripping him of the ranch and of everything else that he owned except what he'd run away with—an old truck and a suitcase full of clothes. I thought about all the times I'd heard my father say he was going to hire a lawyer to get back what she'd taken from him, but how he'd never done it. I thought about his stroke and how his lover had abandoned him shortly thereafter. Then, I tried to create a vivid image of him lying in bed with a broken hip, so frail he only weighed 107 pounds. I thought about the fact that at the end of his life he had no one to love him and nothing to his name but a suitcase full of old clothes and a truck he wasn't able to drive.

As I went through this exercise, I became aware of one of the reasons I resisted connecting with my father: his life was too tragic. In his seventy years on this planet he'd had only two moments of glory: one as a devil-may-care fighter pilot in World War II; the other as a sixty-five-year-old man in love with a younger woman. Both of those interludes had been far too short. Most of his life had been empty and desolate. It was impossible for me to think about my father's life and not grieve for him.

But why not grieve for him? Why was I so afraid to acknowledge the emptiness of my father's life? If grief was the feeling that welled up in me when I was around him, why not experience my grief? I took a deep breath and resolved to show my father more of my feelings, whatever they happened to be. I slowly made my way to his room. His eyes lit up when he saw me enter the doorway. Had he been that happy to see me on other visits? Had I missed that spark of life? I sat beside him and looked in his eyes. "How are you?" I asked, as I had asked him dozens of times before, only this time was different. This time I truly wanted to know.

"Not bad," he said. "I can't complain."

Unlike all the other times, this time I didn't try to maintain a distance between us by talking about sports or the news. I wanted to talk about how he was really feeling. I said, "It must be frustrating to lie in bed and not be able to take care of yourself."

"Yeah," he said. "It is."

"And I know how important your truck is to you," I said. "You've always driven everywhere. Is it hard not being able to drive?"

"Yeah, I miss my truck. But I'm going to get out of here, though."

I reached for my father's hand and told him how much I wished I could help him, but there wasn't much I could do. I wasn't in a mood to give him any false assurances. His hand felt frail and bony to me, and I was surprised to feel him give me a little squeeze. It was one of the few times I had ever felt any love flowing back and forth between us. I looked in my father's eyes and told him I loved him. I'd said those words before, but this time I meant them. My father felt my love for him and tears rolled down the sides of his face. "I love you too, Marvin," he said.

When I left my father that afternoon, I no longer felt resentment toward him. It seemed to have melted away. But I also felt strangely hollow, as if something else was missing inside me. And then I knew what it was. It was hope. My hope was gone. Once I saw my father clearly for who he was—an old man barely able to raise a mound under the blankets—I could no longer hold on to the wish that he would some day repay his debt to me. When I was a little boy, he had taken away my self-esteem, my sense of safety, my pride in being myself. He owed me! He owed me for all those years when I needed him to pay attention to me and value me and look at me with his proud eyes. A little boy in me was still looking for a real dad. As long as I held on to my resentment, as long as I dwelt on the past, a part of me still believed I could force him to make good on his debt.

But now I knew without question that the destitute old man in room

44B was unable to repay me. He had nothing left to give. And the bitter irony was, he now needed me to take care of him. He needed me to ease his suffering and to make his last days on earth more bearable. Regardless of how little he had given me as a child, it was my turn now to look after him.

I gradually began to realize in the following days that even if my father had been a healthy and vigorous man, there was no currency he could have given me to take the place of the gold coins of usable love that he denied me as a child. Gold coins have to be exchanged between a father and a little boy. They only fit in a little boy's pocket. A father can be as loving as Gandhi when his son is an adult, but he can't make up for his failure to be there when his son was young. The emotional debt that an absent, neglectful, or abusive father owes his son can never be repaid in full. The son has to forgive it.

When my father died last winter, I was truly able to grieve for him. Because there had finally been some closeness between us, I was free to mourn his passing. During his memorial service I sat in the almost empty church and listened to a Baptist preacher say meaningless things about him. The preacher hadn't known my father and, apparently, hadn't been able to unearth much information from the people who had. But then there hadn't been all that much to say about my dad. His ashes were in a small urn next to the altar. Beside the urn someone had placed his medals from World War II. That said it all. My father's spirit had died when he had come home from the war. The rest of his life had been marking time.

As the minister talked on, quoting passages from the Bible, I felt the growing need to say a few words about my father. When the minister was through, I stood up and asked if I could speak. I turned to the handful of people who had come to the service and began to talk honestly about my dad. I talked about his hard life. I told them a few things about his difficult childhood and how he'd managed to pass much of his pain on to his kids. I said that for most of our lives the three of us had been either scared of him or mad at him. Then I talked about his years as a fighter pilot and how he had prided himself in flying so close to the ocean waves that he would come back to the base with salt on his wings. I said that that was how I would remember him, as a wild and talented fighter pilot who had helped win the war.

CHAPTER 11

CREATIVE MASCULINITY

By the time a man has been in a men's therapy group for a year or more, he has had a chance to become well acquainted with the other people in the group. He knows the intimate details of their struggles, and he has some familiarity with their childhood histories. Somewhere in the course of acquiring this information he makes a key observation: there are a lot of parallels in the way all the men live their lives and deal with their problems, regardless of how or where they were raised. There seems to be a shared male response to the world.

Joe and Harold, two men in my Tuesday-night group, are a good example of how similar two men can be despite strikingly different childhood histories. Joe's parents divorced when he was six; Harold's parents have just celebrated their fiftieth anniversary. Joe rarely saw his father after the divorce; Harold's father was an active, involved parent. Joe's mother turned to him for her emotional needs; Harold's mother satisfied her needs for companionship and emotional support in her marriage.

Given these differences it's surprising that Joe and Harold would have so much in common. Both of them have been divorced twice. Both of them were in new love relationships within a month of separating from their second wives. Both of them are highly competitive and are constantly worried about money. Both of them work compulsively.

Neither Joe nor Harold has a male friend outside the group with whom he confides on a regular basis. Both of them have drinking problems.

At first Joe couldn't understand why Harold, who came from such a "normal" family, would have so many of the same problems he did. Like many people, he thought all his difficulties came from growing up in a dysfunctional family. Over the course of the year he came to realize that, despite their disparate backgrounds, they both grew up in the same larger "family," the culture in which they were raised. They were both the products of a society that trains men to deal with their difficulties, whatever they may be and from whatever cause they may arise, in the same formulaic way: numb your feelings and focus on external success. Joe and Harold have been shaped by the masculine code as much or more than they have been by their individual families.

THERAPY AND THE MASCULINE CODE

In my years of working with men I have discovered that helping men revise their gender conditioning is an essential part of their therapy. For men to go through therapy but continue to live by the old masculine code would be like going back on the football field with a partially healed broken leg—the leg would surely break again in the very same place.

An all-male therapy group provides an ideal opportunity to start rewriting the masculine code. Hardly a session goes by without some comment leading to a discussion of the similarities between various group members. This, in turn, leads to a discussion of the masculine code and how it has shaped their lives.

In the course of this discussion the men realize that their gender conditioning has not been entirely negative. Some of it has worked to their advantage. For example, it has allowed them to focus their energy on mastering a great number of worthwhile skills. It has given them the ability to work hard and put aside minor problems. It has helped them endure life's many hardships. It has helped them develop courage and leadership skills. But it has caused them great pain as well.

What the men need to do is draw some distinctions between beliefs and behaviors they want to keep and ones they want to discard. For example, they may see that being able to hide their feelings in a poker game or in the middle of a business deal works to their advantage; there are times when it's important not to show your hand. But hiding their feelings from their wives and their friends keeps them isolated and alone. Similarly, ignoring their pain may be entirely appropriate if they've stubbed a toe, but ignoring the warning signs of cancer or a heart attack can kill them. Holding back their tears when they've botched up a job is going to win points with the foreman, but holding back their tears after a divorce is going to keep the grief living on in their souls. Being a perfectionist may be vital when compiling a complex computer program, but applying those same standards to a son's homework can destroy the boy's self-esteem.

What men need to do is create a *flexible code of behavior,* one that allows them a wide range of choices and enhances their ability to find happiness and success. Just the other night an issue came up in my Tuesday-night group that helped the men overcome one key limitation in their gender conditioning. Clint, a man who had been in the group for almost two years, had just returned after a three-week absence. He'd been having back trouble for months and had had to have major back surgery. When we went around the circle for the weekly check-in, Clint said he was disappointed that no one from the group had visited him during his long stay in the hospital. He was surprised because everyone in the group had known how worried he'd been about the operation. He confessed that on the Tuesday night two weeks earlier, when all the other men were in group, he'd been lying in his hospital bed creating an elaborate fantasy: "I imagined that you guys were sitting around talking about me and wondering how I was doing. Then I imagined that you decided to end the session early and come see me. I pictured all nine of you marching into my room."

No one responded for a few moments. They were too ashamed. They'd known Clint for almost two years and had gotten to know him intimately. They'd laughed with him and cried with him. Why hadn't they called or visited?

"I can't believe I didn't call you," said one of the men. "But, to be honest, it never crossed my mind."

"Guys don't do that kind of thing," said another. "It's not the way we are."

"I thought about calling you," said a third, "but when I'm sick or depressed, I just withdraw. I don't want anyone around me. I thought you might feel the same way."

After making their apologies to Clint, the men began to talk about all the ways they failed to reach out to others. They rarely sent greeting cards, whether people were graduating, getting married, having a baby, recovering from illness, or having a birthday; it was a woman's job to maintain those social ties. They forgot birthdays and anniversaries. They put little effort into gift giving. ("It's always a last-minute, Christmas Eve effort.") They rarely wrote thank-you letters, except to a business client. They avoided people who were sick, depressed, or lonely because they didn't know how to help them and because being around them made them feel vulnerable. The men concluded that in most areas of their lives they relied on women to weave the social matrix. If a man happened to be single, as was true for Clint and several of the other men, then there was no one to create that cloak of comfort.

The men wore a look of shame on their faces as they went through this self-examination. They were blaming themselves for their solitary, self-centered ways. I let the discussion continue for a few minutes. Then I voiced my opinion that the shame they were experiencing was yet another crippling by-product of the masculine code. I explained that once men have learned to repress their emotions, once they have learned to become overly reliant on their intellects, once they have developed a warrior mentality—in short, once they have adjusted to life in the MAN BOX—people start telling them how deficient they are for living in those cramped quarters. People criticize them for being insensitive and self-centered, the very qualities that result from having to live by the masculine code. The underside of the MAN BOX is covered with graffiti that denigrates men for being men: "Men can't feel." "Men are insensitive." "Men are arrogant." "All men care about is work." "Men can't commit." Men are attacked and maligned for following all the commandments written on the other sides of the box. After a lifetime of absorbing this condemnation, it's not surprising they would join in with a chorus of self-blame.

Instead of dwelling on their shame I suggested that the men attack the problem at its source and begin challenging the negative parts of their gender conditioning. In this instance their remorse was telling them that they needed to show more support for Clint. A cuff on the shoulder and a few mumbled words had been the macho way to show their concern: "Tough luck about the back, Clint." (Punch.) But Clint had been playing by the new rules when he let them know how worried he was about the surgery. "Real men" don't expose their vulnerability. Clint was asking them to stretch into new behavior and meet him on a higher plane.

The men talked about what they might have done for Clint had they been free of the old programming. One man suggested that they might have brainstormed about all that Clint had told them in the past two years and then gotten him a gift that showed they'd been listening. Another man volunteered that they might have taken Clint something to while away his time as he recovered from surgery. A third suggested that since he was the one who had developed the closest friendship with Clint, he might have visited him before the surgery to try to ease his mind.

To reinforce this new mind-set I gave the men an assignment to do that very week. I suggested that they go to a store and buy an assortment of greeting cards—birthday cards, cards of condolence, graduation cards, get-well cards, thank-you cards. When an occasion called for a card, they would have one right at hand. Buying the cards would take only a half hour of their time, but in this one small area of their lives they would be able to start playing by a new set of rules.

I mentioned that they might feel some resistance to buying the cards, as simple a task as this was. But as they were learning in the group, being able to show love and support, offer sympathy, celebrate other people's success, and reinforce social ties were not just feminine virtues. They were *human* virtues, and being able to exercise them would make their lives more enjoyable.

I gave them an example of how my life had become richer because of the effort I was making to reinforce family ties. A few months earlier I had decided to call an aunt of mine whom I hadn't seen for ten years. Like a lot of men, especially men who've been through divorce, I hadn't been very diligent about keeping up with the family. I'd let some relationships slide so long I was embarrassed to reestablish contact. One night I decided to clean up my act. I picked up the phone and called my aunt. As I was waiting for her to answer the phone, a stream of negative thoughts ran through my head: my aunt and I wouldn't have anything to say to each other; I would be imposing on her; she would wonder why I hadn't contacted her years ago. But as it turned out, my aunt was delighted to hear from me and we had a wonderful conversation. She called me the following month and we chatted some more. I mentioned I was going to be doing some business in her hometown, and she invited me and my wife to stay with her. We took her up on the invitation and had a great visit. During the visit my aunt encouraged me to look up her daughter whom I hadn't seen for fifteen years. It turned out my cousin was living in San Antonio, twenty miles away from where we lived. My wife and I recently spent an afternoon with her getting reacquainted. One simple phone call has helped rebuild the family network.

CHANGES IN THE OLD ORDER

As the old masculine code begins to change, it's going to change in just this way. A growing number of men are going to make alterations in their daily lives, changes that allow them to live a more expansive, more enjoyable existence. Other men will observe these changes and be encouraged to follow suit.

I saw an example of this chain reaction a few months ago. Stan, a physician in one of my groups, announced to the men that he had diabetes. He'd been afraid to disclose this part of his medical history, despite the fact that he was a doctor. He'd been worried that the men might treat him differently if they knew about his disease. The men did, in fact, treat Stan differently after his revelation. But instead of being put off by his announcement, they became warmer toward him. His willingness to expose his vulnerability was the ticket that gained him admission into the inner circle.

It wasn't long after Stan's announcement that Leo, another member of the group, decided to tell his girlfriend that he'd been wearing a toupee, something he'd avoided telling her for a year. Witnessing Stan's openness had given him the confidence to be more forthcoming himself. The old idea that men have to hide their vulnerability in order to be accepted by others was loosening its grip, at least in this small group of men.

As the chain reaction spreads, an increasing number of men will come out of hiding. In reality it's not just gay men who have been forced to hide their true natures—virtually all men are hiding in a closet, afraid to let other people see who they are, afraid to *be* who they are. As more men challenge the rigidity of their gender conditioning, society's definition of masculinity will change to encompass this altered behavior. Just as we now see women as intelligent, powerful, and capable human beings, we will someday see men as empathic, compassionate, and emotionally vital human beings.

THE NEW MASCULINITY

It is likely to be decades before we see a dramatic change in the way most men live their lives, and what shape this "new masculinity" will take is not entirely clear. I like to draw on the all-inclusive definition of masculinity presented in Bernie Zilbergeld's book, *Male Sexuality*. Zilbergeld recounts an anecdote about a famous matador from a part of Spain where the men followed a rigid, machismo version of masculinity. Working, fighting, gambling, and aggressive sexual behavior were considered "manly" virtues. Men who spent much time around the house were highly suspect. One day the matador decided to host a dinner party for his friends. One of the neighbors came by early and happened to see the matador cooking in the kitchen. He said, "My God, sir! You're in the kitchen with an apron on. Isn't that terribly feminine?" The matador looked down his long nose at the guest and said, "I'll have you know, sir, that *everything* I do is masculine."

I applaud this definition. It implies that anything a man chooses to do is naturally imbued with his manliness, whether the activity has been defined as a male or female pursuit. However, I would add a slight clarification. When we are discussing the notion of "masculinity," we're not talking about any particular activity that happens to be performed by any given man. We're talking about ideals and paradigms—a set of standards to inspire men and guide them. In my view an apt definition of the new masculinity is "anything an emotionally healthy man chooses to do." And by *an emotionally healthy man,* I mean a man who is in touch with a full range of emotions and has learned to relate to others in a constructive, respectful, life-affirming manner.

MEN WHO ARE CREATING THE NEW MASCULINITY

It has been my privilege to witness a number of men in my groups beginning to create their own versions of this new masculinity. Through the hard work they've been doing in the groups, their lives have become much more productive, exciting, and joyful. They work less compulsively, laugh more often, and feel more intimately connected to their family and friends.

I am deeply moved by the progress they've made in therapy. I am also pleased to see that they are creating a ripple effect in the larger community. When a man recovers his emotional wholeness, he becomes a change agent wherever he goes—whether that is his intention or not.

A recent incident illustrates this point. Karl, a twenty-eight-year-old member of my Wednesday-night group, had a birthday last week. He invited five of the men from the group and about twenty other men and women to his birthday party. At the end of the party a friend who had never been in therapy before came up to him. He said he'd noticed something different about the men from Karl's group. His friend said, "There's something different about those five men. I can't put my finger on it. But I want it." Soon after Karl's friend joined the Wednesday group.

Some of the men in my groups are making a conscious choice to communicate what they've learned in the group to the outside world. One of those men, a forty-two-year-old pharmaceuticals engineer named Tom, has been leading a men's support group in a nearby state prison for the past six months. Tom is not a therapist. He's just a man with a heartfelt desire to spread what he's learned in his own emotional recovery to other men.

Tom has made tremendous progress in his therapy, a saga that illustrates many of the points in this book. He started therapy with my colleague, Allen Maurer, three years ago. His weight was one of his primary concerns. He'd lost fifty pounds in a weight-loss program and was dismayed to find he was putting the pounds back on. He realized he needed to resolve some underlying issues or he'd gain them all back.

One of the first issues he explored with Allen was the emotional and physical abuse he'd suffered at the hands of his father. He described a traumatic scene that happened to him over and over in his youth. When he would offend his mother, which seemed to happen with regularity, she would insist that he be punished—not by her, but by his father. Tom says, "My dad would pull in the driveway at night. My mother would meet him at the front door and tell him I'd been a bad boy. My father would march me into the bathroom and beat me. He wouldn't let me out of the bathroom until I had hugged him and told him how much I loved him. He gave me a very sick message about love and anger."

In later years Tom found himself unconsciously re-creating this same tense drama with his employers: "In order to win my boss's approval, I'd first do something to make him angry. Then I'd go in and apologize to him. It was a totally destructive pattern, and I did it again and again."

Tom's issues with his mother were equally unresolved. She was raised a strict Catholic. When she was eleven, her own mother died, and she was placed in a girl's school run by nuns. Some years later at age twenty-two, she met Tom's father, a Methodist, and they conceived Tom out of wedlock. The pregnancy gave his mother a tremendous amount of guilt. Says Tom, "I was her mortal sin."

When Tom was a teenager, his mother had an irrational fear that he would repeat her mistake and make one of his girlfriends pregnant. She sent him to a Catholic boys' school to separate him from a close girlfriend. Tom spent the next three years at the school. While there he became deeply involved in religious studies. He had a mystical experience while praying in the chapel that touched him very deeply and convinced him he wanted to be a priest. His future seemed clear.

All that changed when his father arrived at the school unannounced and forbade him to enter the priesthood. "My father said that if I wanted him to put food in my mouth and pay for my schooling, I would have to abandon my plans. He also said that if I disobeyed him, he would divorce my mother. He saw her as the force behind my decision. Divorcing her was a way to punish us both."

Tom was devastated. "I had no options. I had no resources of my own. I had to abandon my dream. I went east to college to study technology, just as my father had done."

In an effort to overcome his troubled upbringing Tom spent much of his adult life creating what he calls an "intellectual survival kit." From the 1960s on he studied a broad range of philosophical and psychological literature, including works by Carl Jung, Alice Bailey, Carl Rogers, and various Eastern mystics. He says, "Nothing opened any doors. I was too emotionally blocked. I know this sounds strange, but I didn't have feelings associated with 'feeling words.' I'd say the word *fear,* but I didn't know what fear felt like. I had no idea whatsoever what grief was. I was quite sure I had anger inside of me, but I wasn't able to experience it. The connection between my head and my gut was severed."

Tom worked individually with Allen for several months. Then Allen suggested that he join a men's group that he and I were coleading. Tom recalls being highly resistant to the notion: "No way was I going to sit in a group of men and talk about my stuff! When it was just me and Allen in his therapy office, I felt I could exert some control. I didn't know what was going to happen in a group. I was afraid I'd feel exposed."

Tom had been in therapy before and, like many men, had discovered he could control the situation rather well: "I was better at the game than the psychiatrists were. One of my issues is being a pleaser. I'd find out what the therapist wanted to hear from me and that's what I'd say. I got nowhere fast. But at least I was in control, which lessened my fear of the unknown."

After months of foot dragging Tom reluctantly decided to join our group. I recall my first impression of him. I saw a bright man with a ready smile that had a hard edge to it. I sensed a lot of hidden anger. He used his intellect as a sword to fend everyone off. He had great insight into human behavior, but no awareness of human emotion.

Tom made little progress in the group for the first three months. He says, "I had no gut-level understanding of what was going on. The other men would call me on being too rational, and I would deny it. I'd get mad at them for attacking me, then I'd deny that I was angry." He resisted all entreaties to use the bat and pillow. "I was too afraid to let out my rage. My fear was that I was going to run amok. When I'd gotten angry before, I'd hurt people. I was afraid if I started swinging the bat, I was going to destroy something or someone." Tom was a Paralyzed Man, repressing a lifetime of rage at his mother and father for fear of the damage he'd do.

I suggested that Tom attend a Wildman Gathering to see if it would help him break through to his anger. He was even more anxious about going to the Gathering than he had been about joining the men's group. Part of his fear was about being around so many men. "I'd felt inadequate around men or fearful of them all of my life," he explains. "And there I was going to be with a hundred of them." Like some men, he also had an irrational fear of being around gay men. He correctly assumed there would be some gay men among the hundred men at the Gathering, and this bothered him. "I didn't know where my homophobia was coming from," he says, "but it was strong."

Tom forced himself to go to the Gathering despite his fears. He was beginning to sense that the men in the group were right: he was living in his head. "I want to change," he told me when he announced his decision to go. "That's what I'm here for."

Tom drove to the Gathering alone. "Which is just as well," he says, "because I was a wreck. I kept thinking, 'Why am I doing this? This is a really crazy thing to do!' " When he got to the Gathering, his fear of gay men was always in the back of his mind. He saw one man hug another man, and he immediately tagged that man as a homosexual. The man turned out to be a therapist and a good friend of mine who was indeed gay. My friend's sexual orientation became clear to Tom later that day when we honored men from various minority groups, including homosexuals.

Tom studied my friend throughout the remainder of the day. To his surprise his fear was replaced with a growing fascination. "I watched this man very closely. I noticed he was very comfortable with himself. He didn't hide his homosexuality, and he didn't flaunt it. He was just who he was. I began to sense that *I* was the one with the problem, not him."

Tom began to feel more comfortable and was able to focus on his reason for coming to the retreat. The part of the Gathering that proved most meaningful to him was a segment Sunday morning called "the Father Quest." During this part of the retreat, I talk about the father-and-son relationship for an hour, then the men are sent off individually to meet with their ghost fathers. Each man is instructed to draw a circle in the dirt, invite his ghost father into the circle, have a conversation with him, and then let out any rage or grief. To help start the flow of anger he can hit the ground with a stick.

"I knew I had a lot of frustration with my father," Tom says. "But I didn't identify it as anger. To see what might happen I picked up a stick and started beating the ground. I felt some anger, but it wasn't directed at my father. It was just generalized anger."

Although not much came of Tom's initial attempt to connect with his feelings, his willingness to participate in the exercise broke through his resistance to anger-release techniques in general. He'd learned that hitting the ground with a stick wasn't going to hurt anyone or destroy any property. Nor was it going to release a torrent of uncontrollable rage.

His fears abated, Tom risked working with the bat and pillow during his therapy group the following week. This time he was able to release some rage. In the following weeks he continued to work with the bat and pillow, and his emotions became increasingly intense. After about six months he was releasing immense rage, rage that was clearly directed at his father. "My rage was so strong that several times I beat the pillow nonstop for twenty or thirty minutes. I would come home exhausted. My muscles would be sore for a week. It was an incredible experience."

As Tom's pool of rage diminished, he discovered at long last that he could express other emotions. "Once I'd released my anger, I began to experience sadness, grief, and love. It was totally spontaneous. Anger is like a hard scab that forms over all the other feelings. Once you break through it, your other feelings are right there."

Tom's father had died eight years prior to this work, so Tom wasn't able to talk with him directly about his childhood years. He had to resolve his issues with his father within the group. His mother, however, was alive and well, so he resolved to have a talk with her to set the record straight. This was extremely difficult for him to do. "I was in therapy for almost two years before I worked up the nerve to confront her. I didn't know whether she would agree with me, deny everything, put me down, or start the whole guilt and blame trip all over again."

Tom finally set up an appointment to have an honest talk with his mother. He spent several hours driving her around to various parts of the city that were symbolic to him. As part of this odyssey he took her to the very spot where his father had made his stand against his becoming a priest. He said to his mother, "I want you to know how much that hurt me to have him control me that way. My dreams weren't important to either one of you. Neither of you cared what I wanted to do." He told his mother that she didn't have to defend herself or apologize to him. He just wanted her to understand how she and his father had made him feel.

As Tom was driving his mother back home at the end of that momentous day, he looked over at her and was amazed to see that she seemed physically smaller. "I looked at her and she looked like a little girl. She looked about the size and age she would have been when her own mother had died and she'd been sent away to the girl's school. This is the first time in my life she didn't seem larger than life to me. She had always been 'The Almighty Mother.' Now she was human. I felt an overwhelming sadness and compassion for her. The little boy in me was finally standing up to her. I was equal to her. I was no longer subject to her control."

The hard work that Tom was doing in the group began to be reflected in his daily life. He felt much closer to his wife. He eased some long-standing tension between himself and his twenty-one-year-old son. He broke out of self-defeating patterns at work.

He also began to look for ways to share what he was learning with other men. He learned that a group of men at a state prison were interested in forming a men's support group and he volunteered to be their leader. A dozen men showed up for the first meeting. Some of the men were facing life in prison. Others had twenty- or thirty-year sentences. As would be expected Tom found it difficult to get the men to open up and talk about themselves during the initial session. Prisoners have to follow an exaggerated version of the masculine code in order to survive. To show any vulnerability is to invite psychological or physical abuse from other inmates.

The second session proved equally frustrating for Tom. During the third session he did something that took a great deal of courage: he let down his defenses and allowed himself to be completely honest with them. "I told them we weren't getting anywhere. I needed their help. I wasn't a guru. I wasn't a magician. I wasn't even a therapist. I was just a guy like them trying to find my way through a maze. I said, 'I need you to tell me if these sessions are helping you. Are you getting anything out of them?' "

After a brief pause one of the men spoke up: "Last week I was walking out in the field and I started thinking about all the times my family moved when I was in grade school. I remembered how painful it was to lose my friends. I haven't thought about that in years." Another man said that he had started writing letters to his son. A third man said that he realized he'd been isolating himself in prison and needed to reach out to his family. He'd called his wife and she was coming to visit next Saturday. Tom looked around him and realized that the ice was broken.

Tom's most recent visit to the prison has been the most rewarding so far. He started the session by telling one man how much more open he seemed since the first meeting of the group. Another man commented that he'd observed the same thing. Tom got the idea to spend the next hour going around the room, giving each man this kind of positive feedback. "The exercise lasted a full two hours, not just one. The men had so many good things to say about each other. My main job was to help each man open up and really feel the compliments the other men were giving him. By the end of the session all of the men were beaming. Some of them acted as if they'd never been praised before. It was deeply moving."

Tom is now looking for some funding so he can expand this work. "The men in prison are just basic people," he says. "Their problems come from the same childhood pain as men everywhere. It's just that they've had more pain, and they've made more self-defeating choices. I look forward to working with them. It's a priesthood of a different complexion."

Ellis—Rediscovering the Joy of Childhood

Ellis, a thirty-six-year-old physician, has been in one of my groups for almost a year. He too is communicating what he's been learning in the group to other people. He gave an example at the last session of his group. The night before, he'd been on duty in the emergency room. A mother brought in her four-year-old boy for treatment. The boy was trembling. He had a cough, a high fever, and pain in both ears. Ellis examined the boy's eardrums and discovered they were so infected they were about to rupture. He said to the boy, "My goodness. Your ears are really infected. That must hurt!"

His mother said, "But he's not supposed to cry. He's a big boy."

The mother's comment helped Ellis understand why the boy was trembling: he was tightening all his muscles to keep from crying. Ellis said to the boy, "It's okay to cry. Big people would cry with that much pain, too. You don't have to hold it in." The mother looked taken aback by his remarks. Meanwhile, the boy continued to tremble. Ellis decided he had to say more: "Boys can cry just like girls can cry. Tears help take away the pain." The boy appeared to relax, but he still wouldn't allow himself to cry.

Ellis went on with the examination. He was concerned about the boy's cough, so he ordered an X ray. Hearing the word *X ray* frightened the boy. Ellis explained to him that an X ray was just a picture of his chest. It wasn't going to hurt him in any way. But if he felt scared, it was okay to cry. Little boys sometimes cry when they're afraid. Ellis added, partly for the mother's benefit, that the people in the X ray room were used to seeing boys cry. He wanted to give the mother a glimpse of an alternative view of masculinity.

The boy was sent off to be X-rayed. When he returned fifteen minutes later, the first words out of his mouth were, "I didn't cry!" Ellis wasn't surprised: "The macho messages were already too deeply embedded in his brain. I wasn't going to change all that with a few comments. But I wanted to plant a seed."

Ellis is also making a deliberate choice to plant seeds with his colleagues. "I'm more forthcoming with my feelings around the people I work with. Sometimes that's risky. Sometimes I get a snide remark. It *always* raises eyebrows. But it doesn't cost me as much as I thought it would. It's a little risky, but it's honest."

Ellis grew up in the South where men are men. "Nobody gave me permission to feel. If I felt sad, I'd get this lump in my throat and cover it up by acting real macho. Just like that little boy." A car accident several years ago convinced him he needed to examine his priorities. He hit a deer and his car rolled over three times. When the car came to a stop, he was relieved to find out that he wasn't seriously injured.

He crawled out of the ditch and looked up at the stars. He thought to himself, "God! I've got to start making some changes in my life. Life is too fragile!"

One of the changes he made was to get some therapy. He'd long felt his life was out of control, but he hadn't allowed himself to get any help. "I was afraid of seeing a therapist. I would have to disclose too much. I had spent years maintaining a façade."

Ellis saw a psychologist for a month, but he made little progress. "I went in there and talked for an hour, and the psychologist hardly said a word. The few remarks he did make were highly analytical. I was spending a hundred bucks an hour. I thought, 'Jeez, I'm not getting any feedback from this guy. I'm not getting my money's worth. This could go on forever.' " Ellis also realized that he didn't feel comfortable with the therapist: "I can't say why, exactly, but it didn't feel good to be there."

At the time, Ellis was reading some books on men's issues, including some books by John Lee. In the back of one of Lee's books was the phone number of the Texas Men's Institute in San Antonio. He called the number and was told that I was putting together a new group. He showed up for the first session.

Unlike Ed, Ellis felt safer in a group setting than in individual therapy. "I didn't have to disclose myself all the time in the group. I wasn't the only one talking." For the first few sessions, Ellis kept in the background. The only contributions he made were analytical comments. "I've always been the expert on the topic. In the group I became an expert on psychology. 'This is what I am. This is why I am doing this.' I'd have all these rational explanations. That kept me from having to feel. But ultimately the other guys wouldn't let me get away with it. They confronted me, and then they drew me in with their own willingness to feel. Gradually, I began to feel safe expressing my feelings."

The primary emotions that Ellis explored in the group were his feelings of anger and sadness about his impending divorce. The tears that he cried were some of the first ones he had cried since he was three or four years old. "It was a tremendous feeling of relief to express those feelings. Before, I would have had to stuff it. Be macho. Be tough. Now I could let them all out."

As has been true for virtually every man in my groups, Ellis found that expressing his grief allowed him to experience his joy. He and two other men from the group have started going to a Mexican restaurant after each group meeting. For the first hour or so they continue to talk about their issues. But then humor erupts spontaneously. "Last week we laughed like three-year-olds. I don't even remember what it was about. But we laughed so hard we nearly fell out of our chairs."

Ellis went to his first Wildman Gathering about six months ago. He drove to the retreat with Greg, one of the men who joins him at the restaurant. They found the Gathering an exhilarating experience. Ellis felt a spirituality that he hadn't experienced since he was a young boy. "There was a magic about being around the campfire and beating drums. I just let myself go."

At the Gathering I read a poem titled "Fuckers," written by a Florida poet named Cal Hosman. Both he and Greg felt that the poem spoke directly to them. It goes like this:

Fuckers

> I don't like myself.
> They set the standards too high.
> Didn't give me what I needed to meet up to them.
> And now, I don't like myself.
> Fuckers.

On the drive home Ellis and Greg would look at each other every few minutes or so and say the word *fuckers.* Then they would burst into uproarious laughter. Says Ellis, "There we were, two professionals. I'm a doctor and Greg is an engineer with a top security clearance from the army. We were wearing shorts and sandals. We had scarves wrapped around our heads like headbands. At one point Greg said to me, 'I don't think the army would give me security clearance if they could see me now!' We laughed some more. I don't know when I've had a better time. The work that I'm doing in the group is helping me reclaim my childhood joy."

Kurt—Learning How to Feel

Kurt, fifty-three years old, has been in therapy with me for three and a half years. He has made as much progress in his work in the group as any man I've counseled. He was raised in a small community where his father had the distinction of being the town drunk. He says, "When I was born, my dad was already a gone alcoholic. He was either at the tavern, drunk, or arguing with my mother." Because his father was emotionally unavailable, his mother turned to Kurt for her needs. She was a Martyr Mother who manipulated him through guilt. "She told me a hundred times that she did without things so I could have more. The implication was that there was a payback due. The payback was that I was going to take care of her for the rest of her life. I was her 'Little Man.' "

His mother used fear to bind him to her as well. "She scared the shit out of me as a behavioral tool. She created all these frightening scenarios to keep me by her side. If I went into the backyard, she told me I was going to be bitten by my dog or spurred by the rooster who was locked up in a pen. If I played in the front yard, a car might jump the curb and run over me. If I didn't obey her, John Lewis, the local constable, was going to take me away and lock me up. I was terrified of John Lewis. He wore a gun that seemed to hang down to his knees. I can remember being four years old and seeing him drive by our house. I ran into the house, hid in my bed, and was sick to my stomach. I was convinced he was coming for me. Because of what my mother did to me, fear and anger have been the dominant emotions in my life."

When Kurt graduated from high school, he managed to break free from his mother's influence and go to a university on the other side of the state, not the one close to his hometown where most of his friends went. "I don't know how I worked up the courage to do it, but it's something I'm still very proud about. It was one of the first times I stood up to her."

While in college Kurt fell in love with a woman named Mary. He had such low self-esteem he was afraid that if Mary knew much about him, she wouldn't want to marry him. "I felt inferior, inadequate, and frightened. When she agreed to marry me, I kept pushing the date forward so she wouldn't have a chance to back out. I was afraid she would get away and there would never be another woman in my life." His low opinion of himself made him extremely jealous throughout their marriage. He was deathly afraid of competition from other men and accompanied her everywhere she went so he could monitor her activities. He says, "I went to a million events that I didn't want to go to. I was on guard." He had an irrational fear that if his wife was allowed to get involved in an extended conversation with another man, she would choose the other man—whoever he was—over him. "I lived in absolute fear and the certain knowledge that she was going to leave me. I tried to control her friends. I tried to control what she did. I literally tried to control what she thought. That was the only way I was going to keep her."

Kurt stayed vigilant for twenty-nine years. "I was still ruled by the fear my mother had instilled in me. I didn't trust the universe. For some reason, being with my wife kept away the fear. With her I felt like a complete person. She was my only support system. I didn't have a single male friend."

On numerous occasions his wife insisted that they get marital counseling. Kurt went on the premise that he, himself, didn't need help. If his wife wanted to go, that was fine. But he thought that what she really needed to do was get a job, get busy. Then life would improve. He wasn't willing to look at his own pain. "I was afraid of therapy. I knew deep down that I needed help, but I didn't trust anyone, certainly not a shrink. The male story on therapy, out in the community, is why pay one hundred dollars for something you can get by talking to a friend? Of course, I didn't have a friend to talk to."

When Kurt's wife finally left him, he was desperate. "I was so traumatized that I had no choice but to start doing some serious work on my own stuff. I had to be hit between the eyes with the thing I feared most before I could allow myself to get any help."

Kurt was fifty-one when he joined one of my groups. "I had lived for half a century, but this was the first time I realized it was permissible to have feelings. And to express them? That was a real shock. Even though I was full of fear and rage, I'd never really expressed them directly. I just let them leak out by being sarcastic, cutting people down, belittling them. Every once in a while I'd blow up. In the group it was safe to express whatever I was feeling."

Kurt started to heal as soon as he began releasing some of his pent-up rage. He resisted using the bat and pillow at first but soon discovered what a tremendous relief it was to disgorge his anger. "Those emotions are still welling up," he says. "It's been over three years and they're still coming up. I have a lot to work through."

In the second year of his therapy Kurt released enough rage about his past that he began to look at some present-day issues, including his obsession with work. At the time, he was heading an economic research team for the government. He worked long hours, often straight through the weekend. He felt pressured virtually all of the time. With the help of the men in the group he realized that it was fear, not financial need, that kept his nose to the grindstone. He had more than enough money to retire, even though he was only fifty-two. For ten consecutive sessions Kurt talked about the fear that kept him chained to his job. One night he said to the group, "How much money is enough? I have enough money to live the rest of my life in comfort. But you never know. Something might come up. I might need more."

Finally, Kurt was able to work up the courage to cut back his hours. He let his contract with the government expire, and began doing private consulting work part-time. But old habits die hard. When his clients pressured him to meet impossible deadlines, he found it difficult to say no.

About six months ago Kurt came to the group and announced that he'd had a breakthrough. He was working on a project that was supposed to be finished that very night. He said, "I told my client that I'm going to have dinner and then I'm going to group. The project's not going to be done until tomorrow afternoon. And you know what? The sky didn't fall in. They accepted my limits." He's been more relaxed about work ever since.

For the last year and a half Kurt has been living with a woman named Janice. His new relationship is a dramatic improvement over his fear-based marriage. Recently, Janice told him she wanted to spend a week in Colorado skiing with a girlfriend. "I didn't bat an eye. For the first time I'm discovering what love is. I never had those tender feelings in my marriage. I was too frightened my wife was going to leave me. I was always controlling her and trying to please her. There was little room for love. Now I sincerely want Janice to enjoy herself. This relationship is light years away from my marriage. Most of the difference is due to the changes I've made in therapy."

Kurt's relationships with his two children have also changed dramatically. "You always want to do something good for your children, give them a lot. I always interpreted love in terms of material possessions. Now I know that the best thing I've ever done for them is getting therapy for myself." He says that his relationship with his twenty-five-year-old son, Julian, has changed 180 degrees. "I rarely spent time with him when he was young. I was too busy with work. I was too busy keeping tabs on my wife. Now we do a lot of things together, including having dinner at least once a week. We openly talk about everything."

Another change for Kurt is that he has reestablished ties with his brother, who is fourteen years older than he is. The two of them were never close. "He was out of the house before I was old enough to be aware of him. When I started therapy, we had never hugged each other, never said that we loved each other." As a part of recovery he felt the need to make a connection with his brother. He invited himself to his brother's house for a weekend visit, and the two of them talked nonstop virtually the whole time. "I think we got three or four hours sleep that entire weekend." Kurt learned that his brother had many of the same childhood experiences that he had, although his father's alcoholism had been less severe in earlier years. "My brother had never dealt with all those issues," Kurt says. "Because of talking with me, he's decided to get some therapy himself. He's sixty-seven, and he's recently joined a men's group. It's never too late to get help."

Kurt says that in his first year of therapy he wasn't aware of all the changes he was making. "People would tell me how different I seemed, but I couldn't see it myself. The change seemed so gradual. I only felt good for a split second, then it was gone. It takes a while for this stuff to work. But things are moving more rapidly now. Every time I am able to express an emotion—and that's what healing is—I'm getting healthier. By the minute. I can feel it."

The one person who is most aware of how much Kurt has changed is his son, Julian. Kurt invited Julian to a recent Wildman Gathering. Kurt stood up in front of a hundred men and talked about how much his son meant to him. He said, "I want to say in public, in front of all you guys, that I love my son and I'm damn proud of him."

Before Kurt could sit down, Julian stood up beside him. He said, "Dad, don't sit down yet. I want to say a few things about you. I've spent twenty-five years with you and my mother and only one of you seemed to care about me, and it wasn't you. When you were around me, it seemed you were preoccupied with anything and everything but me. You were too impatient with me and too critical of me. To be honest, most of the time I didn't enjoy being around you.

"But the last couple of years—Jesus, what a difference. We can talk without getting into a fight. You listen to me, even when I disagree with you. Most of all, you respect what I have to say. I can screw up, and you don't shame me. You're honest with me about how you really feel. You're even fun to be around. I love you, Dad. And I'm even more proud of *you*!"

As Julian finished speaking, father and son met each other in the middle of the circle and hugged. Then Julian stepped back, looked at his father, and said, "Welcome to life, Dad."

APPENDIX

For a schedule of Marvin Allen's lectures, therapy groups, and the date and location of future Wildman Gatherings, send a stamped, self-addressed envelope to:

The Texas Men's Institute
P.O. Box 311384
New Braunfels, Texas 78131-1384

Or call (210) 964-4153
Toll free (800) 786-8584

HOW TO LOCATE A MEN'S THERAPIST OR MEN'S SUPPORT GROUP IN YOUR AREA

There are two general kinds of men's groups: support groups and therapy groups. Support groups are leaderless groups designed to give men a forum to discuss daily issues, support each other, and build community. They are not run by a therapist, and they are not designed as therapy. Therapy groups are run by a qualified therapist. In addition to offering men support and community, they help men resolve a wide range of emotional problems.

A Circle of Men is a good book that helps men create their own support groups. Written by Bill Kauth and published in 1992 by St.

Martin's Press, it gives step-by-step information on how to form and conduct such a group.

To find a men's therapy group or a therapist who works with men on an individual basis, check the listings below. If you do not find a convenient men's resource center, check the community services section of your phone book. Look for a central information and referral number and ask for men's mental health services or resource centers. You can also look in the alphabetical listings of your phone book for headings that begin with "Men": for example, "Men's Resource Center," "Men's Institute," or "Men's Counseling Center." Many men's centers are preceded by the name of a state or city (for example, "Seattle M.E.N." or "the Texas Men's Institute") so check those listings as well. If you cannot find a men's center in your city, look for one in a larger city nearby.

You can also write or call one of the national men's centers or look in the ad sections of men's magazines, both listed below.

MEN'S CENTERS AND ORGANIZATIONS

Note: Many men's organizations operate on a tight budget and do not have full-time receptionists. You may reach an answering machine.

The Austin Men's Center

The Austin Men's Center is a private counseling and psychotherapy practice. The center offers individual and group counseling on an outpatient basis and week-long intensive retreats for men. A wide range of services are available for men, women, children, and families. 4314 Medical Parkway, Suite 200, Austin, TX 78756. (512) 477-9595.

The Father's Network

The Father's Network's goals are: to increase involvement of the father in parenting, encourage mutually fulfilling relationships between fathers and their children, and challenge traditional "provider" roles in order to open greater opportunities for fathers. They provide information and referral services and organize workshops, events, and retreats. P.O. Box 800-MV, San Anselmo, CA 94979-0800. (415) 453-2839.

The Hill Country Men's Center

The Hill Country Men's Center is a cooperative of therapists and visionaries committed to personal discovery and meaningful change. The center offers individual, couple, and group counseling. Clients explore issues of attachment, grief, rage, guilt, boundaries, sexuality, empathy, and personal and relationship excellence. Therapists have certification in imago relationship therapy, neurolinguistic programming, bioenergetics, and massage therapy. They also have training in Gestalt therapy, recovery and codependency, and emotional-release work. 4314 Medical Parkway, Suite 8, Austin, TX 78756. (512) 467-8000.

The Male Health Center

The Male Health Center helps men live healthy lives. It is the first center in the country specializing in treating male health problems. The center addresses issues of impotence, prostate disorders, sexually transmitted diseases, vasectomy, cancer screening, general medicine, and wellness. The center offers a patient network that connects new patients with others who have a similar problem. 5744 LBJ Freeway, Suite 100, Dallas, TX 75240. (214) 490-MALE.

The Men's Council Project

The mission of the Men's Council Project is to bring men together for personal awakening and empowerment and to serve our communities through social and environmental action. The project does this by providing four main services: leadership-training programs, men's-initiation ceremonies, public talks and seminars, and individual mentoring to help create and strengthen local men's councils. P.O. Box 17341, Boulder, CO 80301. (303) 444-7741.

The Men's Health Network (MHN)

The Men's Health Network is an organization committed to promoting men's issues. Based in Washington, D.C., MHN strives to: (1) reduce the premature mortality of men and boys, (2) counteract the cycles of violence and addiction that plague and cripple our male population, and (3) promote the physical and emotional health of men.

MHN plans to implement a national campaign to increase public and media awareness of these issues, develop a national data base for men's resources, maintain a national network of health-care providers, and support local and national government programs that address men's issues. P.O. Box 770, Washington, D.C. 20044-0770.

Men's Resource Center of Portland, Oregon

The Men's Resource Center in Portland offers individual and group counseling for men dealing with issues such as relationship problems, emotional expression, fathering issues, men relating to men, anxiety and depression, and life transition. They have additional programs for gay men, men who have been sexually abused, and for men with anger issues. They offer couples and family counseling as well. 2325 East Burnside, Portland, OR 97214. (503) 235-3433.

Men's Resource Center of Texas Coastal Bend

The center offers men's therapy and support groups, educational and experiential workshops, information and outreach programs. Codependency, anger, father-son wounding, relationships, and spirituality are addressed in their groups. 1735 Third Street, Corpus Christi, TX 78404. (512) 887-8290.

The Menswork Center

The Menswork Center provides individual counseling, men's groups, weekend retreats, workshops, and seminars. The center offers a line of consciousness-raising audiotapes to inspire the exploration of one's images, beliefs, and attitudes regarding masculinity. 1950 Sawtelle Boulevard, Suite 340, Los Angeles, CA 90025. (310) 479-2749.

The National Men's Resource Center

The National Men's Resource Center has worked since 1982 to end men's isolation by developing local men's resource hotlines and calendars, men's-studies programs on college campuses, and men's-studies sections in bookstores. They provide referral and information on: men's books, publications, research, conferences, films and videos, organizations, groups, services, and cultural events. P.O. Box 800-HL, San Anselmo, CA 94979-0800. (415) 453-2839.

The Santa Barbara Institute for Gender Studies

The Santa Barbara Institute for Gender Studies was established in 1989 for the purpose of hosting dialogues and encounters between groups of men and women. In order to gain deeper understanding of one another and reduce conflicts, it is often necessary to meet on neutral ground with the help of trained facilitators. Toward that end, the Santa Barbara Institute conducts research, training, and workshops designed to heal old wounds and support new visions for the mutual empowerment of men and women. P.O. Box 4782, Santa Barbara, CA 93140. (805) 963-8285.

Seattle M.E.N

The goal of Seattle M.E.N. is to contribute to the emergence of healthy, whole men. They support and encourage men in their personal growth and in service to others and the community. Primarily a networking organization, they have a monthly newsletter and provide information about men's therapists, men's groups, lawyers, as well as lectures and workshops of special interest to men. 602 West Howe, Seattle, WA 98119. (206) 285-4356.

South Florida Men's Center, Inc.

The primary goal of the South Florida Men's Center is to bring together men who are interested in exploring a powerful yet humane and nonoppressive masculinity. The center organizes local men's groups and provides legal and referral counseling to assist men in child-custody cases and other men's-rights issues. 801 Brickell Avenue, Suite 900, Miami, Florida 33133.

The Texas Men's Institute

The Texas Men's Institute offers individual and group therapy for men. The staff is trained in masculine relational therapy, a gender-specific therapy for men. They help men resolve problems with love relationships, codependency, anxiety and depression, anger and passivity, fathering, friendships, sexuality, and midlife crisis.

The institute also offers marriage and family counseling, therapist training, Wildman Gatherings, and co-ed wilderness retreats. It is the primary sponsor of the annual International Men's Conference held each fall. Director: Marvin Allen. P.O. Box 311384, New Braunfels, TX 78131-1384. (210) 964-4153.

Twin Cities Men's Center

The mission of the Twin Cities Men's Center is to provide resources for men seeking to grow in body, mind, and spirit. The center offers a variety of educational forums, peer-support groups, and other activities to foster emotional, intellectual and spiritual growth. 3255 Hennepin Avenue South, Suite 45, Minneapolis, MN 55408.

Unisphere

Unisphere offers individual, group, and couples therapy with a primary focus on personal and spiritual growth, relationship issues, and life transition. Also available are weekend seminars on specific issues, including reframing conflict as a creative process. 10212 Fifth Avenue NE, Suite 250, Seattle, WA 98115. (206) 932-2288.

MEN'S PUBLICATIONS

Brother

National Organization for Men Against Sexism, $25/yearly membership. 798 Penn Avenue, Box 5, Pittsburgh, PA 15221.

Conscious Manhood

A quarterly publication of The Texas Men's Institute that focuses on the inner and outer worlds of American men. Covers a broad range of topics from relationships and marriage to sexuality to careers to health to outdoor adventures. Stories, articles, essays, and poetry. $12/year. Texas Men's Institute, P.O. Box 311384, New Braunfels, Texas 78131.

HO! A Men's Journal

An informal little treasury of men's voices about life as a man. Full of articles, poems, and whimsical observations about men. Published quarterly, $12/year. P.O. Box 1029-477, Van Nuys, CA 91408.

Man Alive!: Journal of Men's Wellness

Quarterly journal of men sharing honestly with each other about the challenges and joys of being male. $8/year. Network Press, P.O. Box 40300, Albuquerque, NM 87196.

Men Talk

An informal magazine full of resources about men's events with a few stories about men. Regional quarterly publication featuring local authors, $14/year. Twin Cities Men's Center, 3255 Hennepin Avenue South, Suite 45, Minneapolis, MN 55408.

Men's Council Journal

Excellent little magazine of stories and poems about the male experience. Quarterly with photos and strong mythopoetic content. Published quarterly, $15/year. P.O. Box 385, Boulder, CO 80306.

Men's Health Magazine

Slick, national magazine that is chock-full of tips and short articles about men and their health issues. Informative and easy to read, but doesn't take many chances with cutting-edge issues. Published every other month, $17/year. 33 East Minor Street, Emmaus, PA 18098.

MENTOR: The Oregon Resource for Men

An informal magazine with thought-provoking articles about men. Quarterly printing with exclusively local authors, many their first time in print, $20. P.O. Box 10863, Portland, OR 97210.

The National Men's Resource Calendar

This quarterly calendar is filled with dozens of pages of events, workshops, and services across the nation committed to a positive change in male roles and relationships. Lists hundreds of bookstores with men's sections, men's groups and councils, and men's services plus a listing of over eighty men's publications. Each issue reviews around twenty current "men's issues" books. $10/year. The National Men's Resource Center, P.O. Box 800-MV, San Anselmo, CA 94979.

NetWORK: National Congress of Men and Children

A quarterly newsletter focusing on the protection of the rights of men and fathers. Annual directory of father's/men's rights groups across the U.S. for $82. NCM, 1241 East Chestnut, #D, Santa Ana, CA 92701.

Seattle M.E.N.: Men's Evolvement Network

A newsletter with stories and resources for men from the Northwest. A resource guide, local calendar of events, voice of the Seattle men's community, and an information and referral hotline. $10/year, $35 membership. 602 West Howe Street, Seattle, WA 98119.

THUNDER STICK:
Vancouver Men's Evolvement Network

Articles on mythopoetic issues, ecomasculinity, traditional peoples, with calendar of Canadian men's events. Published quarterly, $10/year. 3392 West 34th Avenue, Vancouver, B.C. V6N 2K6.

WINGSPAN: Journal of the Male Spirit

A national newsletter that has served as an important voice of the men's movement. Mostly mythopoetic in orientation, thrives on the cutting edge. Published quarterly, Free. Donations accepted. Box 23550, Brightmoor Station, Detroit, MI 48223.

MEN'S RETREATS AND SEMINARS

Wildman Gatherings

The Wildman Gatherings are a three-day retreat in a wilderness setting for groups of men. They offer a series of exercises, rituals, and discussions designed to help men explore their full range of feelings. Participants are encouraged to express the emotional pain of childhood in the company of supportive, validating men. Special attention is paid to the way they are wounded emotionally and spiritually by their fathers. The Wildman Gatherings explores "creative masculinity," a masculinity that allows men to be passionate and powerful, yet doesn't oppress women, children, or other men. Led by Marvin Allen. The Texas Men's Institute, P.O. Box 311384, New Braunfels, Texas 78131-1384. (210) 608-9201.

The Wilderness Warrior

A tribal celebration of the deep male spirit in the Sangre de Cristo Range of southern Colorado with experienced men's group and outdoor leaders. Camping, rock climbing, rappelling, peak ascents, and other "warrior skills training" for men of all ages help build a community that lasts well beyond the trip. Limited to fifteen participants. Led by Rick Medrick, (800) 331-7238.

The Warrior's Journey Home

Weekend retreat for men that focuses on recovering from dependency and addictions. Led by Jed Diamond, 34133 Shimmins Ridge Road, Willits, CA 95490.

Men's Vision Quests and White-Water Rafting Trips

Outdoor adventures exploring and celebrating the masculine spirit in the deserts, mountains, and canyons of New Mexico, Arizona, and Utah. Led by Dick "Coyote" Prosapio, 754 Saratoga, Rio Rancho, NM 87124.

Healing the Father Wound

Gordon Clay, creator of the Tantrum Yoga movement and breathwork, uses experiential exercises and emotional-release techniques to help participants experience hidden feelings. There are two separate sessions, one for women and one for men. Gordan Clay also conducts "A Father and Teenage Daughter Rite-of-Passage." Father Wound, P.O. Box 800-HL, San Anselmo, CA 94979-0800. (415) 547-3389.

About the Authors

MARVIN ALLEN, director of the Texas Men's Institute and founder of the Texas Wildman Gatherings, led the First and Second International Men's Conferences. He has been featured in *Fortune, Esquire*, and *The New York Times Magazine*, as well as on *The Oprah Winfrey Show*, *20/20*, and the PBS documentary *Save the Males*. He lives near San Antonio.

JO ROBINSON is the co-author of *Getting the Love You Want, Full House, Unplug the Christmas Machine*, and *The Emotional Incest Syndrome*. She lives in Portland, Oregon.